T0419787

GHOSTLY ENCOUNTERS

TERRIFYINGLY TRUE HAUNTINGS

RICHARD ESTEP

GHOSTLY ENCOUNTERS: TERRIFYINGLY TRUE HAUNTINGS

Visible Ink Press®
43311 Joy Rd., #414
Canton, MI 48187-2075
Visible Ink Press is a registered trademark of Visible Ink Press LLC.

Most Visible Ink Press books are available at special quantity discounts when purchased in bulk by corporations, organizations, or groups. Customized printings, special imprints, messages, and excerpts can be produced to meet your needs. For more information, contact Special Markets Director, Visible Ink Press, www.visibleink.com, or 734-667-3211.

Managing Editor: Kevin S. Hile
Cover Design: John Gouin, Graphikitchen, LLC
Page Design: Mary Claire Krzewinski
Typesetting: Marco Divita
Proofreaders: Suzanne Goraj and Shoshana Hurwitz
Indexer: Larry Baker
Cover image: Shutterstock.

ISBNs:
Paperback: 978-1-57859-812-0
Hardcover: 978-1-57859-883-0
eBook: 978-1-57859-884-7

Cataloging-in-Publication data is on file at the Library of Congress.

Printed in the United States of America.

10 9 8 7 6 5 4 3 2 1

CONTENTS

ABOUT THE AUTHOR

Photograph by Ali Cotton, Bleu Cotton Photography.

Richard Estep is the author of numerous books, ranging from paranormal non-fiction and UFOlogy to history and current affairs. These books include *Serial Killers: The Minds, Methods, and Mayhem of History's Most Notorious Murderers, The Serial Killer Next Door: The Double Lives of Notorious Murderers, Grifters, Frauds, and Crooks: True Stories of American Corruption,* and *The Handy Armed Forces Answer Book.* He is a regular columnist for *Haunted Magazine* and has written for the *Journal of Emergency Medical Services.* Richard appears regularly on the TV shows *Haunted Files, Haunted Hospitals, Paranormal 911,* and *Paranormal Night Shift,* and has guested on *Destination Fear* and *A Haunting.* He makes his home in Colorado, with his wife and a menagerie of adopted animals.

DEDICATION

For MJ, Duncan, and Mum

Peel me a grape,

Save me a sandwich,

Put the kettle on.

INTRODUCTION

We British love our pubs, and we love our pub discussions.

It's a cultural thing. For generations, the public house has been the center of British life, the hearthstone of our local culture. In days of yore, Brits would prop themselves up at the pub bar or congregate around the fireplace with a glass of something that burned on the way down. It was just the thing to while away the cold winter nights, when the darkness closed in outside the windows. Tree branches took on the look of withered, spindly fingers in silhouette against the glass, sometimes scraping against the pane in a way that sent shivers up the spine.

The ghost story is woven every bit as tightly into the fabric of both British and American life. As a son of both worlds—born in Britain, living in the United States, a dual citizen—I've been doubly bitten by the paranormal bug.

Who doesn't love a good tale of spirits returning from beyond the grave or lingering after death in order to complete some unfinished business? Charles Dickens gave us the perfect, eternally spooky Yuletide gift with *A Christmas Carol*. Arguably the greatest ghost story of all time, Christmas or not, this evergreen tale of Ebenezer Scrooge and the four ghosts—not three, for we must count Jacob Marley—continues to resonate almost two centuries after its publication in 1843.

While *A Christmas Carol* is close to perfection, it has at least one flaw that I could never get past.

It is fiction.

Dickens wrote plenty of nonfiction in his time, certainly, but he was primarily known as a writer of fiction. The ghosts of Christmas Past, Present, and Future aren't real. Neither is the lamentable Jacob Marley. All are inventions of the storyteller's keen imagination.

The only thing I love more than a good ghost story is a good *true* ghost story. Even the most adeptly plotted tale—with sublime characterization and flawless prose style—pales in comparison to something that we know is true ... or that we are *told* is true, at any rate.

When the good folks at Visible Ink Press offered me the opportunity to write *Ghostly Encounters*, I didn't have to think twice. As a paranormal investigator, a researcher into claims of ghostly goings-on and haunted houses around the world but primarily in the United States and Great Britain, since 1995, I was aware of hundreds of cases that might fit that description.

Introduction

This was a book that I expected to practically write itself.

Except that it didn't because it wasn't as easy as all that.

For as long as I could remember, I had grown up reading about many of these classic cases. As a young boy, I sat wide-eyed in an armchair that was much too big for me, with a book carefully propped open on my lap. It was here that I learned of places such as Borley Rectory, supposedly the most haunted house in England, and the adventures of one Harry Price, Esq.

Price had the most amazing adventures: poking around haunted houses, testing psychic mediums, even pursuing animals that could talk. It would only be later, when I grew up, that I would learn my hero had feet of clay and may not have been the paragon of ethical ghost hunting he was purported to be.

There was nothing in the way of paranormal reality television in those days, so it was necessary to get one's ghostly fix with a library card. I checked out the books of the great (and greatly missed) gentlemanly ghost hunter Peter Underwood and devoured them, reading and re-reading each one until I had their contents practically memorized. His books remain in print today and deserve a much wider audience, particularly on the U.S. side of the Atlantic, where Mr. Underwood isn't nearly as well known as he ought to be.

I went from Underwood to Colin Wilson, another legend in the field. It was from his work that I learned of the mischievous and malevolent Black Monk of Pontefract, never dreaming that 40 years later I would take up residence in that very house while researching a book of my own about Britain's most violent (and longest-running) poltergeist case.

As a young man growing up in Britain of the 1990s, I was excited at the advent of satellite television. The great appeal came from an American TV show titled *Sightings*, which covered paranormal phenomena such as ghosts, UFOs, and mysterious powers with a sober, rational eye. Unquestionably, my favorite segments of the show centered around what was called "The Heartland Haunting." This was another violent poltergeist case, one that afflicted a young married couple in the American Midwest. I could hardly believe my eyes at the video footage of bloody wounds spontaneously appearing on the skin of one of the residents.

Today, the case is referred to not as the Heartland Haunting, but rather by the name of the ghostly little girl who is said to have caused so much mayhem to the lives of that family. Her name, *Sightings* told us, was Sallie, and the Sallie House in Atchison, Kansas, is a location that rides high on the bucket list of many a paranormal investigator.

The Sallie House has a reputation for being a dark and malevolent haunted location. In the process of researching its story, I spoke with individuals who flatly swore never to return there under any circumstances. I spent several nights investigating the house, consulting with trusted researchers in the field in an attempt to unearth answers to some of the house's many mysteries.

Ghostly Encounters really is a book of two halves, although those halves have been carefully integrated into one coherent, singular entity. On many of the cases, I put actual boots on the ground, investigating the cases in person. Sometimes, those investigations lasted days or weeks. At least one took me three years. When writing those cases up for inclusion in this book, I have striven to convey some sense of what it was like to be there within those haunted places. When it comes to locations such as the Gettysburg battlefield, the Waverly Hills Sanatorium, or the Lemp Mansion, it is definitely a case of "been there, done that."

But what qualifies a haunting to be more notable than another and worthy of discussion in this book? Go to a paranormal convention (or join a Facebook group) and casually start a conversation about the great hauntings of history. Poll a random sample of, let's say, 50 enthusiasts or investigators, and you're liable to find a few commonalities among their opinions—most Americans would agree that the Stanley Hotel deserves a place on the list, for example—but also quite a bit of variance.

What makes a haunting memorably famous is debatable, and that's where the joy can be found: in the debate. This book includes cases from the annals of paranormal research that were either considered groundbreaking at the time they happened or garnered so much attention that they became icons of pop culture. A case in point is the Enfield haunting. This poltergeist outbreak took place in a perfectly normal single-parent British family home during the 1970s. It was extensively studied by two highly adept researchers and documented with great aplomb in Guy Lyon Playfair's masterpiece of paranormal nonfiction, *This House Is Haunted.*

This particular haunting also spawned a TV miniseries of the same name and a Hollywood blockbuster (*The Conjuring 2*), which played *extremely* fast and loose with the facts. By any objective measure, Enfield is a fascinating and important case. Yet there are those skeptics who claim that it was essentially made up, being nothing more than the product of two mischievous and pranksterish little girls who had nothing better to do with their time than spend months trying to fool paranormal investigators, newspaper reporters, and their own family.

Great hauntings stir up controversy. It is inevitable, and there is a lot to be said for the practice of placing them under the proverbial microscope and assessing them with a critical eye.

The cases included in this book that I have not been able to investigate in person, such as Enfield, the Philip Experiment, and the crash of Eastern Airlines Flight 401, to list just three, have been on my list of great cases for many years. It has been a pleasure to revisit them and to apply some of the analytical skills I have worked to develop over the past 30 years in the paranormal field. It is my hope that you will find them as intriguing, colorful, and thought-provoking as I do.

Your list of important hauntings may differ from mine. I invite you to drop me a line at my website, www.richardestep.net, and let me know which cases you believe would fit the bill.

For now, sit back, relax, and enjoy this journey into some of the most fascinating, baffling, and downright spine-tingling hauntings on record.

I hope that you enjoy it.

OTHER VISIBLE INK PRESS BOOKS BY RICHARD ESTEP

Dark Spirits: Monsters, Demons, and Devils
ISBN: 978-1-57859-847-2

Family, Friends, and Neighbors: Stories of Murder and Betrayal
ISBN: 978-1-57859-844-1

Great Hauntings: Terrifyingly True Hauntings
ISBN: 978-1-57859-812-0

Grifters, Frauds, and Crooks: True Stories of American Corruption
ISBN: 978-1-57859-796-3

The Handy Armed Forces Answer Book: Your Guide to the Whats and Whys of the U.S. Military
ISBN: 978-1-57859-743-7

The Handy World War II Answer Book
ISBN: 978-1-57859-810-6

The Serial Killer Next Door: The Double Lives of Notorious Murderers
ISBN: 978-1-57859-768-0

Serial Killers: The Minds, Methods, and Mayhem of History's Notorious Murderers
ISBN: 978-1-57859-707-9

ALSO FROM VISIBLE INK PRESS

The Afterlife Book: Heaven, Hell, and Life after Death
by Marie D. Jones and Larry Flaxman
ISBN: 978-1-57859-761-1

The Alien Book: A Guide to Extraterrestrial Beings on Earth
by Nick Redfern
ISBN: 978-1-57859-687-4

Alien Mysteries, Conspiracies, and Cover-Ups
by Kevin D. Randle
ISBN: 978-1-57859-418-4

American Ghost Stories: True Stories from All 50 Books
by Michael A. Kozlowski
ISBN: 978-1-57859-799-4

Ancient Gods: Lost Histories, Hidden Truths, and the Conspiracy of Silence
by Jim Willis
ISBN: 978-1-57859-614-0

Angels A to Z, 2nd edition
by Evelyn Dorothy Oliver, Ph.D.; and James R. Lewis, Ph.D.
ISBN: 978-1-57859-212-8

Area 51: The Revealing Truth of

UFOs, Secret Aircraft, Cover-Ups & Conspiracies
by Nick Redfern
ISBN: 978-1-57859-672-0

Armageddon Now: The End of the World A to Z
by Jim Willis and Barbara Willis
ISBN: 978-1-57859-168-8

The Astrology Book: The Encyclopedia of Heavenly Influences, 2nd edition
by James R. Lewis
ISBN: 978-1-57859-144-2

The Astrology Guide: Understanding Your Signs, Your Gifts, and Yourself
by Claudia Trivelas
ISBN: 978-1-57859-738-3

The Bigfoot Book: The Encyclopedia of Sasquatch, Yeti, and Cryptid Primates
by Nick Redfern
ISBN: 978-1-57859-561-7

Bigfoot Sightings: True Encounters
by Jim Willis and Joseph Kozlowski
ISBN: 978-1-57859-869-4

Celebrity Ghosts and Notorious Hauntings
by Marie D. Jones
ISBN: 978-1-57859-689-8

Censoring God: The History of the Lost Books (and Other Excluded Scriptures)
by Jim Willis
ISBN: 978-1-57859-732-1

Conspiracies and Secret Societies: The Complete Dossier, 2nd ed.
by Brad and Sherry Hansen Steiger
ISBN: 978-1-57859-368-2

Control: MK Ultra, Chemtrails, and the Conspiracy to Suppress the Masses
by Nick Redfern
ISBN: 978-1-57859-638-6

Cover-Ups and Secrets: The Complete Guide to Government Conspiracies, Manipulations & Deceptions
by Nick Redfern
ISBN: 978-1-57859-679-9

Demons, the Devil, and Fallen Angels
by Marie D. Jones and Larry Flaxman
ISBN: 978-1-57859-613-3

The Dream Encyclopedia, 2nd edition
by James R. Lewis, Ph.D.; and Evelyn Dorothy Oliver, Ph.D.
ISBN: 978-1-57859-216-6

The Dream Interpretation Dictionary: Symbols, Signs, and Meanings
by J. M. DeBord
ISBN: 978-1-57859-637-9

Earth Magic: Your Complete Guide to Natural Spells, Potions, Plants, Herbs, Witchcraft, and More
by Marie D. Jones
ISBN: 978-1-57859-697-3

The Encyclopedia of Religious Phenomena
by J. Gordon Melton
ISBN: 978-1-57859-209-8

The Fortune-Telling Book: The Encyclopedia of Divination and Soothsaying
by Raymond Buckland
ISBN: 978-1-57859-147-3

The Government UFO Files: The Conspiracy of Cover-Up
by Kevin D. Randle
ISBN: 978-1-57859-477-1

Haunted: Malevolent Ghosts, Night Terrors, and Threatening Phantoms
by Brad Steiger
ISBN: 978-1-57859-620-1

Hidden History: Ancient Aliens and the Suppressed Origins of Civilization
by Jim Willis
ISBN: 978-1-57859-710-9

Hidden Realms, Lost Civilizations, and Beings from Other Worlds
by Jerome Clark
ISBN: 978-1-57859-175-6

The Horror Show Guide: The Ultimate Frightfest of Movies
by Mike Mayo
ISBN: 978-1-57859-420-7

The Illuminati: The Secret Society That Hijacked the World
by Jim Marrs
ISBN: 978-1-57859-619-5

Lost Civilizations: The Secret Histories and Suppressed Technologies of the Ancients
by Jim Willis
ISBN: 978-1-57859-706-2

The Monster Book: Creatures, Beasts, and Fiends of Nature
by Nick Redfern
ISBN: 978-1-57859-575-4

Monsters of the Deep
by Nick Redfern
ISBN: 978-1-57859-705-5

Near Death Experiences: Afterlife Journeys and Revelations
by Jim Willis
ISBN: 978-1-57859-846-5

The New Witch Your Guide to Modern Witchcraft, Wicca, Spells, Potions, Magic, and More
by Marie D. Jones
ISBN: 978-1-57859-716-1

The New World Order Book
by Nick Redfern
ISBN: 978-1-57859-615-7

Nightmares: Your Guide to Interpreting Your Darkest Dreams
by J. M. DeBord
ISBN: 978-1-57859-758-1

Real Aliens, Space Beings, and Creatures from Other Worlds,
by Brad and Sherry Hansen Steiger
ISBN: 978-1-57859-333-0

Real Encounters, Different Dimensions, and Otherworldly Beings
by Brad and Sherry Hansen Steiger
ISBN: 978-1-57859-455-9

Real Ghosts, Restless Spirits, and Haunted Places, 2nd edition
by Brad Steiger
ISBN: 978-1-57859-401-6

Real Miracles, Divine Intervention, and Feats of Incredible Survival
by Brad and Sherry Hansen Steiger
ISBN: 978-1-57859-214-2

Real Monsters, Gruesome Critters, and Beasts from the Darkside
by Brad and Sherry Hansen Steiger
ISBN: 978-1-57859-220-3

Real Vampires, Night Stalkers, and Creatures from the Darkside
by Brad Steiger
ISBN: 978-1-57859-255-5

Real Visitors, Voices from Beyond, and Parallel Dimensions
by Brad and Sherry Hansen Steiger
ISBN: 978-1-57859-541-9

Real Zombies, the Living Dead, and Creatures of the Apocalypse,
by Brad Steiger
ISBN: 978-1-57859-296-8

The Religion Book Places, Prophets, Saints, and Seers
by Jim Willis
ISBN: 978-1-57859-151-0

Runaway Science: True Stories of Raging Robots and High-Tech Horrors
by Nick Redfern
ISBN: 978-1-57859-801-4

The Sci-Fi Movie Guide: The Universe of Film from Alien to Zardoz
by Chris Barsanti
ISBN: 978-1-57859-503-7

Secret History: Conspiracies from Ancient Aliens to the New World Order
by Nick Redfern
ISBN: 978-1-57859-479-5

Secret Societies: The Complete Guide to Histories, Rites, and Rituals
by Nick Redfern
ISBN: 978-1-57859-483-2

The Spirit Book: The Encyclopedia of Clairvoyance, Channeling, and Spirit Communication
by Raymond Buckland
ISBN 978-1-57859-790-1

Supernatural Gods: Spiritual Mysteries, Psychic Experiences, and Scientific Truths
by Jim Willis
ISBN: 978-1-57859-660-7

Time Travel: The Science and Science Fiction
by Nick Redfern
ISBN: 978-1-57859-723-9

Toxin Nation: The Poisoning of Our Air, Water, Food, and Bodies
by Marie D. Jones
ISBN: 978-1-57859-709-3

The UFO Dossier: 100 Years of Government Secrets, Conspiracies, and Cover-Ups
by Kevin D. Randle
ISBN: 978-1-57859-564-8

Unexplained! Strange Sightings, Incredible Occurrences, and Puzzling Physical Phenomena, 3rd edition
by Jerome Clark
ISBN: 978-1-57859-344-6

The Vampire Almanac: The Complete History
by J. Gordon Melton, Ph.D.
ISBN: 978-1-57859-719-2

The Vampire Book: The Encyclopedia of the Undead, 3rd edition
by J. Gordon Melton, Ph.D.
ISBN: 978-1-57859-281-4

The Werewolf Book: The Encyclopedia of Shape-Shifting Beings, 2nd edition
by Brad Steiger
ISBN: 978-1-57859-367-5

Werewolf Stories: Shape-Shifters, Lycanthropes, and Man-Beasts
by Nick Redfern and Brad Steiger
ISBN: 978-1-57859-766-6

The Witch Book: The Encyclopedia of Witchcraft, Wicca, and Neo-Paganism
by Raymond Buckland
ISBN: 978-1-57859-791-8

The Witches Almanac Sorcerers, Witches and Magic from Ancient Rome to the Digital Age
by Charles Christian
ISBN: 978-1-57859-760-4

The Zombie Book: The Encyclopedia of the Living Dead
by Nick Redfern and Brad Steiger
ISBN: 978-1-57859-504-4

"REAL NIGHTMARES" E-BOOKS BY BRAD STEIGER

Book 1: *True and Truly Scary Unexplained Phenomenon*

Book 2: *The Unexplained Phenomena and Tales of the Unknown*

Book 3: *Things That Go Bump in the Night*

Book 4: *Things That Prowl and Growl in the Night*

Book 5: *Fiends That Want Your Blood*

Book 6: *Unexpected Visitors and Unwanted Guests*

Book 7: *Dark and Deadly Demons*

Book 8: *Phantoms, Apparitions, and Ghosts*

Book 9: *Alien Strangers and Foreign Worlds*

Book 10: *Ghastly and Grisly Spooks*

Book 11: *Secret Schemes and Conspiring Cabals*

Book 12: *Freaks, Fiends, and Evil Spirits*

Please visit us at www.visibleinkpress.com.

THE CURSE OF THE LEMPS

History is replete with examples of supposedly cursed families. Take, for instance, the Kennedy dynasty. Even setting aside the assassinations of President John F. Kennedy in Dallas, Texas, on November 22, 1963, and Senator Robert F. Kennedy in Los Angeles, California, on June 6, 1968, the family suffered more than its share of untimely deaths.

One of the future president's brothers, Joseph Jr., died while on a top secret military mission in the summer of 1944. The explosive payload in the aircraft he was flying spontaneously detonated while the flight was still in British airspace, killing him and a fellow officer instantly.

Four years later, their sister Kathleen was killed in a civilian plane crash. In 1999, 38-year-old John F. Kennedy Jr. was also killed in a plane crash, along with his wife, Carolyn.

In addition to aviation-related incidents, members of the Kennedy family have lost their lives from drug overdoses, suicide, and a variety of accidents. While it may be a stretch to describe this long string of misfortunes as a "curse," it cannot be denied that some families seem more prone to tragedy than others, and in some of those cases in which tragedy strikes, a haunting may follow.

Such appears to be the case with the Lemp family of St. Louis, Missouri. Like many American immigrants, the Lemps were of German stock. During the mid-1800s, the family trade was brewing beer. They had a talent for their craft, something for which the thirsty population of St. Louis developed a strong appreciation. Starting out from relatively humble

The Lemp family established their St. Louis, Missouri, brewery in 1840 and it stayed in the family for the next 80 years.

origins, patriarch Johann Adam Lemp and his family turned their small brewery into an industrial-scale juggernaut. In those days before technological refrigeration, the Lemps stored their product in caves beneath the city, where Mother Nature would help keep it cool on their behalf.

The name "Lemp" became synonymous with beer in St. Louis, its brand immensely popular and the Lemp logo becoming immediately recognizable by everybody who was old enough to drink. Their European style of beer was known as lager, which derived from a style of brewing known as bottom fermentation. Lemp lager was the talk of the town.

As their business expanded, so did the family fortune. The Lemps grew extremely rich, yet as seems to be the case so often, the money brought them worry and tribulations rather than happiness. The Civil War was entering its second year in 1862 when Adam Lemp died, bequeathing the family business to both his son, William J. Lemp, and his grandson, Charles Brauneck, whose share in the enterprise William went on to buy out in February 1865. (Their business partnership was outlasted by the Civil War.) Nobody outside the immediate Lemp family either owned a chunk of the brewing operation or had a meaningful say in how it was run—which was exactly how William Lemp wanted it.

For the remainder of the nineteenth century, the Lemps lived high on the hog. They moved in the uppermost social circles, wining and dining their contemporaries in high society. Yet, as the old truism goes, the good times wouldn't last forever. The dawning of a new century brought the downfall of the Lemp business and tragedy for the family itself.

In 1901, William's son, Frederick died at the young age of 28 while taking a sabbatical in California. His sojourn to the West Coast had been intended to relieve him of the pressures brought by life in St. Louis and to restore his failing health. He never returned to Missouri alive. The cause of death was heart failure.

The son of German immigrant Johann Lemp, who first started his famous beer, William Lemp bought the property that would become the famous Lemp Brewery complex.

Frederick Lemp's body was brought back to the city by train. Adam Lemp aside, most of the Lemp family would be laid to rest in St. Louis's Bellefontaine Cemetery. This was where the monied individuals of the time tended to be buried; many of those families constructed expensive and sometimes ostentatious mausoleums. The Lemps were no exception.

The family's home and seat of influence was what is today known as the Lemp Mansion and dates back to the 1860s. Then, as now, the grand house is located just a short walk away from the brewery whose brickwork still bears the Lemp name. It was used both as a residence and as an administrative center for the family business and was the scene of several untimely Lemp deaths.

The unexpected loss of his son all but broke William Lemp. As often happens with grieving parents, he was never quite the same man afterward. In 1904, following the death of a dear friend, it all became too much. On the morning of February 12, after completing his ablutions and preparing for the day ahead, he went upstairs, placed the barrel of a revolver to his own head, and pulled the trigger. He died shortly afterward in the presence of his traumatized family members. His body lay in state within the house in order to give friends and employees the opportunity to say their goodbyes and was then interred in the family mausoleum at Bellefontaine.

Two years later, his widow, Julia, died of cancer inside the Lemp Mansion. Unlike the death of her husband, Julia's was anticipated, allowing her family to be at her bedside when she passed. According to the *St. Louis Post-Dispatch* on April 16, 1906 ("Mrs Wm. J. Lemp Dead of Cancer"), she was reputedly the richest woman in St. Louis, with an estimated net worth somewhere between $12 million and $20 million—an incredible sum back then, as now.

William Lemp Sr. would not be the last Lemp to die of a self-inflicted gunshot wound inside the house. His son, William Lemp Jr.—known to all and sundry as "Billy"—worked hard and partied hard. He had a reputation for not only being a ladies' man but also being somebody who was fond of his drink and not afraid to use his fists if he felt the urge to do so. Those who crossed Billy Lemp often came off worse for it. He was a shrewd businessman, one who made plenty of money and liked to spend it freely. His marriage to the sophisticated Lillian Handlan, one of the darlings of St. Louis high society, ended in a humiliating, acrimonious divorce that brought scandal upon the Lemp family.

Four days after Christmas of 1922, Billy took his own life a few feet from his working desk in the Lemp Mansion. Rather than shoot himself in the head, as his father had done, he chose instead to fire a single bullet into his own heart, killing himself quickly. In another commonality between the deaths of father and son, neither William Sr. nor William Jr. had left a suicide note explaining his reasons for killing himself.

After Billy's interment at the Lemp mausoleum, ownership of the house passed to his brother Charles, who promptly decided to move in and call the place home. It's fair to say that Charles Lemp was someone who marched to the beat of his own drum, a man who insisted on things being done in a very specific way within the walls of his mansion. He was strong-willed and had forged his own path in the professional realm rather than tying himself to the family brewing empire. As the years passed, his liking for other human beings deteriorated until it was more of a grudging tolerance and then

Most members of the Lemp family were put to rest in their family mausoleum.

finally something bordering on dislike. In his final days, he had become somewhat akin to a hermit, preferring the company of his dog to that of other people.

Sometime on the night of May 9 or in the early morning hours of May 10, 1949, Charles Lemp killed himself while lying in bed. The cause of death was a single, self-inflicted gunshot wound to the right temple. He was 77 years old. A suicide note left at the scene declared: "In case I am found dead, blame it on no one but me." It bore Charles's distinctive signature.

Breaking with family tradition, Charles insisted on not being laid to rest in the Lemp mausoleum. Instead, he chose to be cremated and have his ashes interred on a farm that he owned. Their exact whereabouts remain unknown.

Many accounts of Charles Lemp's death (including those aired on popular television shows) claim that prior to taking his own life, he first shot his dog, Cerva. Author Troy Taylor disputes the claim in his book *Suicide & Spirits: The True Story of the Rise & Fall of the Lemp Empire*.

To reassure all of the dog people out there (which most definitely includes the author), none of the contemporary newspaper accounts mention anything whatsoever about Cerva being killed. Charles Lemp may have been an eccentric and possibly tortured man, living as he did with chronic pain due to medical ailments, but that doesn't make him a bad one.

Although she did not die in the house, no account of the Lemp family and their misfortunes would be complete without including the sad demise of Elsa, the youngest child of William and Julia Lemp. Born in 1883, she was very much a free spirit and had a strong personality to match. Elsa had a passion for social reform, particularly the growing suffragette movement, which had the goal of earning women the right to vote.

Much like that of her brother Billy, Elsa's marriage—to executive Thomas Wright—was a fiery one, and not in a good way. The pair fought regularly like the proverbial cat and dog. She and Wright divorced, and if they had stayed that way, things might have turned out differently. Instead, they remarried in 1920. Twelve days later, on March 20, 1920, Elsa died at the home they shared of a single gunshot wound to the heart, just as Billy had.

Located in St. Louis's Benton Park, the Lemp Mansion is now a hotel and restaurant that features ghost tours and mystery show dinners.

Although the official verdict was one of suicide, there remains suspicion to this day that she may have been murdered by the only other person present at the time: her husband. Certainly, her death occurred under suspicious circumstances. There was no obvious motive, and Wright's version of the story was somewhat flexible depending on who was asking him what. He also benefited financially by inheriting a significant portion of her money and valuables. She was laid to rest alongside her parents and siblings in the family mausoleum.

Claims that the Lemp Mansion is haunted go back for decades. As a restaurant and an inn since the 1970s, it has had many customers pass through its doors. A common claim is the sensation of being watched or at least accompanied by an unseen presence, particularly in the rooms where the deaths took place. It makes complete sense that these would have been the most paranormally active rooms.

The furniture has a tendency to move around by itself. Then there are the sightings of Charles Lemp, whom visitors have encountered throughout the building. Shadow figures are said to walk at all hours of the day and night, according to numerous eyewitness accounts. An archetypal phantom lady in white has been seen by more than one person. Some have theorized this to be the ghost of Julia Lemp, keeping a watchful eye on her former home.

Phantom odors also abound. In contrast to the more pleasant olfactory phenomena seen in other hauntings, some parts of Lemp Mansion are stricken with a foul stench that is said to be somewhat akin to rotting flesh. While filming the TV show *Ghost Hunters* at the mansion in 2010, a repulsed Grant Wilson noted: "You couldn't make that smell. It's disgusting.… It was almost like a wall of just this phenomenal stench." He went on to describe the smell as being like "someone who hadn't showered in a long time, combined with decomposition. I've smelled a lot of gross stuff as a plumber, but this topped it all."

Although several deaths have taken place within the house, as already noted, none of the bodies were kept inside Lemp Mansion long enough for the process of decomposition to advance. This makes the foul odor reported by Wilson and others harder to explain. If it was attributable to natural causes, then the stink ought to grow steadily worse, until its source was finally located and dealt with. Instead, the smell comes and goes with no apparent rhyme or reason. It's been theorized that the spirit responsible for it is using the stench as a means of pushing people out of its space, essentially as a means of intimidation or control.

A 2014 episode of the TV show *Ghost Adventures* covered the Lemp haunting. Host Zak Bagans opened the show by referencing a 1980 *Life* magazine claim that the Lemp Mansion was one of the most haunted places in the United States. Questioning Betsy Burnett-Belanger, who at the time had spent 18 years at the Lemp Mansion, about her paranormal experiences within its walls, he is told that she sees something "almost every time."

Both she and Bagans report feeling dizzy while recording footage in the room where William Lemp Sr. shot himself. In what is presumably a bad-taste attempt to shock the viewer, there are scenes depicting a William Lemp–look-alike holding a gun to his own head and the bloodsplattered aftermath. Bagans wonders whether the dead man's spirit might have lingered in the mansion and later witnessed the suicides of Billy and Charles.

The wife of the property's most recent owner had a disconcerting encounter with the mansion's resident ghosts while cleaning the upstairs rooms one day. Behind her back, every single painting was turned face down in the span of just a few seconds.

The mansion has been featured in three TV shows about the paranormal: *Living with the Dead, Ghost Adventures,* and *Ghost Hunters.*

Studying a map of the caves and tunnels that underlie the Lemp Mansion and associated brewery complex, host Bagans posits that the caves may first have been used by the Cherokee and that this may be connected with the string of tragedies that befell the family—in other words, some kind of indigenous American curse.

The show's director of photography, Mike Stodden, encountered something disconcerting while shooting footage in the caves. In an apparent case of apportation, the movement of an item from one location to another by paranormal means, the spectacles he tucked into his pocket disappeared, only to reappear 50 yards in front of him on the ground.

This episode of *Ghost Adventures* is notable for the insight it gives into the monolithic interior of the Lemp Brewery. The viewer gains an appreciation of how the massive brick structure, now crumbling and all but abandoned, must once have teemed with hundreds of staff as they hustled to brew gallon upon gallon of Lemp beer for the thirsty drinkers in St. Louis. There are accounts of apparitions being seen and poltergeist-type phenomena taking place inside the old brewery. The sound of what may have been Native chanting and doors slamming of their own accord made for an eventful episode.

Photos of the inside of the mansion show off its period elegance with fine furniture, woodwork, and lighting.

Although I was unable to gain access to the brewery interior, I was fortunate enough to spend a night in the Lemp Mansion during the spring of 2024. Accompanied by two fellow paranormal investigators, Erin and Mike, we took rooms on the top floor, which would once have belonged to the servants who attended on Charles Lemp. Our two rooms were interconnected, separated only by doors, and we spent much of the evening trying to connect with whatever spirits might be around.

My bedroom for the evening is said to be haunted by a child named Zeke. There are several different stories purporting to tell the origin of this physically or developmentally handicapped boy: a child born out of wedlock or the result of an extramarital affair (and therefore a shameful Lemp family secret) is a common theme. Another version has Zeke being an orphan. The only certainty is that no records or documentation has thus far been uncovered that proves his existence.

Zeke's story has been told often enough that it may possibly have taken on a life of its own, in the manner of a thought-form capable of interacting with the living. This spirit—if a spirit it truly is—is sometimes said to knock and tap on the walls of the third floor. After bedding down, I slept soundly throughout the night, lulled to sleep by the sound of traffic passing by the Lemp Mansion on the busy highway outside. There were several creaks and thuds that may have been the building settling down for the night.

On the other hand, they might not.

If Zeke actually exists, he did not speak into the voice recorder I left running throughout the night. My companions and I experienced none of the other ghostly phenomena that are said to take place at the Lemp Mansion, though we did enjoy a delicious meal in the restaurant.

The following morning, Mike and I were carrying our suitcases down to the car. Erin heard the sound of a child speaking, though she couldn't make out any words. Shrugging, she assumed that the guests in the only other occupied room in the mansion that night included a kid.

A few minutes later, one of those other guests emerged from his room and introduced himself to Erin in the common hallway on the third floor. The pair began chatting. Had Erin heard the sound of a baby crying, the man wondered? Because he and his wife just had, clearly and distinctly, a few seconds before he opened his door.

There were no children or babies staying at the Lemp Mansion that night, and none had arrived that same morning. If the sounds that Erin and our fellow guest heard really had come from a kid, then it must have been one who was long since dead.

At its core, the story of the Lemp family is not one of commercial success followed by financial collapse, nor is it one of haunted mansions, caves, and breweries. The true focus should be on those members of the family who took their own lives because of the intense grief and undoubted mental illness that they suffered. We can only hope that the Lemps have finally found the peace that so eluded them during their lifetimes.

GEF, THE TALKING MONGOOSE

The annals of psychical research are littered with instances of animal ghosts. The Tower of London is said to be haunted by a phantom black bear, the appearance of which has shocked even the most hardened guards at this famously haunted fortress.

It has often been remarked that the British are a nation of dog lovers, which may be why tales of ghostly dogs abound. Although many of them appear to be the spirits of faithful companions, often sticking around after their earthly lives have ended in order to keep a watchful eye on their grieving humans, not all such hauntings are quite so nice.

Tales of supernatural black dogs such as the Barguest, the Shuck, and the Shag have long been a part of the folkloric tradition, where they are said to lurk in cemeteries and prowl the coast at night. Legend has it that the appearance of these hellhounds may herald death, though it must also be pointed out that smugglers encouraged such stories as a means of keeping particular stretches of the coast clear of human interference, enabling them to engage in their illicit activities after dark. On the other hand, encounters with black phantom dogs have been reported for hundreds of years and have taken place under circumstances that have nothing to do with smuggling or any other illegal activity.

The black dogs are sometimes said to have glowing red eyes, and, even more bizarrely, to shape-shift into another animal form right before the astonished witness's eyes. This subset of accounts strongly implies that, whatever these entities are, they are unlikely to be the spirit of man's dearly departed best friend and may be something altogether stranger.

An equally bizarre animal-centric haunting was investigated by Harry Price, who would gain infamy from his association with the haunting of Borley Rectory. Even by Price's standards, what came to be called the haunting of Cashen's Gap (known also as Doarlish Cashen) was unprecedented, and all because of a mysterious creature named Gef, the Talking Mongoose.

James and Margaret Irving stand in front of their house in Cashen's Gap.

The Isle of Man can be found in the channel athwart the British mainland and Ireland. In 1931, it was a lonely and windswept place. Although not a part of the British Isles, its population was British citizens. Many of them made a living by farming. Such was the case with the Irving family: James Irving; his wife, Margaret; and their 13-year-old daughter, Voirrey. The Irvings lived in a farmhouse situated halfway up the slope of a small mountain. They lived with a menagerie of farm animals and their faithful sheepdog, Mona. Cashen's Gap was an isolated place, with no other houses for at least 1 mile in any direction. One is forced to wonder what effects this had on the mental health of the Irving family.

In the fall of 1931, a strange animal suddenly turned up at the farm. Initially, the Irvings mistook it for a weasel. At first, the creature could not speak, but the newcomer proved to be a skilled mimic, imitating the clucks, moos, and screeches of the nearby farmyard animals.

According to the Irvings, the mongoose then finagled its way into the structure of the house, where it took up residence in the walls and the ceiling. The sounds of its claws skittering against wood could be heard as it ran around the house at all hours of the day and night.

Using nursery rhymes as a guide, Voirrey set about teaching the creature to speak, something at which it quickly became adept. In a shrill, high-pitched voice, the mongoose declared its name to be Gef (pronounced *Jeff*, in the same way that *gif* is pronounced *jiff*). Gef had quite the story to tell. According to the mongoose, it had been born in India back in 1852, then traveled on to the Isle of Man aboard a ship.

1932 brought the first newspaper reporter to Cashen's Gap. Having come a long way from the mainland in order to cover a decidedly oddball story, the reporter interviewed the Irvings and was subsequently rewarded by hearing the sound of Gef's voice speaking from somewhere behind the walls. At that time, Gef was still being referred to as a weasel rather than a mongoose. In order to get attention (or, sometimes, apparently just for the hell of it), Gef pounded loudly on the walls and ceilings, startling the Irvings out of whatever they happened to be doing at the time.

The mongoose would sometimes up and disappear out of the blue, claiming later to have been making its rounds of the island by hitchhiking on the vehicles of unsuspecting drivers. When it returned to the Irving household, Gef regaled them with gossip and the latest goings-on in the vicinity.

As time went on, the Irvings discovered that Gef had a most un-mongoose-like taste for human food, including the pickings from hearty fried breakfasts and sweet treats. As Gef became more talkative, it showed a propensity for switching in and out of different languages at will. Even by the standards of a human being, it would have been a polymath. For a mongoose, this level of intelligence was simply unbelievable.

Voirrey Irving took it upon herself to teach the mongoose-like creature to speak.

Presumably in an attempt to cause mischief, Gef had a penchant for throwing stones at the Irvings when they were trying to sleep. In addition to being an uninvited houseguest, it was also far from well behaved. While the entity did hurl and smash crockery and sometimes threatened to hurt the family, its behavior never escalated beyond the level of being a nuisance.

Equally remarkable were the reports that Gef had taken to reading the newspapers whenever Mr. Irving left them lying around. By 1936, Gef had become the darling of the very same print media it so eagerly consumed. The reality (or charlatanry) underpinning the case of the talking mongoose was the equivalent of water cooler talk. Skeptics pointed out that during efforts to objectively investigate the case, Gef had never put in an appearance for any outside observer when they came to visit. Gef seemed to reserve that for the family with which it lived and to whom it was a constant source of both wonder and bewilderment—or so they claimed.

"Gef, Talking Mongoose, Stirs England, Has London Adither," declared the Saturday, November 14, 1936, edition of the *Louisville Courier Journal,* shrewdly noting that "when the reporters swarmed down to

Irving's cottage to see the little animal, he was extremely reticent. In fact, he was completely absent, even though they waited all night to see him."

Why would such an extraordinary entity reveal its existence to the Irvings but not to the world at large? Interviewed for the same article, Mrs. Irving noted that "he has often told me he doesn't like newspaper reporters."

Fair enough, yet Gef apparently also had a dislike for scientists and psychic researchers, as it refused to show itself to Harry Price or Nandor Fodor when they came to Cashen's Gap to investigate the claims in person. Indeed, Gef was apparently no fan of Harry Price, telling the Irvings that the famous ghost hunter was too skeptical for its liking and should not be allowed near the house. Price came anyway. There was neither hide nor hair of the entity until he left, at which point Gef returned in full force, gleeful now that the object of its ire had gone away empty-handed.

Price had initially been reluctant to visit Cashen's Gap in person and had sent a fellow psychic researcher to scout out the case in his stead. That researcher heard the voice of Gef talking to him inside the house (though he never saw the mongoose itself) and was impressed that the entity seemed privy to information it could not have known through conventional means. It could recount specific actions that

A drawing of Gef, the talking mongoose, made in 1936 by artist George Scott.

Price's emissary had taken while far away from the farmhouse. This had bolstered Price's willingness to go Gef-hunting in person. Although Gef failed to put in an appearance for the great ghost hunter, Price would ultimately benefit in other ways from his involvement with the case.

1939 brought Britain's entry into the Second World War. On the Isle of Man, the new focus on wartime life took the spotlight away from Gef. Within two years, the talking mongoose was gone—seemingly for good.

Today, almost a century after Gef put in its first appearance, students of the case are left with the question: what exactly was going on in that run-down farmhouse at Cashen's Gap? Some considered Gef to be some sort of ghost or trickster spirit, though that seems unlikely considering the fact that the creature left hairs behind for scientists to examine. When analyzed, they turned out to belong not to a mongoose but to a dog—possibly Mona, the sheepdog.

Mr. Irving dismissed out of hand the notion that he was living in a haunted house. Yet if the powers and faculties attributed to Gef are to be believed, then how best to explain a talking mongoose that was supposedly able to read minds and learn multiple languages in a very short period of time?

Gef itself played both sides against the middle. At one point, it denied being a spirit or ghost. The mongoose attributed its precognitive abilities (knowing what was going on far outside the walls of the farmhouse) as being simply "magic." Yet on another occasion, Gef claimed the opposite, admitting to being a spirit that haunted the Irving family. Gef's story was nothing if not consistently inconsistent. The entity, whatever it really was, was by no means a reliable historian.

In 1945, Mr. Irving died in the farmhouse. Margaret, his widow, moved out. Gef completely ceased to speak after the remaining Irvings had moved on to pastures new, leaving the next tenants of the house undisturbed. The farmhouse was demolished in 1971, with hardly a trace left of its ever having existed. For quite some time, Doarlish Cashen had developed the reputation of being a dark and haunted place, a stigma that the house could never shake off. Locals tended to avoid it whenever possible, even some of those who dismissed the idea of a talking mongoose.

In 1947, the owner of the property trapped what he thought might have been Gef and killed it with a sharp blow to the head. Photographs of him holding up a very large, slender creature's body were taken for

This photo shows plaster casts of Gef's footprints and teeth marks. The photo was published in *The Haunting of Cashen's Gap: A Modern "Miracle" Investigated* by Harry Price and R. S. Lambert.

posterity and published in the local newspaper. Yet the dimensions of the dead animal, which was never positively identified, did not match the Irvings' descriptions of Gef.

Was Gef real or simply a contrivance of the Irving family? In his written account of the case, Harry Price made note of the lonely upbringing that Voirrey Irving underwent. With the exception of school, she had little in the way of friendship from children her own age or anywhere close to it. Most of her formative years were spent in the company of her parents and the family dog. Not given to losing herself in books, once her chores were done, Voirrey instead occupied herself with long and regular hikes across the nearer parts of the island. Lacking attention and human interaction, who could blame her if she had made up the colorful Gef in order to draw the spotlight of the outside world upon herself and her family?

One possible explanation for the vocal phenomena is ventriloquism: at least one observer accused Voirrey Irving of creating Gef's utterances herself via trickery—"throwing her voice," in the parlance of the time. However, it must be noted that Gef's voice was heard by multiple different witnesses, and on some occasions, this happened when Voirrey was not inside the house.

While ventriloquism may seem like a reasonable hypothesis with regard to the vocal phenomena, throwing one's voice is a skill that needs to be learned and practiced repeatedly if it is to stand a chance of fooling an audience—especially if they aren't in on the joke. How likely is it that Voirrey Irving had the means and the opportunity to master this skill in 1931? There was no internet, no YouTube lessons for her to study. Nor do we have any evidence to prove that somebody coached her on the art of ventriloquism. This wasn't something she or anybody else in her circumstances would simply be good at from the outset.

The haunting of Cashen's Gap—if a haunting it truly was—bears many of the hallmarks of a poltergeist case.

There is also the matter of the pounding on the walls of the Irving home. One possible explanation is that offered up by the Fox sisters of Hydesville, often credited as the pioneers of the Spiritualism movement in the 1920s. They claimed to have cracked their joints, primarily their toes and knuckles, in order to generate the loud knocks and raps that purportedly came from spirit communicators.

The haunting of Cashen's Gap—if a haunting it truly was— bears many of the hallmarks of a poltergeist case. The focus would appear to be the youngest member of the Irving household, Voirrey, who, like so many poltergeist foci, was on the cusp of puberty when the phenomena began. The disembodied voices, knocking, stone throwing, and other disturbances fit the established poltergeist parameters remarkably well. The fact that no subsequent tenants of Doarlish Cashen were plagued by Gef once the Irvings moved out is also suggestive that something about their family dynamic acted as a catalyst for the strange occurrences.

In the Enfield Poltergeist case, which is covered elsewhere in this book, the titular entity was said to be the spirit of a former resident of the house who had died of a brain hemorrhage while sitting in a chair downstairs. Could "Gef" have been something similar—the discarnate spirit of a human being who either appeared in the form of a mongoose (i.e., a psychic projection) or had somehow possessed the body of a flesh-and-blood animal?

Doarlish Cashen, the farmstead, and Voirrey Irving.

CLUE TO MYSTERY OF "TALKING" WEASEL.

Schoolgirl May Have Powers of Ventriloquism.

FROM OUR OWN REPORTER.

Peel (Isle of Man), Monday.

DOES the solution of the mystery of the "man-weasel" of Doarlish Cashen lie in the dual personality of the 13-year-old girl, Voirrey Irving? That is the question that leaps to my mind after hearing the piercing and uncanny voice attributed to the elusive little yellow beast with a weasel's body.

An article published in the January 11, 1932, issue of the Manchester *Dispatch* declared the whole story of a talking weasel to be nothing more than a trick involving ventriloquism.

Alternatively, was Gef an *egregore*—a thought-form created and given form at the behest of one of the Irving family (most likely Voirrey) or the collective beliefs of them all?

While these hypotheses may sound far-fetched, it must be borne in mind that none of them is significantly stranger than the notion of a talking mongoose!

The tufts of hair that were ostensibly donated by Gef for analysis turned out to be nothing remotely like those of a mongoose, being instead of canine origin. Neither is photographic analysis helpful in determining the validity of this phenomenon. None of the photographs purporting to show Gef, two of which show some kind of animal sitting on a wooden rail fence, are of sufficient resolution to prove the identity of the creature. It could just as likely be a cat, a stoat, a weasel, or a number of other animals as opposed to a mongoose.

Even Harry Price, the consummate showman who loved nothing more than to be involved with any outlandish story that might generate publicity on his behalf, remained unconvinced of Gef's reality. In true Price style, that didn't stop him from cashing in by coauthoring a book on the subject. *The Haunting of Cashen's Gap* stops short of declaring the Gef phenomenon to be truly paranormal in nature, something that Price would do in other cases, such as his works on Borley Rectory.

At the time of writing, Gef is enjoying a modest resurgence in popularity due to the release of the 2023 movie *Nandor Fodor and the Talking Mongoose*, starring Simon Pegg and Minnie Driver. Gef is voiced by the author Neil Gaiman. The film is something that would almost certainly have mortified Voirrey Irving, who relocated to the British mainland and did everything she possibly could to distance herself from all things relating to Gef. Far from cashing in on her intimate connection with the case, after leaving the Isle of Man, she maintained a low profile for the rest of her life, right up until her death in 2005.

Had the Cashen's Gap case arisen in the twenty-first century, it would have been an easy one to confirm or dispel. After supplying the

Irvings with something as simple as a cell phone, we could have high-resolution still images and video footage of the notoriously camera-shy mongoose and audio recordings of its voice. On the other hand, we might have absolutely nothing at all if the so-called haunting was as fraudulent as some people were convinced it truly was.

Yet, if the whole thing was a hoax, then it should be noted that none of the Irvings ever confessed to it. So far as the record goes, not one member of the family deviated from their story to their dying day. There is no longer a farm at Cashen's Gap to be investigated. All of the principal participants are long dead. The only thing that remains is the mystery and the ongoing speculation that surrounds it.

Perhaps that is for the best. One suspects that Gef, for one, might have preferred it that way.

THE PHILIP EXPERIMENT

Question: When is a ghost not a ghost?

Answer: When it has been intentionally created.

As someone who has been investigating claims of the paranormal for 30 years, I've come to believe that many field researchers are in danger of becoming a little bit lazy when it comes to theories and hypotheses concerning the nature of ghosts.

The default explanation most of us tend to jump to is that "ghosts equal dead people."

To be fair, we grow up biased, steeped in spooky stories of restless spirits and vengeful specters. We read about haunted mansions and castles in books such as this one. We watch TV ghost hunters creep through dark hallways, tinted green in night-vision lenses or other colors through the multicolored spectra of the thermal imaging camera. When voices turn up on audiotape or digital recorders, seemingly talking to us out of thin air, we assume that these are the disembodied voices of the dead. It makes sense. Based on the steady diet of ghost stories on which many people are raised, there's a logical consistency to thinking that.

But there are other explanations, no less outlandish than the possibility of communication with the spirits of the deceased. During the 1970s, a team of Canadian researchers set out to explore one of those possibilities in detail by literally creating a ghost out of their collected imaginations.

Thus was the so-called Philip Experiment born.

The Toronto Society for Psychical Research was a group of volunteers with a passion for all things paranormal and a common goal. They came together with the intention of engineering a haunting of their very own in as controlled an environment as it was possible to create. No actual human being, living or dead, would be involved. The process was more akin to creating a character in a role-playing game such as Dungeons and Dragons, but rather than rolling for stats that would define the character's various strengths and weaknesses, the eight participants in the Philip Experiment would instead write their titular entity's backstory as though they were plotting a piece of short fiction.

Philip Aylesford would be a thought-form, or thoughtform, willed into life by sheer concentration and focus. The blueprint that the team worked from was an outline of Philip's entirely fictional life. He was conceived as a nobleman who lived in England during the seventeenth century. Spicing things up a little, Philip was given both a wife and a mistress. This love triangle turned ugly when Philip's wife found out about his lover, accusing her of witchcraft and causing her to be burned alive at the stake. (The Philip Group was apparently unaware that during the English witch trials, most of those convicted were hanged rather than burned.)

In the researchers' fabricated story, the fictional Philip had a mistress who was accused of being a witch by Philip's wife to give the tale a tragic spin.

Philip had stood by and done nothing while his girlfriend was accused, tried, and executed. Racked with grief and self-loathing at having done nothing to prevent his wife from exacting her revenge, he could finally stand it no longer: he jumped from the upper story of his home and was killed instantly on hitting the ground.

It was a tragic tale, and intentionally so. The remorse, guilt, and violent death by suicide were all fodder for a haunting. Students of the paranormal have long believed that such intense emotions—particularly in the context of a life ending so abruptly and brutally—can be key factors in the creation of a ghost. Why should the imaginary Philip's story be any different?

Once the broad strokes of his life and death were written down, the participants gathered together and got to work. The first order of business was for them to collectively visualize Philip in their minds' eye, trying to picture the dead nobleman with as much detail and clarity as they could muster. Some readers do this instinctively, conceptualizing characters and settings in the novels they read down to the most minute detail: clothing, hair, expression, skin tone, and much, much more. Behavior and mannerisms were decided upon. Philip's personality and temperament were discussed in depth, along with his various tastes and proclivities.

Consensus was key. In addition to his physical, intellectual, and emotional characteristics, the participants formed opinions on his financial and business affairs, his religious beliefs, and even his medical history.

By the time the process was fully underway, the eight sitters knew more about this imaginary man of the seventeenth century than they did about some of their own friends. Had they chosen to do so, the men and women who originated the Philip Experiment could have written a historical novel based on the sheer amount of research and preparation they did before trying to bring their subject to life.

The practical phase of the experiment began with the group members entering a state of meditation, a state in which they focused their concentration on Philip and attempted to infuse him with the energy he would need in order to manifest.

At first, there was little progress. If anybody was hoping that Philip would materialize out of thin air as a fully formed full-body apparition, they were to be disappointed. With hindsight, it is easy to see how the lack of developments could have been disheartening. Nonetheless, they persevered. In an effort to reach out to Philip, the group began to hold regular séances.

Their perseverance paid off.

Philip arrived with little fanfare, coming in the form of a knock on the table around which they all joined hands. More knocks followed. Although the group trusted one another implicitly, it was noted that the knocks happened when the hands of all participants were clearly visible. When

After thoroughly crafting their fictional seventeenth-century Englishman's backstory, the researchers meditated on their creations and then held a séance to see if they could generate a spirit out of literally nothing.

his name was spoken aloud, "Philip"—if that's who was knocking—responded with a loud bang on the tabletop.

With Philip now knocking enthusiastically, the next logical step was clear: using those knocks to answer yes/no questions. This allowed for a primitive form of communication, in the vein of the once popular game 20 Questions. Philip would be asked certain things and would respond in the affirmative or negative with either one knock or two. Rather than sounding from the same place consistently, Philip's knocks seemed to follow the questioner around the table. Whoever was asking something at any given time would feel the response coming from the table in front of them, often on the underside of the table itself.

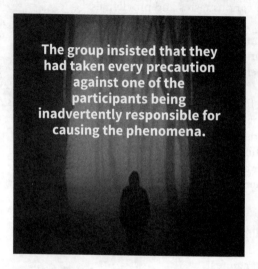

The group insisted that they had taken every precaution against one of the participants being inadvertently responsible for causing the phenomena.

The Philip Experiment group took care to keep the atmosphere lighthearted and convivial rather than solemn. It wasn't a case of them not taking the situation seriously. Rather, they believed that the positive energies created from joyful moods were more conducive to fueling the phenomena. Some paranormal investigators still adopt this attitude today, separating themselves from those who choose to explore the darker side of the paranormal realm.

Among the several methodological flaws that call the Philip Experiment into question, arguably the most obvious involves the true identity of the communicator. For argument's sake, if we stipulate that the knocks and raps were paranormal in nature (as opposed to being consciously or subconsciously produced by one or more of the participants), then it becomes problematic that nobody knows for sure who or what was making them. Was this Philip, the paranormal construct? Possibly. Certainly, the Philip Experiment group thought so, which was probably a product of their bias, at least in part. The group insisted that they had taken every precaution against one of the participants being inadvertently responsible for causing the phenomena. However, having invested more than a year's worth of time and energy into the project, the members were primed to *want* Philip to make contact with them. Nobody likes having their time wasted, nor do they like having the perception of egg on their face. It is possible that in their own subconscious ways, one or more of the participants may have been "helping the phenomena along." If this was the case, it was less likely to have been conscious fraud but, rather, subconscious wish fulfillment at work.

Back in the late 1990s, internet chat rooms were all the rage. For readers who are too young to remember them, these were private websites used for text-based conversations with friends and strangers. Yahoo hosted thousands of wildly popular chat rooms that allowed people to virtually meet others, all from the comfort of their own homes. It seemed like a great idea at first. However, the big flaw was that the communicators had to take one another on faith. Adults sometimes posed as children and vice versa. Men pretended to be women. Sometimes there were bad outcomes, as the chat rooms were used by stalkers, pedophiles, and even murderers to connect with their victims. (Ultimately, Yahoo shut the chat rooms down for good.)

By the same token, the entity that answered to "Philip" was of an equally unproven identity. While it's possible that it was indeed what the experimenters intended it to be, a thought-form or *tulpa,* it is also possible that Philip was in actuality a guise for an opportunistic entity that was role-playing the part for its own amusement or to further its own goals. After all, at the end of the day, there is only so much that can be gleaned from yes/no answers. Writing in *Conjuring Up Philip: An Adventure in Psychokinesis,* Iris M. Owen and Margaret Sparrow nailed their colors to the mast by declaring that the Toronto group members "do not believe that their communicator was a discarnate spirit. Their common focus of attention was an invented character, a product of their own imaginations."

As time went on, Philip seemed to grow in strength. He arrived quickly when summoned. The table that was used to communicate with him seemed to take on a life of its own, dancing and standing up on one or two legs in the manner of the Victorian-era table-tipping craze. Video footage of these sessions is available on YouTube, and the reader is invited to make up their own mind about the paranormality of what took place.

Might it be that the spirit of the fictional Philip was reified by the collective thoughts of the experimenters as a kind of *tulpa* or thought-form?

The group used these sessions to add further nuance to Philip's backstory, asking questions about his personal and professional life, then integrating this new data into

Philip's imaginary history, just as a biographer would fill in details about the life of their subject. Essentially, that is what the group finally produced: Philip's biography, as partially dictated by the entity itself.

As it seemed to grow in power, the entity no longer restricted itself to the table. Philip started to affect electrical devices, accepting responsibility for causing the lights to flicker upon request.

Despite their best efforts, the group never achieved their Holy Grail: getting Philip to physically materialize in front of them so that they might capture his image on camera. Unfortunately, the Philip Experiment ended not with a bang but with something of a whimper. The participants were convinced that something truly anomalous had occurred, most likely involving psychokinesis or telekinesis—the notion that objects can be moved or touched by the power of the human mind, either directly or indirectly. Afterward, other groups went on to conduct similar experiments, replicating the results of the Philip Experiment to some extent. Yet ultimately, it led nowhere, and despite the optimism of those involved that it would lay the groundwork for a major breakthrough in psychic research, that has yet to be proved correct. The Philip Experiment remains one of the more interesting dead ends in the paranormal field, though it may not stay that way forever.

The existence of tulpas, egregores, and other types of thoughtforms has long been a part of the spiritual philosophy of many cultures, particularly those of Tibet. The concept has been slowly gaining traction in the West for decades. Paranormal investigators now consider such artificially created entities as a potential explanation in certain cases of so-called haunting. This paradigm shift owes a great deal to the pioneering work of the men and women of the Toronto Society for Psychical Research and an enigmatic being by the name of Philip Aylesford.

TO THE LAST BREATH

More than a century before COVID-19 tore a swath through the global population, another deadly pestilence stalked the face of the Earth. It, too, took lives by the millions. That disease was tuberculosis, and, contrary to popular belief, it remains a significant health threat today. It kills more people annually than AIDS, an estimated 1.25 million deaths in 2024. In 2020, the only other infectious disease that claimed more victims was COVID-19.

Tuberculosis is a particularly cruel malady. It is spread by tiny aerosolized bacterial droplets in the form of coughing, sneezing, kissing, and even spitting. When one of these droplets enters the unsuspecting victim's mucous membranes, they become infected.

The disease can lie dormant within the body for an extended period of time. Once it is activated, tuberculosis can spread through the lungs to the spine, the brain, the joints, and other parts of the body. The infected person begins to lose weight at an accelerated rate, gaining a wasted, sallow appearance, a symptom that led to TB's historical name of consumption.

Fevers, chills, and night sweats are common symptoms. As the disease progresses, a productive cough can appear, resulting in the spitting up of frank red blood as the body attempts to clear the lungs of tubercles, masses of tuberculosis-induced tissue that form in the lower airway. Death is usually caused by septic shock or respiratory failure, and it can be an ugly death indeed, with the patient expelling streams of blood from the nose and mouth as they fight to breathe.

Fortunately, in the present day, we have treatments and preventative measures to help combat tuberculosis. In addition to vaccination, there is personal protective equipment to help safeguard those who may be exposed to the disease and medications such as rifampin that are highly effective against it.

The situation was very different a hundred years ago. Tuberculosis was a familiar and feared presence among turn-of-the-century Americans. A string of dedicated healthcare facilities called sanatoriums sprang up across the country, offering care specifically for those suffering from the so-called wasting disease, consumption. Sanatoriums could be found in places reputed to have clean air and a revitalizing environment, towns such as Glenwood Springs, Colorado, where the notorious gunfighter John "Doc" Holliday of O.K. Corral fame breathed his last.

The state of Kentucky was hit particularly hard by tuberculosis. In 1910, after suitable land was located and funding secured, one such facility was established in Louisville. It inherited a name, Waverley Hill,

Opened in 1910 as a hospital to accommodate 50 to 60 tuberculosis patients at a time, the Waverly Hills Sanatorium closed in 1961, thanks to the advent of streptomycin to stave off the disease.

from the former landowner but would become known as the Waverly Hills Sanatorium. This was not at first the iconic behemoth of a structure that so many are familiar with today. It was a smaller hospital with multiple pavilions, caring for men, women, children, and African Americans separately.

As time passed, there came a greater influx of patients, causing the facility to expand in order to meet the need until it was more akin to a small village than a hospital. With the necessity for further growth, in 1924, work began on a much larger, million-dollar sanatorium at the same site. Although it was meant to have a 400-bed capacity, that very much depended upon staffing, and Waverly Hills saw some lean times over the years. It weathered the storms of two world wars and the Great Depression when both financing and adequate staffing were problematic.

Caring for those who suffered from tuberculosis could be a risky endeavor. The physicians, nurses, medical staff, and support personnel at Waverly Hills were exposed to an increased risk of infection. Some contracted the disease themselves and became patients at the very same facility in which they had until recently worked.

Between 1926 and the late 1940s, treatment for tuberculosis was either rudimentary or experimental. The basic mainstays were fresh air, fresh air, and still more fresh air. Patient beds were pushed out onto the balcony after sunrise, allowing their occupants to partake of as much natural ventilation as possible. In many cases, the patients were directed to lie flat on their backs for most of the day, with the intent of relieving as much pressure on the lungs as possible.

A healthy diet of fresh foods was the norm. Patients were fed well when they could stomach it, and those who were capable were permitted to walk around and exercise.

Sunlight was believed to be another weapon in the arsenal against tuberculosis. The uppermost floor at Waverly Hills (the fifth) contained the solarium. It was a place for patients to bask in the sun's rays when the weather was suitably accommodating. When it was not, there were sunlamps on hand to mimic the effects of natural sunlight.

Not all procedures aimed at treating the disease were as harmless as the triad of fresh air, supine bed rest, and sunlight. Sandbagging was the name given to attaching bags of sand to either side of the patient's chest. The logic behind this was that it would help to develop the muscles of respiration, strengthening them in a similar manner to that of

Richard explores the solarium at Waverly Hills.

performing bench presses at the gym. A patient could be sandbagged for hours at a time with little or no respite.

Waverly Hills possessed an operating theater in which a range of different surgeries were carried out at the discretion of physicians. These included deliberately introducing air into one side of the chest in order to collapse the lung, thereby generating a condition called pneumothorax. The hope was that by doing so, the deflated lung would be able to rest and recuperate. (There is also the small matter of the patient losing half of their ability to exchange oxygen and carbon dioxide—hardly conducive to good health.)

More ominous still was the surgical removal of multiple ribs on one side of the chest, a procedure also intended to allow the tuberculosis-infested lung to heal. This was of questionable value at best and carried risks of its own, such as bleeding, infection, and potential septic shock.

The x-ray, a relatively new medical technology that became widespread after 1900, was used to monitor the spread of tuberculosis within the lungs. It was an invaluable tool on which clinicians based a number of their treatment choices.

Waverly Hills was equipped with a morgue. Autopsies were routinely performed on deceased patients by the same physicians who staffed the sanatorium as part of their medical duties. Elements of it still survive today. Visitors have developed a habit of crawling into the same enclosures that were once used to store the bodies of the newly dead.

By the end of the Second World War, America's need for the institution of the sanatorium was beginning to wane. Tuberculosis deaths were going down. The advent of dedicated medications to combat the disease meant that the spread of TB was also diminishing. In the summer of 1961, Waverly Hills closed its doors as a sanatorium for the last time. They opened again soon after in a different capacity: a care home for senior citizens stricken with dementia. It operated in this capacity for the next 20 years until being forcibly shut down by the State of Kentucky because of unacceptable conditions for those who were living there.

> Anybody who has ever stood in front of Waverly Hills and looked up at the blank, sightless windows knows that the building looks sinister.

The property went through several different owners in succession. Each subsequent owner had their own plans for the site, but none ever came to fruition—not even the one intended to build the world's largest statue of Jesus. Inevitably, with the building devoid of occupants, the condition of the once state-of-the-art facility continued to deteriorate.

Anybody who has ever stood in front of Waverly Hills and looked up at the blank, sightless windows knows that the building looks sinister. The sanatorium wings branching out on either side of the main section appear to be enfolding you. It's almost as if they're preparing to sweep you up in an embrace.

If ever a building looked like it ought to be haunted, this is the one.

Ghost stories have swirled around Waverly Hills for at least the last 20 years. Some of them are built on the false premise that upward of 60,000 people died at the sanatorium during its active lifetime, a number floated by the television show *Ghost Adventures*.

This ludicrously inflated figure was questioned in 2017 by researcher and author Shannon Bradley Byers. Through her own research, assisted by others, Byers placed the estimated death toll at closer to 6,000—an entire order of magnitude less.

In the excellent *Waverly Hills Sanatorium: A History,* after reviewing records and death certificates, then crunching the numbers, historian Lynn Pohl cites the even lower figure of 3,486 deaths at Waverly Hills between 1911–1915, 1923, 1926–1940, and 1943–1960. Admittedly, there are 11 years of data missing, but even so, extrapolating from the data she has unearthed, Pohl's final total for deaths at Waverly Hills would be much closer to Byers's approximation of 6,000 than *Ghost Adventures'* 60,000.

Both Byers and Pohl deserve kudos for attempting to dispel some of the many myths surrounding Waverly Hills and to tell its story in an accurate light. One of the most reputedly haunted parts of the sanatorium is the 500-foot tunnel that slopes downward toward the base of the hill. Over the years, it has attained such nicknames as the Body Chute and the Death Tunnel, based on claims that it was dug out because of the sheer number of deaths taking place at the sanatorium; the constant parade of dead bodies was having a detrimental effect on the morale of patients and staff alike, so the tunnel was put in to serve as a clandestine method of getting the corpses of the newly deceased out of Waverly Hills with a minimum of people seeing them.

It's a creepy and ghoulish story and one that has a partial basis in fact. Bodies were sometimes sent out of the facility via the tunnel,

winched down in a cable car. Yet this was not the reason for the tunnel's existence, and according to Pohl's research, it didn't happen nearly as often as most people seem to think. The practice was stopped after the winch broke, causing the runaway car to race out of control down the tunnel and through the door and careen into the outside world.

In reality, the tunnel was installed to provide a link between the sanatorium and the power station that supplied it. In heavy rain or snow, it was also a convenient way for staff to enter and leave the sanatorium without getting soaked.

A grim view of the body chute at Waverly Hills, a 500-foot tunnel said to be riddled with ghostly presences.

With so many deaths having taken place there, it would be truly remarkable if a place like Waverly Hills was not haunted. Even so, it has developed a reputation for paranormal activity to rival that of any other place on Earth. Predictably, many rumors and legends have become interspersed with the known history, making it a challenge to separate fact from folklore where some of the stories are concerned.

One particularly outlandish story involves what's known as "the Creeper," a sinister, shadowy figure that's said to creep through the shadows along the now empty floors. On some occasions, the Creeper has even been spotted scurrying along the walls and ceilings in complete defiance of gravity. If the Creeper bears any resemblance to a human being in shape, the stories claim, then it's at best a grotesquely warped and distorted one. Its behavior is said to be predatory in nature, as though the Creeper is sneaking up on those who encounter it as a hunter would stalk their prey.

It might be tempting to simply dismiss these accounts out of hand as being nothing more than campfire-type stories, yet Waverly Hills Sanatorium isn't the only place that's said to harbor such an entity. The Randolph County Infirmary in Indiana has similar claims, as does the Graber Olive House in California. Some investigators believe that the Creeper-type entity is fast becoming a specific classification of its own. Quite what they may be, or where they might come from, remains undetermined, yet overall, the reports are increasing in number.

More common are sightings of shadow figures, both adult- and child-sized. Some appear to be playful children. Others behave in a manner consistent with medical staff, apparently still making their rounds of the sanatorium many years after it closed—and, presumably, after their own deaths. There have been a handful of non-tuberculosis deaths. Some are verifiable from records and newspaper reports. Others are not, and because some of the unproven accounts pertain to the alleged suicide of employees, I will not repeat them here.

I have been fortunate enough to investigate the sanatorium on multiple occasions. By far the biggest challenge is the sheer size of the building. Even with the luxury of having numerous personnel, it's impossible to cover everything, and one is forced to be se-

A deserted hallway at the sanatorium, an ideal place for the shadowy figure known as "the Creeper" to lurk.

Richard exploring the spooky spaces at Waverly Hills, something he has done on several occasions.

lective. Like many who are faced with the daunting opportunity of investigating Waverly Hills, I focused a great deal on the fifth floor and on the tunnel. The former solarium sits at the highest part of the building and therefore garners more than its fair share of wind, which rustles the plastic sheeting covering parts of the exterior. Despite the near-constant flapping sounds, my group connected with what purported to be several different spirit entities, including patients and a physician who claimed to feel duty bound to care for them. Interestingly enough, a handful of them denied having died at Waverly Hills, implying that what we were communicating with was some kind of remnant of a human personality, a fragment that was somehow left behind when the physical person left.

One of the more bizarre phenomena encountered at Waverly Hills is the doppelganger—an apparition of a living person. Folklore holds that if a person encounters their own doppelganger, they will die soon after. Some prefer to refer to these sightings as mimics. Whatever one chooses to call them, phantasms of the living have been documented in paranormal literature for many years. There is usually a sinister connotation, though this isn't always the case. My own doppelganger was spotted in the old Teller County Jail in Cripple Creek, Colorado, several years back; to the best of my knowledge, no harm befell me after the encounter, in which one of my colleagues saw what he swore was me standing on the upper cell block. He was shocked to find that I had been inside one of the jail cells the entire time, with another investigator guarding the door.

Doppelgangers could be phantasms that mimic a person's appearance, and they are often considered harbingers of doom.

I was mimicked again at Waverly Hills. While I was leading a small group up on the fifth floor, the other part of the team set out to explore the tunnel. As they made their way toward its entrance, which lies at the opposite end of the sanatorium and five floors down, they heard my voice speaking somewhere in the darkness up ahead. It was quite clearly me, as I was the only person with an English accent in the building that night, and all of the investigators present recognized it. How on Earth, they wondered, had I gotten down from the roof and across to the tunnel so fast?

The answer was, of course, that I hadn't. I was still up there. As the small group approached the entrance to the tunnel, my voice suddenly stopped. They shone their flashlights down into the darkness. Apart from one particularly disgruntled bat, there was nothing noteworthy down there. Whoever had spoken, it hadn't been me.

The former South Pittsburg Municipal Hospital is one of the more active locations it has been my privilege to investigate on numerous occasions.

At the time of writing, Waverly Hills remains paranormally active. It is as popular with paranormal enthusiasts and ghost hunters as it ever has been. The ghost stories bring in legions of visitors each year, yet the real point is the heroic and compassionate care that was given to so many patients during the sanatorium's life span. The old building on Paralee Drive is a crucial part of U.S. history, a time capsule that stands testament to the valor and commitment of twentieth-century healthcare workers. Fortunately, repairs and restoration work are ongoing, which means that (all being well) future generations will get to appreciate Waverly Hills Sanatorium by walking its haunted hallways in person.

In my capacity as both a paranormal researcher/author and active paramedic, I love nothing more than a haunted hospital. I feel a natural kinship with the medical professionals who dedicated their lives to serving their fellow human beings. The notion of service underpins every aspect of the healing profession, and it therefore makes complete sense why some of those doctors, nurses, technicians, and even janitors, are still making their rounds in the afterlife.

The former Old South Pittsburg Municipal Hospital is one of the more active locations it has been my privilege to investigate on numerous occasions. Situated in Tennessee, Old South Pittsburg saw limited skirmishing during the Civil War, though no grand set piece battles ever took place there. South Pittsburg retains that small-town feel, with

Southern charm and courtesy very much the order of the day. Around 3,000 people call the place home.

Seeing the need for a generalized medical facility, a trio of local physicians banded together and established the community hospital in 1959. It remained open until 1998, taking care of every medical complaint imaginable. From paper cuts to cardiac arrests, from gunshots to gut pain, the hospital saw and treated it all.

The sun finally set on the hospital in 1998. Once the last of the patients and staff were gone, the building was left to its own devices and those of its ghosts. It fell into a state of disrepair. Local children predictably knew it to be a haunted place and would break in on a dare, sometimes running up to the roof and hurling rocks down into the parking lot below.

The ghost stories that circulated around town went as far as the local police, who responded to such a call one night and spotted a shadowy individual in one of the upstairs windows. Determined to arrest the trespasser, the officers made entry (only afterward did they realize that the building had shown no signs of already having been broken into) and made a beeline for the uppermost floor.

It was empty.

Also known as Old South Pittsburg Hospital in Pittsburg, Tennessee, this is one of the most haunted places in the American South. You can book daytime or nighttime tours, too, by visiting the Old South Pittsburg Hospital Paranormal Research Center website at http://osphprc.com.

Methodically, the cops went from room to room, floor to floor, searching every nook, cranny, and stairwell for the intruder's hiding place. They found nothing at all amiss. There was no way that a living person could have gotten past them, yet the crumbling, old hospital was utterly deserted. They left nonplussed, with no explanation for the figure they had seen looking back at them from above.

Ghost stories began when the hospital was still operational. One of the doctors suffered a sudden cardiac arrest in the elevator while he was working a shift. His colleagues attempted to resuscitate him—a horrifying and traumatic experience for all concerned— but were unsuccessful. Everything that could possibly be done was done. Regrettably, resuscitative efforts ceased, and he was pronounced dead.

Completely unaware of this, a nurse returned from her vacation several days later. After stepping into the main lobby, she encountered the aforementioned doctor while entering the elevator, which was the same elevator in which he had died. She offered him a cheery greeting. There was no response. After riding the elevator up, she got out and went to her duty station—only to be hit with the emotional sledgehammer that the doctor had died while she was away.

That wasn't possible, the nurse insisted. She had just ridden the elevator with him. The sad and disbelieving faces of her colleagues told her that it was true. She had just encountered one of the hospital's resident ghosts.

The nurse turned in her notice that day. She never returned.

> **One of the most active hot spots is the nurses' station on the second floor. It is here that I saw a tall shadow figure, completely solid and larger than life, standing behind the counter where the charge nurse would have coordinated the shift....**

Not all of the spirits are as benevolent as that of the good doctor. On the third floor, individuals have been attacked by an aggressive, invisible entity that some believe to be the ghost of a former psychiatric patient. Profane electronic voice phenomena (EVPs) have been recorded in the same part of the building, implying that whoever or whatever haunts the vicinity is far from friendly.

The ground floor apartments are haunted by a former tenant of the building, who lived there with the permission of a previous owner and filled the role of security guard, handyman, and janitor all rolled into one. Jim was a happy-go-lucky type of guy, one who enjoyed smoking pot while listening to, and sometimes recording, music. He has been falsely maligned as having been an intravenous drug abuser, largely due to hypodermic needles that were discovered in his residence after his death. In reality, according to his best friend, Jim was a diabetic. His spirit likes to interact with visitors in the wing that is now known as "Jim's Area," particularly if somebody fires up one of his favorite tunes and cranks up the volume.

One of the most active hot spots is the nurses' station on the second floor. It is here that I saw a tall shadow figure, completely solid and larger than life, standing behind the counter where the charge nurse would have coordinated the shift while other nurses completed their charting and bustled about taking care of the patients' needs. The figure was simply standing there, looking right at me. It appeared to be male and stood quite still before taking a step back into the shadows and disappearing right in front of my eyes.

I needed no further convincing that the old South Pittsburg hospital was haunted. I had just come face-to-face with one of its resident spirits.

Many hospitals have a dedicated morgue. This is often located in the basement, the coolest part of the building, where members of the public are least likely to trespass. Not so South Pittsburg. Located next to the waiting room for the emergency department is a relatively small anteroom that was used to store the corpses of deceased patients. Known informally as the Body Box, it was accessible only from an exterior door that opened out to the back lot. Ambulances or hearses could back up to the door, allowing their attendants to quickly and discreetly load up the body of the deceased with minimal risk of anybody noticing what was going on—shades of the Death Tunnel at Waverly Hills Sanatorium.

The Body Box has a reputation for being paranormally active. The most common communicator is a foul-mouthed male entity named John, who likes to respond provocatively with profane responses to male questioners and crude, sexualized comments to females. My fellow in-

There have been numerous reports of verbally abusive spirits at the hospital. One of the notable ones is called "John," who shouts profanities at men and sexual comments at women.

vestigators and I tried to connect respectfully with John. His response was an unequivocal "F*** off!"

Profane, verbally abusive EVPs are common at the hospital, even when paranormal investigators are polite and friendly. Somewhat more alarming are the sudden episodes of chest pain and breaking out in a cold sweat that some visitors have experienced while in the proximity of the emergency department waiting room and the Body Box; clearly the symptoms of a heart attack, they can be extremely distressing to anybody who suffers from them. Fortunately, they tend to be resolved by putting some distance between oneself and the makeshift morgue.

> Those who say they sense a presence in this room only report good emotions; there is no darkness or negativity to be found....

Stories of monstrous dark entities are associated with the upper floors of the hospital, particularly the previously introduced Creeper; my colleagues and I uncovered no evidence to support the existence of such a thing. While there are angry and aggressive spirits at the former Old South Pittsburg Hospital, there are also welcoming and friendly ghosts with whom visitors can try to connect. Take the sweet little old lady who had a room at the far end of one wing. A long-term memory-care patient, this gentle and kindly soul was afflicted with dementia and was known to climb into the beds of other patients. There was nothing sexual about this behavior; she simply wanted to hug and cuddle, to share some love and affection with another human.

Sadly, she is said to have passed away on the floor of her hospital room one day. Her room has been kept in a very similar condition to the way it was during her lifetime. The bed is still there, along with some furniture and a few sentimental items. There are also numerous gifts, small tokens of affection brought along by well-wishers, flowers, ornaments, framed pictures, and so forth. If there's a room at the hospital where the haunting is fueled by positive emotion, such as love or affection, this would be the room.

Accounts abound of visitors lying on the bed and feeling the soft, gentle caress on their body, as if they are being stroked by a caring, reassuring hand. Those who say they sense a presence in this room only report good emotions; there is no darkness or negativity to be found in that particular section of the hospital as there tends to be in some other rooms in the psychiatric and behavioral wing.

Why is the hospital so haunted, particularly as it stands empty for long periods of time? It's easy to discount the lazy and ubiquitous explanation of the building having been built on land that originally belonged to indigenous people. This alone doesn't account for a haunting, as it applies to vast tracts of North America, whether they are reputed to be haunted or not.

Others have credited the presence of ley line junctions as a possible source for the haunting. Yet despite the fact that belief in them has long been widespread in metaphysical circles, there is no objective proof that such mystical intersections actually exist—or that, if they do, they are correlated with paranormal activity.

Some researchers have posited that underground streams and pools beneath a haunted location may play a role in significant hauntings such as that of the old South Pittsburg Hospital. Others have credited the presence of certain types of rock and stone, which underpins the famous "Stone Tape Theory." As the hospital was built in very close proximity to a mountain, that is certainly a potential explanation; so too is the near-constant influx of visitors. The hospital is kept clean and maintained by a small staff of individuals, primarily volunteers, who also chaperone regular paranormal investigations for the public and conduct research of their own.

In many ways, this location is a long-term experiment for the study of ghostly phenomena. As time goes on, the archive of documented evidence continues to accumulate. New aspects of both the history and the haunting continue to emerge, lending fresh perspective and helping to humanize the spirits of the men, women, and children who spent part of their lives within the walls of the old South Pittsburg Hospital and those who continue to do so in the afterlife.

THE ENFIELD POLTERGEIST

For most people, simply saying the words "haunted house" conjures up a set of very distinct mental images. We think of a ramshackle old mansion high on a hill, with a ghostly lady in white gliding soundlessly from room to room. Or perhaps we think of a castle, dark and forbidding, its stone hallways adorned with suits of armor and festooned with cobwebs. Of such things are classic ghost stories (not to mention a fair few Halloween decorations) made.

Yet when we look at some of the more intense, if not downright terrifying, haunted locations of the twentieth century, some of them are made all the more frightening because of their sheer *ordinariness*. One such example was an utterly ordinary-looking house: 284 Green Street in Enfield, a suburb of London. There are tens of thousands of homes just like it on housing estates all across the United Kingdom. In Britain, these domiciles are referred to as "council houses"—relatively small but affordable homes that are owned by the local government rather than the people who live in them. Collectively, they are built on council estates, and tenancy is prioritized for families with low incomes or medical conditions.

By the time summer arrived, 1977 had already proved to be a turbulent and colorful year. Punk rock band the Sex Pistols were dumped by their record label, EMI, because of their shocking behavior. On August 16, superstar singer Elvis Presley died in his bathroom at his mansion, Graceland. The cause of death was a sudden heart attack. He was 42 years old, and the world mourned his loss. Later that year, at Christmas, a science fantasy movie titled *Star Wars* would break box office records at British cinemas.

The house at 284 Green Street in Brimsdown, Enfield, London, England, looks unremarkable and not at all intimidating. Who would have guessed it is home to a terrifying spirit?

As a single parent trying to raise four children and struggling to make ends meet, 47-year-old Peggy Hodgson and her children qualified for a council house of their own.

At 13 years of age, Margaret was the oldest of the Hodgson children. Next in line was her 11-year-old sister, Janet. The girls had an 8-year-old brother named Billy. (A fourth sibling, John, was not living with the family at the time.)

There was no shortage of stress at 284 Green Street. Peggy Hodgson was doing her best under difficult circumstances, but there was no mistaking the upset and resentment that tend to accompany the breakup of almost any family. The first indicators that something strange was going on in the house began to manifest at the end of August. The poltergeist's arrival was heralded by the sound of movement in an upstairs bedroom, which Mrs. Hodgson heard and was unable to explain. It seemed relatively minor, perhaps vermin skittering across the floor, or even simply "just one of those things," as people like to tell themselves.

It was far more than that.

Approaching the bedroom, Peggy watched as a chest of drawers slid slowly across the room, completely under its own steam. Unless it was being pushed by superpowered (and invisible) mice, the rodent explanation was now out the window. By her own admission, she was terrified, and understandably so. Yet Peggy Hodgson was made of stern stuff. Refusing to be intimidated in her own house, she pushed the piece of furniture back into place. The chest of drawers slid back toward her. It became a contest of wills until, finally, whatever motive force was shoving it dug its heels in; the chest suddenly refused to be moved, no matter how hard she shoved.

Once she had calmed down a little and had some time to think things through, Peggy Hodgson came to the inescapable conclusion that her house was haunted. Matters only escalated from there. The uninvited presence in their house was an intrusive one, banging and clattering at all hours of the day and night. At her wits' end, Mrs. Hodgson brought in friends and neighbors. None could offer a rational explanation for the strange goings-on, much less help, but they did add to a steadily expanding pool of eyewitnesses. These witnesses were sympathetic, for the most part. They also had the luxury of returning to their own undisturbed homes whenever they felt like it. The Hodgsons, on the other hand, were now living in fear.

Exasperated, Peggy Hodgson picked up the phone and dialed 999. A nonplussed police officer named WPC Carolyn Heeps responded to what must have been the strangest emergency call of her career. It would be difficult to find a more credible witness than the down-to-earth constable, who later recalled having seen a chair move across the room seemingly of its own volition. Heeps looked the chair over carefully, checking for an attached fishing line or any other signs of a hoax. She found none.

Journalists came next. After a period of silence when the house was empty, the return of the Hodgsons heralded a sudden flurry of poltergeist activity. Objects flew through the air all around the terrified children. Later, skeptics and armchair quarterbacks would accuse the Hodgson children—particularly Janet and Margaret—of being behind it all, yet those who were there at 284 Green Street during the most violent outbursts were convinced that the girls were utterly petrified. If they were acting, they must have been incredibly good actresses.

Those who confidently state that the whole thing was a fraud tend to ignore the caliber of professional witnesses. Police officers and veteran news reporters ought to be capable of telling the difference between children larking around and something genuinely inexplicable. These individuals, who had based their careers upon the skills of careful observation and rational analysis, could find no cause for the strange goings-on. None of them came forward during or after the fact to say that the Hodgson family were faking the haunting.

The activity wasn't restricted to number 284. The house was a duplex. The loud knocks and forceful pounding could be heard in the house next door, a fact that was confirmed by its residents, the Nottinghams. It was the Hodgsons who bore the brunt of it all, however.

Objects would fly through the house, terrifying the children and astounding adults.

The story hit the newspapers and public radio shortly thereafter and attracted the attention of the London-based Society for Psychical Research. Formed in 1882, the SPR took on the responsibility of investigating claims of paranormal phenomena. Enfield was practically on their doorstep, and the society had just the man for the job.

Maurice Grosse was a respected engineer and inventor. Following the untimely accidental death of his daughter, Grosse had been fascinated by the subject of life after death and believed that she had been trying to communicate with him. His interest in the paranormal had led Grosse to attain membership in the Society for Psychical Research.

The scientific approach espoused by the society made it an ideal fit for Grosse and his own technical worldview. The investigator was open-minded but also maintained a healthy degree of skepticism, tending to look for a rational explanation before broaching a paranormal one. So frequent were the phenomena, however, that it didn't take long for him to become convinced of the haunting's authenticity.

Shouldering the investigative workload alone was exhausting. Grosse sought help from within the SPR's ranks and found it in the form of an author named Guy Lyon Playfair. The writer entered the picture not a moment too soon, as the frequency and intensity of phenomena at Enfield continued to escalate.

The two researchers spent more and more time at 284 Green Street, often staying late into the night. Sometimes little if anything happened at all. At other times, they were hard-pressed to keep track of everything that was going on.

Fortunately for the sake of posterity, Maurice Grosse recorded much of the alleged paranormal activity as it unfolded. Guy Playfair took extensive notes, which would later form the basis of his book *This House Is Haunted*. Given these two sources and the fact that both Grosse and Playfair were a part of the haunting from the outset—and not only stayed through the ending but also maintained contact with the Hodgsons afterward—Enfield is arguably the best documented poltergeist outbreak on record.

The tapes themselves make for fascinating listening. Grosse narrated events in a tone of voice that more often than not was both level and steadfast but occasionally became raised when stress levels rose in the household. It is difficult to listen to those recordings without feeling a thrill, caused by the possibility that one is hearing an exceptionally aggressive poltergeist manifestation at work.

One of the more alarming incidents occurred when the poltergeist yanked a gas fireplace appliance from its wall mount, pulling the metal supply pipe out along with it. Playfair heard the incident taking place and came running, only to find the fireplace lying askew on the bed. The possibility that one or even all of the Hodgson children could have been responsible for this was laughable. It required a prodigious amount of strength, such that it would have been challenging even for a fully grown man to perform.

Billy was in the room at the time and narrowly avoided being hit by the flying object. Had the 25-pound hunk of solid metal struck him, the injuries he sustained could have been catastrophic.

This raises the ominous question of whether Billy was the target—if the poltergeist had been *trying* to harm him and thankfully missed the mark, or if it was simply trying to scare the boy, in which case, the degree of finesse it had shown in missing

One of the more alarming incidents occurred when the poltergeist yanked a gas fireplace appliance from its wall mount, pulling the metal supply pipe out along with it.

him by mere inches was truly remarkable. Either way, it was a heart-stopping occurrence for all concerned. The Hodgson family had quite understandably come to fear for their safety.

Because of the pressure cooker environment within the house, it was arranged for the family to go away for a few days on a much deserved holiday. Tellingly, while the Hodgsons were away from home enjoying some fresh air and recreation, nothing paranormal happened to them or around them. The same was not true back at Green Street. Mr. and Mrs. Nottingham heard the now typical loud banging sounds coming from within the empty house next door, perhaps an indication that the poltergeist was venting its fury at being separated from its victims. On the other hand, was it possible that the entity actually just *missed them?*

In either case, when they returned, the activity came back with a vengeance. The knocks experienced by the Nottinghams were louder and more intrusive than ever. Maurice Grosse decided to use the knocks as a form of communication, using them to answer yes/no questions—one knock for no and two for yes. In this manner, strange conversations ensued. The investigators could feel the force of the knocks on the

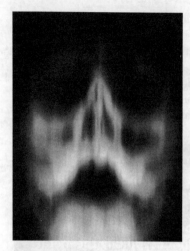

When the poltergeist spoke through Janet, he had the gruff, raspy intonation of an old man.

floorboards and in the walls. Grosse quickly ascertained that the invisible communicator might once have died inside 284 Green Street, a claim that would soon be further solidified when the poltergeist began to speak.

When the poltergeist spoke through Janet, he had the gruff, raspy intonation of an old man. Much like the case of Gef the Talking Mongoose, the question of whether Janet was putting the voice on herself has been the subject of much debate. Certainly, at least one professional ventriloquist thought so. (This explanation conveniently ignored the plethora of other physical phenomena that took place at Enfield.)

For her part, Janet vehemently denied having done so. Maurice Grosse was convinced that there was no way that a child's vocal cords could possibly have sustained that voice for any length of time, let alone repeatedly.

The voice claimed to be that of a former resident of the house, a man named Bill Wilkins, and said that he had died in a chair downstairs of a massive stroke. Bill claimed to be buried in a nearby cemetery. He professed to be looking for his wife, who was nowhere to be found.

Researchers discovered that a man of this name was indeed buried in the Lavender Hill Cemetery, just a short distance away from Green Street. He died on June 20, 1963. His wife, Ethel, died in 1972 and is buried alongside him.

Speaking through Janet, Bill acknowledged freely that he was now a ghost.

It is curious to note that Bill's spirit would have the wherewithal to know that he was buried in the local cemetery and yet remain ignorant that his wife had also passed and was interred there too. It challenges the beliefs some people hold that spirits are essentially omniscient. However, there are also multiple incidents on record in which spirits seemed to be confused regarding events in the material world, seemingly ignorant of some of the goings-on after their deaths.

The rules associated with the living do not always apply to the dead.

"Bill" apparently had a foul mouth, rarely missing an opportunity to throw out a profanity, a personal insult, or a smutty comment. Some skeptics have pointed out that the alleged poltergeist would have been a "get out of jail free card" for Janet, letting her get away with saying things to adults that would have gotten her into hot water under ordinary circumstances.

These were most assuredly *not* ordinary circumstances.

Like most poltergeist cases, as time went on, the Enfield haunting seemed to lose energy. The phenomena became less frequent and less intense. A semblance of normality returned to the house.

All these years later, the great unresolved question remains: were the events at 284 Green Street in Enfield fact, fiction, or a mixture of both?

If Enfield was indeed a genuine poltergeist case, the focus was undoubtedly Janet. She was the Hodgson child who was most tormented by the malicious force. (In fairness, it should also be pointed out that she and her sister were both caught out embellishing or outright faking activity by Playfair and Grosse.) Although some have charged either Janet herself or the entire Hodgson family of making up the whole thing—a charge that seems preposterous when viewed in light of how much evidence and how many witnesses are involved—the family gained nothing but notoriety and stress from the experience.

After the poltergeist outbreak dissipated, the Hodgsons became reclusive, granting few interviews. Had this happened today, it's entirely possible they would have cashed in on the paranormal reality TV circuit.

In Playfair's book, the family was given a pseudonym ("Harper") in order to help protect their anonymity to some degree. Clearly, they weren't seeking fame or fortune. After the poltergeist outbreak dissipated, the Hodgsons became reclusive, granting few interviews. Had this happened today, it's entirely possible they would have cashed in on the paranormal reality TV circuit. In 1979, once the case stopped making headlines, the troubled family faded into the background.

Their lives did not get any easier.

Poltergeists often channel their energies by focusing on a prepubescent child.

Janet was hit particularly hard. She had spent time in children's homes, on the rationale that with her away from Green Street, the paranormal activity might stop. By and large, it did. She later revealed in interviews that this scarred her emotionally, instilling a deep sense of rejection in the young girl. Children can be cruel, and when her schoolmates learned that she lived in the Enfield poltergeist house, they teased her mercilessly at every opportunity. That teasing sometimes crossed the line into outright bullying.

Interviewed by journalist Emma Pietras in 2017, Janet revealed that she blamed herself for the haunting. "It was my fault because I was the epicenter. Why did it happen to me? Our family, why?"

Such is often the way with poltergeist cases. The focus is on a child on the verge of puberty, either a teenager or just about to enter that particular stage of life, when hormones swirl and emotions run strong. An atmosphere of fear pervaded the Hodgson household for months on end. In an attempt to make the phenomena stop, Janet was placed into a care home for a period of time, further isolating her and presumably fracturing the family even more than they already were. She has done a number of interviews over the years on television, radio, and in print. The interviews leave the impression of a woman who is still processing and, to borrow a phrase, is deeply haunted by what happened to her in her childhood home. Bullied in school, not wanted by her own mother (or so she was firmly convinced)—it should come as no surprise that Janet suffered greatly from being the "ghost girl." So why would she want to make it all up and then go on to perpetuate that lie for the rest of her life? Unlike other individuals, Janet and the rest of the Hodgson family made practically no money at all from the media furor that surrounded them.

Others reaped significant financial benefits from the Enfield haunting or tried to. A case in point: self-proclaimed demonologist Ed Warren and his wife, Lorraine, turned up at Green Street in person, uninvited, after hearing about the haunting. Interviewed by radio host Dave Schrader on his show *Darkness Radio* in 2016, Guy Playfair pulled no punches, saying that "all I can remember is Ed Warren telling me that he could make a lot of money for me out of it. So, I thought, that's all I need to know from you, and got myself out of the way as soon as I could."

Playfair's testimony is consistent with the New England–based Warrens' approach, which usually meant involving themselves in cases of alleged hauntings and monetizing their involvement afterward. The Warrens stayed at Green Street for less than a day and should have been nothing more than a footnote until *The Conjuring 2* happened.

The second movie in the blockbuster, multi-billion-dollar-grossing *Conjuring* franchise spins out that one day in Enfield into an entire film, making Ed and Lorraine Warren the stars, sidelining Grosse and Playfair—the investigators who did all the actual work—and inserting demonic entities for added scares and chills. As Hollywood drama, *The Conjuring 2* is an entertaining scary movie; as a dramatic representation of something that actually happened, it's a gross distortion of the facts and an insult to the

Lorraine Warren made an appearance at the 2013 WonderCon in Anaheim, California. The paranormal investigator was famous for her work with her husband, Ed.

hard work of Grosse and Playfair. According to the website *boxoffice mojo.com*, the movie made $322,811,702 worldwide for New Line Cinema and Warner Bros.

Some of the controversy associated with the case involves photographs taken of Janet Hodgson flying through the air across her bedroom, supposedly propelled by the poltergeist. Skeptics say that it's more likely she had simply used her bed as a springboard. The cameras had been placed in the children's bedroom by photographer Graham Morris and could be triggered remotely from another room in the house. Morris and Grosse were sitting downstairs, listening to goings-on in the bedroom via microphones and tape-recording everything. This prevented wasting film, as Morris would only click the shutter control if it sounded like something interesting was going on.

Suddenly hearing a loud ruckus, Morris started snapping picture after picture. The resultant images show Janet rising from her bed; the camera caught her in mid-flight. Bizarrely, there's no setup taking place: Janet is never seen preparing to spring up from her haunches. She goes from lying flat on her back beneath the blankets to being apparently propelled through the air. The look on her face is one of sheer terror.

Talking to reporter Matt Strudwick of the *Daily Mail*, Morris said that he didn't believe the house on Green Street was a haunting at all

Poltergeists means "noisy ghosts" in German, a name that comes from the fact that these spirits like to wreak havoc on items around the house.

but, rather, a case of psychokinesis that centered upon Janet. "I think this girl has some sort of force," the photographer said, that "she is desperate to get this ... whatever it is. This energy, this power, whatever she has, across and out to communicate with people. And it's coming out in different ways in a sort of force. Like a kinetic energy where things are shifting around."

Although the word means "noisy ghost" in German, the fact of the matter is, although poltergeists tend to be lumped in with ghosts and hauntings in books such as this, nobody is entirely sure *what* they are. The spirits of the dead? The subconscious of a living person? Some kind of energy or power, a force of nature that science doesn't yet understand? The jury is still out. We'll cover several different poltergeist cases in this book and examine the similarities and contrast the differences between them.

As a baseline, the classic poltergeist outbreak occurs in a place of tension and disruption. They're much rarer in calm, stable environments. Usually, a form of emotional distress is involved. Many, though by no means all, seem to center around young people such as Janet Hodgson—individuals who are dealing with multiple stressors and often struggling to adjust and cope with major life changes such as the breakup of a family. Females are more commonly poltergeists than males.

Maurice Grosse believed the Enfield haunting to be the most compelling poltergeist case of the twentieth century, if not of all time. If one finds even a fraction of the eyewitness testimony to be convincing, then the claim is a credible one. Almost 50 years later, the debate still rages. Was this the work of an aggressive, vengeful intelligence of some sort, or an extended prank pulled on the adults by bored children? Though the truth most likely can be found somewhere in the middle, this author at least believes that there was far more truth than fiction at work in that anonymous-looking house.

At the time of writing, 284 Green Street is still a private residence, and it is owned by the local council. On October 27, 2023, presumably looking to run a spooky story for Halloween, Britain's *Daily Mail* gained access to the infamous house. Reporter Paul Thompson's article featured numerous photographs of the interior and an interview with the current tenant—a Nigerian mother of four children who wants absolutely nothing to do with stories of poltergeists. A woman of strong faith, she is heartily sick of would-be ghost hunters turning up uninvited and knocking on her front door at all hours of the day and night. In a somewhat unusual move, the council apprised her of the house's haunted past prior to her moving in.

"I am a Christian woman, and I know that God will protect me," she told Thompson. "If there are any ghosts here, they will have been banished by the power of prayer. The spirits will not triumph over God, and when we are here, we pray."

Much like the former DeFeo house in Amityville, New York, it seems that the most frightening thing happening on Green Street these days are unwanted gawkers, who stand outside the house and take pictures. The ghost of Bill Wilkins, or whatever else the entity may have been, seems to have long since moved on, or so it would appear.

THE TOWN TOO TOUGH TO DIE

Growing up as a young boy in the Midlands of Great Britain, I never quite understood my father's love of Western movies—not at first. He was obsessed with all things related to the Old West. As I grew into a teenager, things changed. I somehow developed that same passion, and at the age of 50, I'm an avowed lover of all things Western.

Which brings us to Tombstone, Arizona.

They call it the town that was too tough to die, and everybody knows its name. Most also know something of its story, or at least they've heard of the infamous 30-second gunfight that took place there on October 26, 1881. Two sets of adversaries squared off close to a place whose name is now written in blood in the annals of history: the O.K. Corral.

In the summer of 1881, arguably the most iconic lawman of all time, frontier marshal Wyatt Earp, along with his brothers Morgan and Virgil and a malcontent, drunken dentist named John "Doc" Holliday, feuded with a gang of outlaws named the Cowboys. Although Wyatt gets most of the publicity (nobody named a movie after any of his brothers), it was Virgil Earp who held the position of authority, being the town marshal. It was he who was the law in Tombstone.

In response to a cycle of escalating violence that gripped Tombstone, Marshal Earp had declared the possession of firearms within city limits to be illegal. It was an ordinance that he and his deputies enforced scrupulously.

Wyatt (left) and Virgil Earp. Most people don't know that it was actually Virgil in charge of his brothers, Wyatt and Morgan, because he was the town marshal, not Wyatt.

Predictably, this did not go down well with the Cowboys, who took every possible opportunity to cause trouble. They saw the Earps as being stuck up and full of themselves. The Earps, on the other hand, believed the Cowboys were nothing but trouble. Both sides were right, in their way. The difference was, the Earps were on the right side of the law, but they wouldn't stay there for long.

Then there was the matter of Doc Holliday, a true wild card in every sense of the term. Slowly dying of tuberculosis, the dentist-turned-gambler had a hot temper and was quick to anger, particularly when drunk—which was most of the time. Holliday thought nothing of goading the Cowboys. His close friend Wyatt Earp always backed Doc's play, even when his actions could be considered questionable.

Matters came to a head on October 26, 1881, when word got out that members of the Clanton and McLaury families, prominent members of the Cowboy faction, were arming themselves in a part of town named the O.K. Corral. Deputized by his brother, Wyatt accompanied Virgil, Morgan, and Doc to the scene despite attempts by local sheriff John Behan to talk him out of it.

The stage was set for blood.

In the gunfight that ensued, three of the cowboys were killed, and both Morgan and Virgil Earp were wounded. Doc Holliday was grazed by a bullet, and Wyatt escaped without a scratch. Despite what Hollywood would have us think, the exchange of gunfire took place at terrifyingly close range—a distance of just 6 to 8 feet.

The bodies of Frank McLaury, Tom McLaury, and Billy Clanton were put on display in Tombstone in an attempt to sway public opinion against the Earps.

When the dust settled, Wyatt Earp and Doc Holliday found themselves tried for murder. They were subsequently acquitted and launched what became known as the Vendetta Ride, hunting down members of the Cowboy gang and killing them one by one.

John Henry "Doc" Holliday was a dentist and gunfighter who was a close friend to Wyatt Earp. Legends say he killed a dozen men, but historians say it was no more than three at the most.

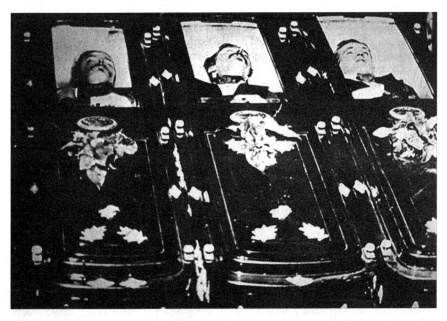

Left to right are the departed Tom McLaury, Frank McLaury, and Billy Clanton. This is the only photo known of the 19-year-old Billy.

Unsurprisingly, the most infamous corral in North America is said to have its ghosts. When the powers that be in Tombstone offered me the chance to get locked in at the O.K. Corral overnight and investigate, I didn't hesitate to say yes.

Tombstone is a surprisingly small town, but each and every block and street corner just bleeds history. Wandering down its main thoroughfare, Allen Street, I stopped every few paces simply to appreciate standing in the same spot where historical events had taken place that I'd read about over and over in history books.

It's not commonly known that the gunfight at the O.K. Corral didn't actually happen in the corral itself but rather in a vacant lot a few doors down from it, facing Fly's photography studio. That spot is currently enclosed and locked off, but I was given access to investigate all of it, along with a handful of fellow investigators.

Standing in the lot now are pistol-toting mannequins representing the Earps, Doc Holliday, and their opponents, all arranged as closely as possible to their positions on the day of the gunfight. For the visitor, it can be hard to believe that one is standing right there, visualizing what it must have felt like when the fusillade of gunshots rang out on October 26, 1881. At the rear of the lot is Fry's studio and boarding house, in which Doc Holliday lodged while staying in Tombstone. His girlfriend, the unjustly named "Big Nose" Kate, took cover there and watched the gunfight happen.

I never did quite get over the sense of awe that came from being in that historic place, where the sense of history is so palpable it feels as if you could reach out and touch it. However, my fellow researchers and I had an investigation to perform. One common claim of paranormal activity is people reporting the sound of horses neighing and moving about within the corral when it is empty at night. There's a toy mechanical rocking horse that makes those noises on a cycle set at 4 minutes and 16 seconds. It goes off whether there's anybody near it or not and would easily explain why passersby would report the sounds of phantom horses.

Although I can't swear to it, my colleagues and I might be among the first people to use a talking board at the O.K. Corral. It was slow to respond at first but gradually gained energy. Rather than communicating with one of those who died in the gunfight, it appears that we were actually talking with a woman who was one of Tombstone's 2,500 ladies of the night. Based on her playful responses, she was remarkably chipper and seemed happy to have some new company to spend a little time with.

According to the locals I spoke with, there have been multiple sightings of ghosts in this bloodstained corner of Tombstone. Witnesses have reported seeing the apparition of a man in old Western-era garb walking slowly across the corral. Other apparitions, believed to be those of the fallen Cowboys, have also been seen several times, pistols in hand, about to meet their fate in the shootout. They're seen inside the O.K. Corral and on the streets that surround it. Little wonder that they might be restless, given the sudden and violent manner in which they met their deaths.

The O.K. Corral site has a particularly poignant atmosphere about it in the middle of the night.

One final piece of evidence was particularly sad and poignant. During an EVP session, one of my fellow investigators, a man named Brad, asked the spirits where they would like to venture if they left the O.K. Corral. The answer, very clearly heard on playback, came from an unidentified male voice, who simply said the words: "Go home."

We wondered whether this was the voice of a miner, a prospector, or maybe even an outlaw, someone who had come to Tombstone during its heyday only to die there, far from home and family. One thing was certain: the message tugged at our heartstrings. It was impossible to not feel compassion for this lost soul, whoever he may have been.

The O.K. Corral is the reason everybody knows Tombstone today, but how did the town first get its start?

In 1877, a prospector named Ed Schieffelin arrived in southern Arizona and set about making his fortune. This was Apache country, so he prospected by day in the shadow of the Dragoon Mountains and spent his nights in relative safety within the confines of a nearby U.S. Army fort. One of the soldiers derisively told Schieffelin that all he'd find out there would be his tombstone.

How wrong he was. Schieffelin struck it big with several major claims, the first of which he named Tombstone. When a settlement began to spring up around it, the name stuck. Other claims received the equally colorful monikers of the Good Enough and the Toughnut. (Indeed, Tombstone has a street that was once full of miner's homes, named Toughnut Street.)

The Good Enough Mine is reputed to be haunted by two miners, both of whom are said to have died there in violent accidents. Their apparitions have been seen by multiple independent witnesses, who have reported their sightings to the mine's manager, Robert. He was kind enough to allow me and my fellow investigators to descend into the depths of the Toughnut to see what paranormal evidence we might obtain there.

My grandfather was a coal miner during World War II, and I have nothing but respect for what has always been a hazardous, dirty, and yet vital occupation. Chains bolted into the rock wall of the tunnels helped guide and steady us down into the darkness, which was illuminated primarily by the light from the helmet-mounted flashlights we all wore. Before long, we were a hundred feet below ground and still descending.

The subterranean passage wound and dipped, the air growing noticeably cooler the deeper we got. One of our investigators had to stay behind. He was suddenly overcome with a feeling of intense nausea and dizziness. As a paramedic, those symptoms always concern me, particularly when I know that the person is hydrated and has eaten. The simplest explanation would be claustrophobia, but I wasn't going to take any chances. Hundreds of feet below the ground is a bad place to try to get medical attention if you need it. He wisely chose to stay on the surface, sipping water while the rest of us kept going.

It was amazing to think about the hundreds of miners who had once worked this claim, using picks and other mining equipment to extract silver and other precious minerals from the rock. Then they'd go back up to the surface, get paid, and blow that money on wine, women, and song. The unluckier ones ran afoul of a six-gun or a knife. They ended up dead and buried in the town's graveyard.

The primary tunnel opened out into a large cavern. A wooden platform had been set up at the far end, and scattered about were a series of wooden explosives crates, which we were happy to discover were empty. Lanterns flickered eerily in the gloom, allowing us to switch off our headlamps and appreciate the silence of being so far below ground. Robert gave us some history on the Toughnut Mine. It first opened in 1880, and in addition to silver, it produced zinc, copper, lead, and even gold.

As our investigation progressed, we quickly connected with what claimed to be the ghost of a man who had died on the streets of Tombstone in the first half of the twentieth century. He had no connection to the mine and had simply taken an interest in our activities and fol-

The author stands at the grave of Ed Schieffelin (Schieffelin shown inset).

The author and fellow investigators conduct a Ouija board session at the O.K. Corral.

lowed us down here out of curiosity. Our invisible communicator seemed friendly and jovial, and he promised to pop back in and keep an eye on Robert every once in a while. "Just don't be giving me a fright," the miner answered gruffly, with a twinkle in his eye. I couldn't have agreed with him more. As if he didn't have enough to concern him without adding the ghosts of dead miners to the list.

And where might those dead miners be buried? None other than the most famous (some would say infamous) graveyard in the West: Boothill.

So—why "Boothill"? The name came about because many of those buried in the graveyard died with their boots on: cowboys, outlaws, lawmen, and workers who were killed on the job, shot down in vicious firefights, or murdered in cold blood. Yet there are also those who died of illness and suicide buried in Boothill. For six years, this was the city's primary burial ground. It was shut down in 1884, after Tombstone made an effort to turn respectable, and many of the townsfolk had qualms about being laid to rest alongside robbers, thieves, rapists, and killers. There's another cemetery within city limits, the one where those "respectable" Tombstoners are laid to rest. Even today, it tends to get fewer visitors.

A photo of the grave markers for the McLaurys and Billy Clanton at Boothill.

Boothill remains the best-known cemetery in the Old West, and thanks to concerted restoration efforts that saved it from falling into complete disrepair, its appearance hasn't changed much since the days when bodies were being laid down with depressing regularity. Let's meet a few of Boothill's residents.

John (age 11) and Frank (12) were inseparable brothers in life. One drowned in a natural pool outside Tombstone. When the other went into the water to try to help his sibling, he drowned, too. In death, the Brady Brothers share a common grave and are among the most tragic of Boothill's occupants, two complete innocents whose lives were cut short much too soon.

Little is known about the death of "Chink" Smiley other than that the cemetery records give his cause of death as "shot" sometime in 1884. Buried in the plot behind him is a gravestone that simply reads "Two Chinese." Life was cheap in Tombstone back then, and it was even cheaper for those who were from minority groups. There was a significant Chinese population, which was a source of constant friction with the white residents, most of whom thought nothing of hypocritically using the Chinese laundry services and restaurants whenever it suited them.

A rare exception to this was Mrs. Ah Lum, who was known all about town as China Mary. She was a highly influential figure in Tombstone during its wildest years, not least because of her connections with Chinese organized crime throughout the land. With two strikes against her—being both Chinese and female—she nonetheless prospered, having her fingers in many pies, most especially those involving prostitution and other vices. Nothing got done in Tombstone's Chinese district without her approval. Ah Lum died in 1906 at the grand old age of 67 and was given a massive funeral procession, with more than 1,000 mourners accompanying her coffin to Boothill. This reflected her standing as a very tough woman with a heart of gold.

Three-Fingered Jack Dunlap was so called because—you guessed it—he was missing two fingers on one hand. A thief and cattle rustler, he was trying to rob a train in 1900 and was shot dead by armed guard Jeff Milton. Dunlap most definitely died with his boots on and presumably still wears them to this day.

After his wife had initiated divorce proceedings, John King went out and got blind drunk, then chased the liquor with a bottle of strychnine, fatally poisoning himself. He lived at the intersection of 4th and Toughnut in Tombstone. In a macabre and tragic coda, four days later, King's neighbor Delia Williams committed suicide by poisoning herself with arsenic. She, too, is buried in Boothill. Neighbors in life, neighbors in death.

The killing of German miner Ernest Brodines was a case of murder most foul. He was shot in the head with two weapons, a shotgun and a pistol, both at close range. He wasn't missed for six days. When Tombstone residents went to check on him at his cabin, they found poor Ernest's body decomposing in the summer heat. Suspicion immediately fell on a fellow miner with whom Brodines had recently quarreled, but he was subsequently acquitted in court. The murder remains officially unsolved. The fact that two different weapons were used suggests that there may have been multiple killers.

One of the most insightful and thought-provoking inscriptions on any of Boothill's gravestones belongs to the marker of Frank Bowles. Bowles was riding the trail outside of Tombstone when he fell from his horse. When he hit the ground, Frank's gun went off, shooting him in the kneecap. The injury was so severe that the town doctor saw no option but to amputate. Unfortunately, this was an era in which the surgical procedure often had as high a mortality rate as the condition it was intended to treat, and Frank Bowles died shortly after having been separated from his leg.

Town records tell us that John Rook was "shot by a Chinaman" on 5th Street outside a candy store. This is just one of Tombstone's many violent secrets that are lost to the pages of history.

There are a number of fake grave markers on Boothill, placed there decades ago by those with a macabre sense of humor. John Heath is one such example. Heath was convicted of masterminding the so-called Bisbee Massacre, in which five of his associates tried to rob a Bisbee, Arizona, store of its payroll. The store's safe was empty, however, and the robbers went on a murderous rampage, shooting indiscriminately and murdering a pregnant mother along with several innocent men. The five outlaws were rounded up by a posse, convicted of murder, and hanged. Their bodies are buried on Boothill.

The grave marker for Frank Bowles at Boothill.

Heath was sentenced to life imprisonment, which did not sit well with the people of Tombstone. A lynch mob stormed the jail, tied the sheriff up, and promptly lynched John Heath in the street outside the courthouse. Heath is not really buried in Boothill, however. His body was taken to his hometown in Texas and buried in an unmarked grave. Who is buried beneath his marker in Tombstone—if anybody—remains a mystery.

Although wary of snakes and scorpions, my team of researchers and I were only too happy to conduct an overnight paranormal investigation on Boothill. We wanted to focus much of our attention on the most infamous graves of the three men who were killed in the shootout at the O.K. Corral.

Billy Clanton, Frank McLaury, and Tom McLaury are buried alongside one another. Next to the triple grave is that of Old Man Clanton himself, the patriarch of the family, who had been killed while cattle rustling earlier that same summer—possibly by a posse led by the Earps.

Boothill is a noisy place no matter the time. As night fell, traffic along the road leading out of town never really abated. Dogs barked, coyotes howled, and the sound of people talking carried on the evening breeze. My small team and I settled in to investigate next to the Clanton and McLaury grave. We soon began to hear from what purported to be the spirit of a man named Frank—hmmm—who had a definite foul mouth on him, calling me stupid (guilty as charged) and telling me in no uncertain terms to "f*** off." Frank also took exception to the presence of my colleague Greg, who is a Tombstone marshal, and made his opinion of the law very clear. While it's tempting to conclude that this was the spirit of Frank McLaury, I don't want to jump to conclusions. He refused to give his last name or discuss the specifics of his demise, and there are several other Franks buried on Boothill. Still, our proximity to Frank McLaury's grave was suggestive.

In addition to its haunted gift shop, which sees poltergeist-like activity in the middle of the night when everything is locked up tight, Boothill Graveyard is said to be home to a multitude of ghosts.

Dowsing rods were particularly effective on Boothill, readily answering a series of yes/no questions that you'll read all about in my future book about the ghosts of Tombstone. The loud, ambient noise meant that almost all of our audio evidence was contaminated and unusable, which is par for the course when investigating outdoors.

In addition to its haunted gift shop, which sees poltergeist-like activity in the middle of the night when everything is locked up tight, Boothill Graveyard is said to be home to a multitude of ghosts. According to local lore and legend, the ghost of Billy Clanton rises from his grave at sundown, walking into Tombstone and wandering the streets with a six-shooter in hand. I can state categorically that young Billy stayed in his grave during our night at Boothill, and we did not encounter him on any of our nocturnal wanderings throughout Tombstone. Nor did China Mary's apparition put in an appearance, as she is said to do every once in a while.

That's not to say we didn't experience anything strange. While we were investigating the McLaury-Clanton grave, one of my fellow investigators saw what appeared to be a head and shoulders peek out from the darkness farther along the track before ducking back again when she went to investigate. Were her eyes playing tricks, or had she truly seen something uncanny in the graveyard that night?

We ended our investigation by pouring a small offering of whiskey over the grave of Billy, Frank, and Tom, a small token of respect for the three men who had met their ends at the hands of the Earps and Doc Holliday.

One of the lesser-known hauntings in the Tombstone saga can be found outside the city limits in a place many call the most blood-soaked cabin in Arizona history. As was previously stated, the town of Tombstone came into being to service a number of mining claims made by prospectors in the desert. Ed Schieffelin was one of them, a man who struck it rich on more than one occasion. Others were less well known, such as Frederick Brunckow. German by birth, after coming to the United States, Brunckow struck out to make his fortune in the mining business. In the late 1850s, he built the cabin that still bears his name, using it as a base of operations for his prospecting. This was right in the middle of Apache territory, and it's said that Apache warriors killed approximately 17 men in and around the cabin over the years.

After striking it lucky in the vicinity of his cabin, Frederick Brunckow opened up a mine and began hiring employees, including a supervisor, a cook, and a crew of Mexican men to work the mine for him. This ended violently when the mining crew turned on Brunckow and two of his colleagues, butchering them all in cold blood. Brunckow's body was thrown down the mine shaft. When U.S. troops found him, what was left of the prospector had been impaled on a rock drill.

All three men were buried in unmarked graves just outside the cabin.

After robbing a Wells Fargo stagecoach, a gang of thieves rendezvoused at Brunckow's cabin to divide the loot. They set to squabbling. Matters turned violent, guns were drawn, and in the ensuing gunfight, all five members of the gang were killed. They, too, are said to be buried outside the cabin.

The violence didn't end there. A retired marshal named Milton B. Duffield took up residence in the cabin in 1873. He lasted less than a year. After arguing with a man named James Holmes over which of them was the legitimate owner of Brunckow's cabin, Holmes drew down and shot the unarmed Duffield dead. Holmes fled Arizona territory and escaped conviction. As for Milton Duffield, he was buried—well, I'm sure you can guess.

By 1880, ghost stories began circulating about the cabin. Prospectors are a hardy breed, but even they began to avoid the place, particularly after dark. They believed it to be both cursed and haunted. The apparition of a man was seen in the cabin, along with the sound of disembodied voices and the clinking of tools used by miners who were long since dead.

Today, the ruins of the cabin are not easy to find. It lies on land owned by the BLM (Bureau of Land Management). The closest road is privately owned, and rather than trespass, my crew and I hiked in cross-country across the desert, picking our way through every thorny plant you can think of and watching warily for rattlesnakes and other varmints along the way. When we finally reached Brunckow's Cabin, it was close to sundown. The place was in considerable disrepair, with only the walls and floor still somewhat intact. One can still see where the oven was, an oven that Tombstone founder Ed Schieffelin used to melt metal when he stayed at the cabin.

Not much remains of Brunckow's cabin, but you can still see where the oven that Ed Schieffelin used for melting metal was.

We established contact with somebody rather quickly, but whoever it was adamantly refused to identify him- or herself. In addition to being evasive with responses, the communicator seemed to want nothing more than to get us out of there. We were told in no uncertain terms to get off and get out, over and over again.

As night fell over Brunckow's Cabin, I stood and pondered the sheer number of bodies—22 is a commonly accepted count—that are said to be buried here. Little wonder that their souls would be restless. As Brad continued to talk, the voices kept telling us to get the hell out of there. Having all but lost the light, that's exactly what we did. It's difficult to avoid feeling like an interloper there, hardly surprising considering all the turmoil and bloodshed the cabin has seen in its 160-year life span.

Does Brunckow's Cabin have its ghosts? The voices we encountered seem to suggest so. Are they the spirits of Frederick Brunckow and his colleagues, the murder victim Milton Duffield, the gang of desperadoes who preyed upon one another in a fit of anger, or someone else, such as those who are said to have been murdered by the Apache here?

Unless one of them decides to share some details, it is impossible to say. This lonely stretch of Arizona desert continues to guard its secrets jealously, as does the City of Tombstone itself. Who knows if they will ever be given up?

THE BLACK MONK

Legend has it that what some claim to be the most violent poltergeist case on record began innocuously enough, one afternoon in the summer of 1966, when a strange, chalky powder began falling from the living room ceiling of what until then had seemed to be a perfectly ordinary house.

Not quite.

The house labeled 30 East Drive, Pontefract, was like tens of thousands of similar homes in Great Britain, called "council houses" because they were built and subsidized with government funding. During the late 1940s and early 1950s, there was a postwar baby boom, and entire estates filled with such homes sprang up across the nation.

The first occupants to move into Number 30 after construction were a family named the Farrars. Like many northerners, they were down-to-earth people who worked hard and took pride in their home and what few possessions they had. Some accounts mistakenly date the haunting as beginning with the subsequent tenants, the Pritchard family, but in reality, the Farrars experienced strange phenomena during their earlier residency. The house was unnaturally cold. Wallpaper refused to stick to the walls, no matter how much glue Bill Farrar slathered on it. It was as though some invisible prankster took delight in pulling it down just as soon as he thought the job was done.

Objects took to moving around of their own accord. At first, Bill's wife, Barbara, blamed her husband, yet his own possessions took to dis-

The author stands behind the house at 30 East Drive in Pontefract, Yorkshire, in the early evening. The unassuming abode is home to one of the most frightening ghosts in the region.

appearing and then reappearing later in different parts of the house. Their two-year-old daughter, Jane, refused to settle down. She was perpetually disturbed and crying. The only cure: taking her out of the house, at which point she calmed down and slept peacefully. Examination by a pediatrician confirmed that there was nothing medically wrong with young Jane. The problem seemed to be the house itself.

Then the wounds began to appear. Bloody scratches marred the little girl's face when she was left alone. There was no family dog or cat to explain them. Although she did not have sharp nails, Barbara put knitted mittens on Jane's hands whenever she put her down to sleep, to make sure she wasn't scratching herself.

The marks kept on happening regardless. Similar scratchlike tears showed up in the fabric of the couch and baby Jane's pram.

Taking on some of the hallmarks of a classic haunting, disembodied voices were heard calling out from rooms that Bill and Barbara knew to be empty.

As time went on, Barbara's personality began to change. She became more nervous, always on edge inside the walls of 30 East Drive.

Years later, Bill recalled that something always felt "off" about the house, particularly the staircase and the smallest upstairs bedroom.

Fortunately for the Farrars, help was at hand. Barbara got talking to Jean Pritchard one day. Jean also had a council house in the vicinity and wasn't particularly keen on the place. (Only later would it come to light that the Pritchards' home was haunted by the ghost of a little girl—shades of things to come.)

In those days, it was permissible for tenants to swap houses if both parties agreed. Jean liked the look of Number 30—it was more spacious than their current abode—and Barbara couldn't wait to get out. May of 1955 saw the Farrars moving out and the Pritchards moving in.

With the benefit of hindsight, Joe Pritchard noted that whatever it was that had infested 30 East Drive, it was "undoubtedly cruel."

In the years to come, the Pritchard family would learn that lesson the hard way.

Joe Pritchard and his wife Jean had two children, Diane and Phillip. Much like the Farrars, the Pritchards were regular working-class folk not given to super-stition or flights of fancy. When young Phillip and his grand-mother witnessed the strange powder falling from somewhere just beneath the ceiling, they were at a loss to explain it—but it's unlikely that the possibility of ghosts entered their minds.

Years later, Bill recalled that something always felt "off" about the house, particularly the staircase and the smallest upstairs bedroom.

After the powder came mysterious puddles of water. Such liquid appearances have occurred in other poltergeist cases. A case in point: this author was once involved with a case in which pools of what would turn out to be animal urine appeared at different points in an ordinary family residence, without any sort of human intervention.

From that point on, no electrical or mechanical device seemed to be safe. Some took on a life of their own, switching themselves off and on over and over again with wild abandon. This included the light switches and anything that was plugged into a power outlet.

Objects would appear and disappear out of nowhere, and in the kitchen, Jean Pritchard experienced a rain of keys pouring out of the chimney.

Footsteps began stomping through the house, the loud, dull thump of a heavyset individual thudding up and down the stairs or from room to room. As the days passed, the haunting of 30 East Drive took on many of the characteristics of a classic poltergeist outbreak, as previously discussed in the chapter covering the Enfield Haunting.

Particularly bizarre were the apports—objects appearing from (and sometimes disappearing into) thin air. Stranger still was a rain of keys that came down the chimney and through the kitchen fireplace, showering a startled, unsuspecting Jean Pritchard, who was kneeling beneath it at the time. Recovering her wits, Jean gathered the keys up and counted them all. There were 19 in total, dumped on her by the mischievous paranormal force that plagued the Pritchard family home. One of the keys was much older and larger than the rest. Despite Jean's best efforts to identify it, this master key's origin remained a mystery.

As the haunting intensified, the poltergeist started to behave like an out-of-control child. When the family was all downstairs, the invisible resident took to opening the windows of upstairs bedrooms and tossing the contents of those rooms out into the street or the backyard. These bizarre goings-on were witnessed by friends of the family and neighbors alike.

Next came the violence.

By no means do all poltergeist outbreaks escalate to the point at which living people are harmed, but some cases do. Certainly, an element of danger is not uncommon when it comes to their activities. For example, some poltergeists seem to delight in starting fires. Yet rather than burn down the houses in which they have taken up residence, the poltergeist prefers to keep these mini-blazes small and self-limiting. It's almost a case of "Here's what I can do. Can you imagine how much worse I *could* do if I really wanted to?"

> Jean sustained actual harm when the poltergeist somehow contrived to place a small swarm of bees inside the wardrobe in the bedroom Jean and Joe shared.

In more intense cases, there appears to be an intent to generate as much fear as possible. It may be that some poltergeists feed on strong emotion, of which terror is one of the most primal and most intense.

At 30 East Drive, the fear factor increased dramatically on the day that a large, heavy grandmother clock was pushed down the stairs from its position at the uppermost landing. Constructed of brass and solid wood, the clock had sat in the same spot quite contentedly for years. Jean Pritchard and her neighbor narrowly avoided serious injury by leaping out of the way before the tumbling clock could hit them.

Jean sustained actual harm when the poltergeist somehow contrived to place a small swarm of bees inside the wardrobe in the bedroom Jean and Joe shared. The bees stung her on several different parts of her body. The ghost's pranksterism, if indeed that's what it once was, had now descended into outright malice.

Next to be targeted was Joe Pritchard. Old-school and tough to the core, Joe had stubbornly refused to believe that 30 East Drive was haunted. He scoffed at the very idea of ghosts and phantoms, laughing it off when stories about his haunted house began to circulate around the Chequerfield Estate.

Joe was forced to eat his words one day when he had an up close and very personal encounter with the poltergeist in what was called the "coal hole." This was a narrow but deep brick enclosure next to the downstairs bathroom, a dank storage closet that contained the family's supply of coal used to heat the house. The door refused to open, trapping the burly man inside.

Although he remained tight-lipped about what went on for the few minutes he was stuck inside that dark, enclosed space, Joe did reveal that he emerged a few minutes later as a changed man. He had joked about the ghost for the last time. Joe Pritchard was now a believer.

Nobody in the Pritchard family was immune from the poltergeist's attention. The teenage Diane was pinned down by a heavy, wooden hall stand one night, her life almost frightened out of her. On another night, she was said to have been forcibly dragged upstairs by the same invisible force. She sustained bruising to her throat during what was clearly a vicious paranormal attack; one can only imagine the emotional trauma she suffered afterward.

Up to this point, the poltergeist hadn't shown its face. That changed late one night when Joe and Jean Pritchard saw the unmistakable silhouette of a monk in the doorway to the master bedroom. No facial features were visible beneath the cowl it wore. The monk simply stood there, seeming to stare at them both. It is interesting to note that while most apparitions have the ability to pass through solid walls and doors, the door to the master bedroom had swung open all by itself before the monk put in his first appearance. It was nothing if not theatrical.

The entrance to the master bedroom, where the Pritchards saw the distinct silhouette of a monk appear in the doorway.

Perhaps in an attempt to humanize the poltergeist and thereby reduce some of the fear it caused, the family had taken to calling it "Fred." It is a name that stuck and remains so to this day. In 2018, when this author moved into 30 East Drive in order to investigate it, current owner Bil Bungay arrived at the house and made a point of greeting "Fred" first, by name. The poltergeist, spirit, or whatever it is seems to have lost none of its ability to intimidate the living.

The story of the Black Monk of Pontefract was comprehensively chronicled by author Colin Wilson in his landmark 1981 book *Poltergeist: A Study in Destructive Haunting*. The Black Monk's legend grew. Wilson, a prolific and respected chronicler of the paranormal, highlighted the theory of a local man named Tom Cuniff.

Cuniff seems to have been more of a keen amateur enthusiast than a trained historian. According to Wilson, Cuniff interviewed Jean Pritchard, who dropped a bombshell: a family friend recalled reading in a library book that several hundred years before, a monk was hanged for the crime of molesting a girl (*Poltergeist*, pp. 146–147). The execution was said to have taken place on the stretch of ground that would one day occupy 30 East Drive.

To his credit, Wilson makes it clear that this was all hearsay. He was never able to track down the book, and it seems more likely that Jean's friend simply had her wires crossed. No subsequent researchers have been able to locate written evidence to support Cuniff's contention either. Yet the story of the murderous, molesting monk is a pervasive one. It has appeared in numerous different places, and it is often told as if it were established fact. One version holds that the monk dropped the girl's dead body down the well that supposedly lies beneath 30 East Drive and its neighboring house. The townsfolk then threw the monk's corpse in after it once they had hanged him. This flies in the face of all logic: why would they have intentionally poisoned a well they relied upon for their survival?

There has been much debate about the presence or lack of that medieval-era stone well that supposedly lies underneath the floor of 30 East Drive. Although some adamantly deny its existence, there are accounts from those who saw it with their own eyes at a time when it was necessary to pull up the floorboards in order to fix a problem with damp in the house. The well was subsequently sealed and the floor replaced. It should be noted that no human remains were discovered within its depths. No murdered girl, and no sign of a monk.

It's more likely a case of not letting the facts get in the way of a good story.

Although one hears often about hauntings associated with the American Civil War, the same does not seem to be true for the English equivalent, which took place over a 10-year period beginning in 1642. The conflict between the monarchy and parliament was bloody and set family against family, as civil wars tend to do. Pontefract had a castle, which still stands today, and was a Royalist stronghold. Blood was almost certainly shed in some form on the land where 30 East Drive would one

Joe Pritchard died in this bathroom on the house's second floor, but it was after the paranormal activity had apparently stopped.

day be built, and this was the final house to be constructed on that particular street. Ghosts of war are relatively commonplace. Perhaps therein lies the key to the haunting, though no historian or other researcher has been able to prove that yet.

Fred's reign of mischief and occasional terror ended shortly after he first appeared in Joe and Jean Pritchard's bedroom doorway. It was as if the invisible intruder finally showing himself brought the outbreak to a dramatic climax.

Afterward, a sense of normality hesitantly returned to 30 East Drive. If this was a typical poltergeist case, the story would most likely have ended here. But it did not. Once the children grew up and moved out, Joe and Jean continued to live at 30 East Drive, no longer plagued by paranormal activity. On June 21, Joe Pritchard died in the bathroom at the top of the stairs.

Now a widow and living alone, Jean long refused to move out despite the frightening experiences she and her family had undergone inside the house. She finally moved out and put the house up for sale four years prior to the 2012 release of the movie *When the Lights Went Out,* a fictionalized account of the haunting. Looking for a novel way to publicize the movie he had produced, Bil Bungay looked at the status of 30 East Drive and was surprised to find the property was on the market. He wasted no opportunity in snapping it up, figuring he would use it to promote the film and then sell it on. Indeed, Bil arranged for the premiere to take place in the house itself, lending the event a uniquely scary frisson.

Of course, the key question for the skeptical producer became: was the house still haunted after all those years? After asking neighbors about it, Bungay learned that Fred the Poltergeist had been far from quiet since Jean moved out. Heavy footsteps were heard stamping around the empty house. Loud bangs and thuds. Voices were heard speaking through the dividing wall between houses, the words indistinct but plainly human speech. The upstairs bedroom that had belonged to Diane was ransacked, as though somebody had gone through it while angrily searching for something.

After the movie was released, 30 East Drive underwent something of a resurgence. Paranormal investigators visited. So did TV news and documentary crews. Most suffered strange equipment malfunctions and inexplicable battery drains, all of which spontaneously resolved themselves once they were clear of the house.

Bil Bungay, formerly skeptical, was now absolutely convinced that his new real estate acquisition was haunted. This view was only strengthened on the day that the poltergeist began flinging small items at him, such as marbles and dominos—some of which appeared out of thin air right before his incredulous eyes and flew right past his head, narrowly missing him.

The living room as seen through the doors that Jean Pritchard kept locked for years until she finally left the house for good.

The Black Monk made national news again when paranormal investigator Claire Cowell snapped an intriguing photograph of the staircase. The image showed what looked to be the sleeve of a black robe and a hand descending on the right side of the stairs, the hand being held out almost laconically over the handrail. It was clutching what Claire believed to be a set of rosary beads.

Nor was this the only strange image to be caught on camera at 30 East Drive. A plethora of shadowy figures and what might have been faces began to turn up in pictures taken by visitors to the house. Soon, Bil had enough of an archive to plaster several walls of a downstairs room with them.

Following a visit from the controversial TV show *Most Haunted,* which aired a live show from 30 East Drive on Halloween night of 2015 that descended into dramatics and histrionic behavior, the house's reputation as an evil place was even further cemented in the consciousness of the British public.

Yet is it really? Although some of Fred's behavior has been aggressive—the scratches, the physical attacks—it is a relatively small percentage of the paranormal activity that has taken place inside the house in front of countless eyewitnesses. The majority of this belligerence took place at the height of the outbreak, when Jean and Joe Pritchard were singled out for the terrifying attention of the poltergeist.

TERRIFYINGLY TRUE HAUNTINGS

The mirror that dropped and broke while the house was empty and locked.

Can this all be laid at the door of the mysterious Fred, or are there, as some researchers have posited, multiple spirit entities inside the house? One hypothesis holds that 30 East Drive is a kind of way station, a place in which multiple beings can come and go as they please. It is an intriguing notion and one that bears further research.

As an author and paranormal investigator, I was ecstatic to receive an invitation to move into 30 East Drive and experience it for myself. I had grown up having read Colin Wilson's book and knew the story of the Black Monk cold. The opportunity to move into the house with a small team of paranormal investigators was one I simply couldn't pass up.

Our visit was an eventful one. We had been in the house for less than an hour when the mirror that hung on the wall facing the staircase fell and smashed. 30 East Drive had been locked up and empty at the time, and a top-to-bottom search of the house revealed no sign of an intruder. Closer inspection revealed that the length of rope from which the mirror had hung had snapped in two. Bil Bungay assured me that it had been on the wall for years. While it was possible that it had been gradually weakening over all that time, the fact that it broke so soon after I arrived at the house made it feel like a personal welcome from the Black Monk himself—his way of saying, "Welcome to 30 East Drive."

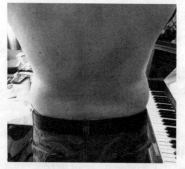

This photo clearly shows a wide swath of scratches on the back of Charlie, one of the team members investigating the house.

After being warned that Fred had gotten into the habit of trying to push people down the stairs, we all took care to hold on tightly to the handrail. Fortunately, none of us were the target of such behavior, but a team member named Charlie seemed to have aroused the ire of one of the spirits one evening as he was standing at the sink washing up dishes. Charlie felt a burning sensation just above the small of his back. His ankles were somehow being held in place, preventing him from moving.

On lifting up his shirt, the rest of the team could see a series of long, angry scratches marring Charlie's skin. Was this simply the ghost making its presence felt in the only way it knew how or a targeted attack? We never did find out.

Over the span of several days, the team experienced several long lulls, interspersed with periods of paranormal activity that nobody could explain. The entirety of the case is documented in *The Black Monk of Pontefract* by Richard Estep and Bil Bungay.

At the time of writing, 30 East Drive remains one of the UK's most popular paranormal tourism sites. Tour companies run guided events there, allowing members of the public to experience a few hours inside the infamous Black Monk House. It is also available to individuals and research teams for private hire.

Some nights, the house is quiet and very little happens.

On others, the place all but explodes with paranormal activity.

Feast or famine. With 30 East Drive, one never knows quite what they're going to get.

THE BELL WITCH

There's a widely accepted belief among paranormal enthusiasts and researchers that relates to potentially dangerous hauntings. A ghost may, in certain cases, physically harm somebody. It may be capable of scratching, bruising, or burning them, even shoving them down a flight of stairs. But however much harm an entity does, it never kills.

Supposedly.

One possible exception involves a nineteenth-century Tennessee haunting in which a mischievous and malevolent spirit is said to have taken the life of the Bell family patriarch.

In many ways, what has come to be known as the Bell Witch case is the classic great American haunting. It really does have all the elements of a truly creepy ghost story, which may be why it was fodder for a 2005 movie titled *An American Haunting*. Unfortunately, the movie was mostly forgettable. Yet the Bell Witch itself remains very much an active point of debate among paranormal scholars and historians. The people of Robertson County, Tennessee, certainly have strong opinions about it.

Today, the land on which the Bell Farm sat is still a rural place. In the early 1800s, it was even more so—a wild place that, while home to a few settlers, had little in the way of infrastructure or amenities. Those who called it home in those days were hardy people. They had to be. It was a hard life, where danger was commonplace, and death was never too far away. People were, generally speaking, strong in their faith. It gave them solace during the long, dark winter nights and helped them cope with the stresses and strains of an uncertain existence.

So it was with the Bell family, who had established their homestead in the region in 1804. Family patriarch John and his wife, Lucy, were of hardy stock, being exactly the type of robust individuals who could thrive and prosper on the newfound Tennessee frontier, the kind of place where the right people could carve out their destinies in the wilderness—if their luck held, that is.

Unfortunately for the Bells, they had not reckoned with the denizen of an old cave that sat on their property. After having spent 13 relatively stress-free years establishing and growing their Tennessee estate, their peace was shattered in 1817 by the arrival of a supernatural entity that would plague them for many years to come.

Members of the family began to see strange creatures, such as odd-looking birds and dogs. British folklore is replete with stories of phantom canines, particularly black dogs, which were often seen as harbingers of impending doom or death. If this is the case with the strange dog seen in the vicinity of the Bell farmstead in 1817, then the death being presaged was to be none other than that of John Bell himself.

What happened next fit the description of a classic poltergeist outbreak. Pounding on the walls of the home became so intense that the

The Bell Witch Cave is located at 430 Keysburg Rd. in Adams, Tennessee, which is about a 40-minute drive from Nashville. Open to tourists, it is on the National Register of Historic Places.

building itself shook. Yet when the Bells tried to identify its source, they found nobody or nothing that might be responsible. Scratching sounds in the walls may at first have seemed like the work of rats, but no such vermin were ever found to account for them. The scratching intensified as time went on. This is not an uncommon characteristic of poltergeist cases; indeed, the alleged 1949 possession of Maryland teenager Ronald Hunkeler, on whom the novel and movie adaption *The Exorcist* was based, also began with similar scratching sounds. The Hunkeler family brought in an exterminator, who found no signs of rats, mice, or raccoons either within or immediately outside of their house. So it was with the Bells, who grew concerned when the scratching sounds migrated into the confines of their home.

The nocturnal disturbances grew steadily worse and began keeping the family awake throughout the night. Objects such as housewares and personal items were flung around the home by some invisible force. The same force physically assaulted members of the family, hitting them and shoving them around. The unseen assailant did not confine its callous attention to the adult occupants of the household. The youngest Bell children were also tormented by it despite their absolute innocence.

Paranormal lore holds that poltergeist cases usually have a focus, an individual upon whom the haunting appears to center. In this particular instance, that focus seems to have been 12-year-old Betsy. That was in keeping with the hypothesis that poltergeist foci often tend to be either teenagers or preteens, children that are usually on the cusp of puberty or have just entered that state of physical maturity. It has been theorized that the intense emotions and whirlpool of hormones that come into play during the process of puberty may provide fertile ground on which the poltergeist can wreak havoc. The prepubescent individuals more often than not tend to be female. Notable examples include Esther Cox, from the 1878 Amherst, Nova Scotia, haunting; Diane Pritchard in the Black Monk of Pontefract case; and Janet Hodgson of Enfield.

The Bell haunting predated them all, and the physical abuse inflicted upon young

The Bells' daughter Betsy was tormented by the witch's spirit for several years, as were the other members of the family, but the witch seemed to focus particularly on her.

Betsy was crueler and more intense than that suffered by any other member of the family. The slaps and blows she sustained seemed indicative of pure malice, though what a 12-year-old girl might have done to bring such attention upon herself was never made clear.

At first, not wanting to become figures of curiosity or amusement, the Bells could do little other than watch as their home life spiraled increasingly out of control. Eventually, perhaps seeking some validation that the paranormal maelstrom taking place inside their home was real and not an indication they were losing their minds, they invited some trusted friends into their confidence. The ghost was not shy about performing for an audience, and inevitably, the Bells' "secret" soon became a matter of public knowledge. The family became the talk of Tennessee, attracting hordes of visitors—the majority of whom were uninvited. All of them wanted to experience the ghostly activity for themselves.

Fortunately, the friends of the family closed ranks around them. This showed their good nature; there was a real possibility that the Bells might have been ostracized by the local community and left to fend for themselves, had their neighbors been so inclined.

There were no easy explanations for the weird supernatural siege that was being endured by the Bells. However, answers were clearly needed, and some of their friends took it upon themselves to try to communicate with the malevolent entity at the heart of it all. They hit upon the idea of using knocks and raps as responses for questions. The limitation was that the only questions that could be answered would have to be phrased as yes or no.

Spirit communication can often be a frustrating endeavor, not least because one has to take the unseen communicator's word that they are who they say they are. Paranormal investigators with experience using yes/no questioning, or devices such as Ouija boards and spirit boxes, frequently encounter messages that are at best disingenuous or misleading and at worst outright deceptive and fraudulent. Given the spiteful behavior of this entity—which those involved had now taken to calling the Bell Witch—we should ask ourselves why anybody would ever have taken it at its word.

Still, the Bells and their friends craved answers and continued to ask questions of the Witch. Perhaps because of their perseverance, the knocking sounds eventually were supplanted by an actual voice that, seemingly out of thin air, spoke to those assembled. The Witch claimed to have been buried in the vicinity and to have grown restless when its grave was somehow disturbed. The desecration of a grave is a valid reason for a haunting to begin, so it is not difficult to see why this answer was taken at face value. The group's next question was: how could the wayward spirit be mollified? Perhaps the grave could be located and the remains, which the voice said had been moved, could be restored, bringing with it some semblance of peace to the Bell farmstead.

A sketch of the Bell home. Unlike other spirits that seem to be limited to a location, the witch was seen in places as far away as England.

Although the attacks upon members of the household—primarily the Bell children—continued, not all of the physical phenomena were violent. In one particularly curious incident, a neighbor who asked that the spirit shake his hand was rewarded with the sensation of an invisible palm and fingers being pressed gently against his own.

There was no shortage of skeptics willing to pit their wits against the so-called Bell Witch. For every member of the community that trusted the Bells and believed their story to be genuine, there seemed to be a potential debunker who wanted to prove that they were making it all up. Several of them visited the Bell home, and it is notable that none of them ever succeeded in uncovering fakery or fraud of any kind. Then there is the question of the motive. Even if the case truly was fraudulent, why exactly would the Bells put themselves through the emotional wringer? There was no material benefit to them. They did not get rich on the basis of the haunting. John and Lucy Bell were initially reluctant to even discuss the matter beyond the walls of their home for fear that they might be ostracized from the church and the local community due to the "dark spirit" that seemed to infest their home.

Claiming fraud also ignores the logistical challenge of convincing numerous eyewitnesses of the ghostly goings-on. Several of them not only heard the Witch speak but actually experienced some form of physical contact with the entity. Even today, this would be difficult if not impossible to fake. In the nineteenth century, pulling the wool over so many sets of eyes would have been all but impossible. Equally difficult to believe is the notion that this was some form of vast conspiracy, once again without any appreciable gain to the local community. Although the influx of visitors may have boosted revenue slightly, as it currently does, thanks to the popularity of the Bell Witch Cave as a tourist destination, the same was not true at the time of the haunting. Although we take paranormal tourism for granted today, the Bell family never dreamed of asking for a single cent from anybody who crossed their threshold in search of the Witch that plagued them.

Some of the would-be truth seekers got a lot more than they bargained for. The Bell Witch could sometimes be playful and mischievous, but it was equally capable of being mercurial and downright vicious. One visitor, a self-professed detective by the name of Williams, repaid the Bells' hospitality by running his mouth. He was loudly skeptical, despite the fact that John Bell allowed him to spend the night in their home. He was an expert in getting to the bottom of such bizarre matters, Williams claimed, and was confident he could solve what was clearly a case of fraud.

Once the family and their guest had lain down for the light and turned out the lights, the Witch struck. Williams was held down by an invisible force, and while he was helpless, he was slapped and scratched until he howled in pain and fright. He was gone once the sun rose the next morning, presumably no longer quite the skeptic that he had been.

Clearly, it did not pay to cross the Bell Witch.

Yet for all of the spite and viciousness of which it was capable, there was also a softer side to the entity. Although it seemed to hate John

Signs draw tourists in to the Bell Witch Cave in Adams, Tennessee.

GHOSTLY ENCOUNTERS

Bell intensely, the opposite proved to be true for his wife, Lucy. Indeed, when she fell ill, the Witch not only expressed sympathy for the Bell family matriarch but is even said to have sung for her and brought her hazelnuts. The dichotomy of how the Bell Witch treated some family members kindly and others so brutally is striking, expressing compassion one minute and utter hatred the next, depending on who was involved.

In many ways, the Witch was the ultimate nosy neighbor. It knew things that took place behind closed doors, not just in the immediate vicinity of the Bell household but also throughout the community. It appeared as if the entity was eavesdropping on the people of Robertson County, learning their secrets and then publicly revealing them with gleeful delight. The Witch knew the whereabouts of individuals when those whereabouts should have been known to only those involved and was willing to accurately recount them when questioned. If true, this is another nail in the coffin of the hoax theory. The entity was suspiciously well informed of people's private business, even the embarrassing little matters that, while not exactly spicy or sordid, would not have been voluntarily shared.

The Bell Witch was not constrained within geographical limits. It roamed far and wide collecting news and gossip, then returned back to the homestead in order to reveal it. In one particularly puzzling case, the Witch's activities are said to have reached as far as England when the Witch allowed a visiting Englishman to hear the voices of his parents, who were thousands of miles away at the time. They, too, heard their son's voice, apparently speaking out of thin air to them. This may be the first documented paranormal trans-Atlantic "phone call"!

The Bells' quest for answers continued. After they enlisted the aid of a preacher, his combination of coaxing and prodding finally drove the Bell Witch to identify itself by name: it claimed to be one Kate Batts.

This name was well known in the locality, having belonged to a woman who lived nearby with her husband, Frederick. It's fair to say that Mary Catherine "Kate" Batts was not a popular woman and had a reputation for being something of an odd bird. Some even believed her to have been a witch, although there is scant evidence to support this claim. Whether they were true or not, these peculiarities did not necessarily make her a bad person, however, and it may simply be that the Witch was lying about its identity, using Kate Batts as a convenient scapegoat.

There was also the small matter of her not being dead at the time of the Bell Witch incident. Although most open-minded paranormal

Although most open-minded paranormal researchers accept that a haunting can be caused by other things than spirits of the dead, it is unclear how the alive and well Kate Batts could have been behind the phenomena.

researchers accept that a haunting can be caused by other things than spirits of the dead, it is unclear how the alive and well Kate Batts could have been behind the phenomena. Playing devil's advocate, could she have conjured up some kind of entity in order to do her bidding? Was Kate Batts capable of astrally projecting, becoming the Bell Witch when it suited her purpose? If so, she did herself no favors. Once her name became associated with whatever it was that tormented the Bell family, Kate found herself frozen out even further from the local community, being eyed with even greater suspicion than she had been before. Her denials and protests of innocence availed her little.

While it is possible that Kate Batts was connected to the Bell Witch in some way, it seems more likely that she was unfairly maligned, her name dragged through the mud in a manner similar to that of Bathsheba Sherman, a victim of historic character assassination in the so-called Conjuring case.

While being able to put a name to the Witch may or may not have provided the family with some reassurance, when the entity stated its goal, the result was terrifying. The Bell Witch said it was bent on tormenting the head of the family, John, to death. He continued to suffer the indignity of repeated physical assault, as did his daughter Elizabeth. Her siblings were not spared the attentions of the Witch either, but the majority of the abuse was focused on her.

The Bells owned several enslaved persons, as did most families in the region at that time. Far from having sympathy for the plight of those who were already faring poorly in life, the Bell Witch seemed determined to add to their suffering. It played mean-spirited tricks on the enslaved, showing a malevolence toward them that suggests that if the entity was the spirit of a dead human, as it claimed to be, then it was almost certainly that of a white person.

Only Lucy Bell was completely safe from the entity's malice; if anything, the Witch seemed to be very fond of her.

Claims that the Witch politely shook hands with a visitor named Calvin Johnson, and even spat in the face of Joel Bell, raises the important question of materiality. How exactly is it that something that should have no physical presence is able to touch the living? The ghostly handshake implies the existence of a phantom palm, fingers, and thumb at the very least. Things are even sketchier when it comes to the claim of the Bell Witch spitting; to do so requires a mouth, along with surrounding anatomical structures, along with the ability to produce and expel saliva. If true, this raises serious questions about the composition of what we currently think of as being a ghost, spirit, or whichever term we wish to use.

> Claims that the Witch politely shook hands with a visitor named Calvin Johnson, and even spat in the face of Joel Bell, raises the important question of materiality.

With regard to those who were enslaved, the Witch claimed that part of its disgust for them was rooted in their odor, which it found repellent. Assuming this is accurate, then the entity seemed capable not only of seeing and hearing events taking place in our material plane of existence but also of smelling them. A ghost with a functioning olfactory sense is all the more remarkable.

As time went on, the haunting ebbed and surged like a storm. Always at its center were Elizabeth Bell and her father, John. We can only speculate as to how much credence the head of the family gave to the Witch's death threats against him, but his health undeniably deteriorated over the next few years. By the winter of 1820, his health was in serious decline. To be fair, Bell was no spring chicken. Born in 1750, he had just entered his seventh decade of life. Although he had the benefits of fresh air and relatively clean country living in his favor, at the age of 70, he had already outlived many of his peers.

Five days before Christmas, John Bell died in his bed. When the contents of his medicine cabinet were examined, a mysterious vial of liquid was discovered. The odor emanating from the liquid could also be smelled on John Bell's mouth. Nobody present seemed to know what it was or where it had come from, not even the family doctor—nobody, that is, except the Bell Witch. In a voice that apparently came from thin air close to the dead man's bed, it triumphantly claimed re-

In this illustration of the death of John Bell, several people gather around what looks like a dog. Throughout the years involving the witch, strange dogs and other animals appeared on the Bell property. A weird-looking dog also was seen shortly before John Bell's death.

sponsibility for having fatally poisoned John Bell, thereby fulfilling the promise it had made long before.

Evidencing a practical manner that was offset by a complete lack of compassion, those present tested the liquid by giving a few drops to the family cat. It promptly died. Suspiciously, the contents of the vial were never submitted for chemical analysis. Whether or not it was a poison was never conclusively proved—but the rather heartless "cat test" suggests that it probably was.

As the Bell family, along with their friends and neighbors, mourned the death of John Bell, the Witch celebrated. It sang loudly and gleefully, starting at the dead man's bedside and resuming just in time to spoil his funeral service. The Bell Witch is even said to have hooted and hollered while soil was being shoveled on top of his coffin.

That should have been the end of it. The death—some said murder by poisoning—of John Bell meant that the Witch bearing his name had achieved its stated purpose. Yet matters did not end there. The Bell Witch stuck around for another year, continuing to disturb the Bell family. It successfully drove a wedge between Elizabeth Bell and her beau, Joshua Gardner. The pair had been set to marry, but after the Bell Witch loudly demanded otherwise, claiming that their offspring would be cursed for generations, Elizabeth and Joshua reluctantly broke off the engagement and went their separate ways.

The paranormal activity did weaken in both intensity and frequency now that the entity had gotten what it wanted. The following year, 1821, the Bell Witch disappeared just as abruptly as it had first arrived four years prior. If the Bells expected it to be gone for good, however, they were to be rudely disappointed.

Seven years later, the entity came back like the proverbial bad penny. It had predicted as much when it had vanished and was true to its word, returning in February of 1828. Elizabeth had married and moved out of the family home, but Lucy still lived there, along with her sons Richard and Joel. The Witch confined itself to some light poltergeist activity, never again resorting to the violent attacks that had been a mainstay of the initial haunting. The Bells refused to initiate conversation with the entity, which seemed to quickly grow bored and moved on to pastures new.

Also receiving multiple visits was John Bell Jr., who was more than willing to spar verbally with the entity. A prosperous businessman who made his home close to the original Bell family residence, John Jr. had no fear of the Bell Witch. He refused to be intimidated despite all that it had done to his father, and the Witch eventually moved on once again, but not before making a number of predictions and prophecies concerning the future of global events and the role that would be played by the United States. The Witch also prophesied what sounds a lot like worldwide environmental collapse, complete with global warming, droughts, and other natural catastrophes—which sound all too plausible today, given what we now know about climate change.

> A prosperous businessman who made his home close to the original Bell family residence, John Jr. had no fear of the Bell Witch. He refused to be intimidated despite all that it had done to his father....

A few years after Lucy's death in 1838, the Bell residence was demolished. The site has maintained its reputation for being haunted to this day.

Writing for *The Tennessean* in October of 1986, reporter David Jarrard set out to spend a night in the cave, with a view to write an article about the Bell Witch for the Halloween season. He was accompanied by photographer Bill Wilson. These two grown men believed they were dealing with a piece of long-established Tennessee folklore, nothing more.

In the end, they got more than they bargained for.

The fact that the then-owners of the Bell Witch Cave refused to ever spend the night there themselves ought to have served as a warning. Indeed, the two veterans of the media world were more worried about snakes and spiders than they were about evil spirits.

The pair were soon beset by strange noises, coming from somewhere within the darkest recesses of the cave. Then came the growls. Tennessee is known to be the home of bobcats, which are not uncommon in the state. Coyotes are also frequently encountered. Both animals may growl if they feel threatened or cornered. It is possible that one of these beasts may have made its way into the depths of the Bell Witch Cave, and on hearing the two men talking, they growled in order to defend its territory.

On the other hand, the men may have had an encounter with the infamous Bell Witch.

When they explored the cave further, however, no animal was found. They considered the possibility that their home for the night had been wired for sound, with concealed speakers playing growling noises in order to spook them—and to drum up publicity for the commercial venture that the Bell Witch Cave had become (tours were and are given for a fee). The newspaper team checked carefully. The only wires they found were tied into the lighting system that had been installed for safety purposes. Of speakers, there was absolutely no sign.

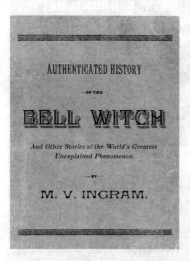

The 1961 reprint of M. V. Ingram's 1894 book, *An Authenticated History of the Famous Bell Witch. The Wonder of the nineteenth century, and Unexplained Phenomenon of the Christian Era. The Mysterious Talking Goblin That Terrorized the West End of Robertson County, Tennessee, Tormenting John Bell to His Death. The Story of Betsy Bell, Her Lover and the Haunting Sphinx.*

The straw that finally broke the camel's back was a blood-curdling scream that echoed from the walls of the cave, terrifying in both volume and shrillness. It was unmistakably a cry, not an animal sound.

Both men fled.

Whether they really did have an encounter with the dreaded Bell Witch or whether a human being was hiding back there playing tricks on them can never be known for certain.

The Bell Witch case arguably qualifies as the quintessential American haunting. It therefore comes as no surprise that the legend has endured for more than 200 years and has lost absolutely none of its capacity to enthrall and fascinate. Yet it is not without problems.

Separating fact from myth has become all but impossible. M.V. Ingram's 1894 book *An Authenticated History of the Famous Bell Witch* gets credit for outlining much of the story. It, in turn, relied heavily upon Richard

Williams Bell's *Our Family Trouble*. Present in the household during the haunting itself, Richard Williams Bell represents a primary source of information. There's just one problem. Doubt exists as to the authenticity of *Our Family Trouble*. In other words, he may not have been the true author of the book.

Ingram was a journalist who was friends with Joel Egbert Bell. Writing in 2014, researcher Joe Nickell notes the fact that there isn't a single manuscript for *Our Family Trouble* to be found anywhere. Its first appearance was as the backbone for M.V. Ingram's text. After scrutinizing the book, Nickell observed that Ingram and Richard Williams Bell write in a very similar style—almost suspiciously so. There are a number of phrases in what purports to be Bell's account that are anachronistic as if they were actually written decades later, probably by Ingram. Although not definitive proof, Nickell's case for Ingram having passed his writing off as Bell's is a compelling one. The matter can never be settled definitively, but there is certainly good reason to view Ingram's book skeptically.

That isn't to say that Ingram made the whole thing up; rather, it's likely that he embellished the pre-existing stories and legends when writing *An Authenticated History of the Famous Bell Witch*. What's up for debate is just how far that embellishment went.

Equal skepticism should apply to the claim that President Andrew Jackson encountered the Bell Witch when visiting the family home. It's a pervasive story but one for which there is not a lick of supporting evidence.

All of which evokes the question: was this a genuine haunting?

Your mileage may vary, but the "it was all a hoax" holds little water with this author. For one thing, there were simply too many people who witnessed the paranormal activity taking place within the Bell household. Not to mention the fact that many of them heard the Witch speak, and none were able to debunk it as an act of trickery or ventriloquism.

In 2021, chemistry professor Dr. Meagan Mann offered up an intriguing hypothetical explanation for what happened to John Bell: poisoning. She told *The Tennessean's* Katie Nixon:

A historical marker on U.S. Route 41 heading to Adams, Tennessee, is placed just south of the Bell homestead site.

He would have trouble swallowing, and his tongue felt weird … he would start getting this weird twitching sensation in his face, and eventually it grew to the point where it was kind of impacting him in other parts of his body—and if that happened to someone now, and you went to your doctor, they would send you to a neurologist.

In other words, he had been exposed to a neurotoxin. One possible candidate for that specific toxin is arsenic, which Dr. Mann points out would have explained the facial tics John Bell suffered in the days leading up to his death. It was the sort of poison that would have been readily available on a place like the Bell Farm because it was used to kill vermin. It's a reasonable explanation for his death, particularly if the patriarch was poisoned slowly and repeatedly over a period of months or years. If true, then a thornier question involves the identity of the mysterious poisoner.

"It could have been anyone," Mann admits. Of course, the definition of "anyone" could also include the Bell Witch herself, particularly as the Witch gleefully claimed responsibility for the old man's death.

There is a middle ground to be walked between the "it was all a hoax" and the Hollywood horror story that the Bell Witch has become: the possibility that what the Bell family experienced was a classic poltergeist case not at all dissimilar to those that occurred in Pontefract and Enfield in England. Many of the reported phenomena mirror those of poltergeist outbreaks, and the pattern of a major episode (1817–1821) followed by a prolonged period of less intense paranormal activity also tracks.

One thing is for certain. Many of the residents of nearby Adams believe that the Witch never truly went away. It is wise to tread carefully, especially after dark, or you might encounter her in some lonely place in the woods. To this day, weird occurrences in the vicinity are often ascribed to "Old Kate," as some like to call her.

If you're brave enough, dear reader, why not find out for yourself? Although the Bell family home is long since gone, at the time of writing, the cave is still there and is replete with claims of paranormal activity. Visits can be arranged by going to www.bellwitchcave.com or emailing bellwitchcave@gmail.com.

I wish you the very best of luck.

BORLEY RECTORY

From the quintessential American ghost story (the Bell Witch), we now move on to that most British of haunted houses, the so-called Most Haunted House in England—Borley Rectory.

At first glance, this one has it all. A dark, haunted manse with a fearsome reputation. A ghostly nun, seen gliding along the grounds so often that her path came to be known as the "Nun's Walk." A phantom coach and horses, steered by a headless driver. Poltergeist activity of all varieties, sometimes playful, sometimes violent. Disembodied footsteps heard walking, not just in empty rooms but also on the lanes and pathways outside the rectory. Mysterious writing appearing on the walls, begging for help. The list goes on and on.

Last, but by no means least: a terrible fire, and an ending that wasn't really an ending. The Borley Rectory case checked all of these boxes and many more besides. Yet, as with most of the cases detailed within these pages, it remains mired in controversy to this day. Borley Rectory went up in flames in 1939, but some claim that the ghosts migrated just across the road to Borley Church.

In church parlance, a rectory is the home of a priest ("rector"); essentially, it is the residence and seat of religious authority for a parish. Some parishes, and their associated rectories, are more prestigious and sought-after than others. Located in rural Sussex, Borley Rectory was in a somewhat isolated location. The building of its sturdy brick structure spanned the years 1862 to 1863.

The rectory was spacious, with more rooms than any rector and his family could possibly find use for. The grounds came complete with stables and an attached cottage, ideal for the use of a groundskeeper. There was a pair of summer houses, one on either side of the lawn. As time went on, a pet cemetery took form just beyond the stream. It was populated with successive family cats after each one passed away.

It is impossible to say for certain when the first episodes of paranormal activity occurred at the rectory. According to eyewitness testimony gathered by researchers such as the late Peter Underwood, strange things began to happen almost as soon as the first occupants—the Bull family—moved in and made themselves at home.

When trying to explain a haunting, one of the first factors that researchers look for is the number of deaths that have taken place at the location. The original rector of Borley, the Reverend Henry Bull, died inside the rectory in 1892 at the age of 59. His wife, Caroline Sarah Foyster Bull, also passed away within its walls in 1914. She was 77.

After Henry Bull's death but prior to the death of Caroline, the rectorship of the parish was taken over by their son, the Reverend Harry Bull. He, too, would die in his sleep at the rectory in 1927 after a protracted period of ill health. A popular man in the locality, the Reverend Bull would soon be reputed to haunt his former home. If this was true, it may have been because, like many individuals who possess a strong

The Reverend Henry Dawson Ellis Bull built the rectory and moved into it when he was made rector.

sense of faith and duty, Bull felt compelled to continue "making his rounds" after his death. Phantom clergymen are not unknown in the annals of psychic research. In life, Harry Bull had given the parish of Borley 35 years of faithful service.

On the other hand, perhaps Harry Bull haunted the rectory because of the way things transpired after his death. The Reverend was quoted by a friend as having said that, should he not like the approach taken by his successor, he would make it clear in no uncertain terms by throwing objects around inside the rectory. After Harry Bull's remains were buried in the cemetery across the road, that's exactly what happened to the next tenants—criticism from beyond the grave.

There is also a third possible explanation—one that is potentially much darker in nature. Author Sean O'Connor notes in *The Haunting of Borley Rectory* that the Reverend Bull's sisters believe he had been intentionally and fatally poisoned. This would provide a strong motive for the dead man's spirit to stick around after his death, a classic case of unfinished business.

Whichever was the case, the Borley ghost stories long predated the Reverend Harry Bull's demise. Almost from the outset, Borley Rectory was alleged to be haunted by numerous phantoms, the most prominent of which was said to be the apparition of a nun. She was seen by the Bull family on numerous occasions, often at sunset, passing along the stretch of rectory grounds that the Bulls informally referred to as the Nun's Walk.

The origin of the Borley Nun was straight out of a gothic ghost novel. She supposedly lived at a nearby nunnery and met with a monk for illicit romantic trysts. When their forbidden love was uncovered, the nun was bricked up alive within the walls of the nunnery, left to slowly starve to death in the darkness.

It's a tragic tale, and the chances are that it is exactly that—a tale. Despite multiple record searches by experienced investigators, no evidence whatsoever has been found to back it up. Historians haven't even been able to cite a nunnery in the region, which makes it even harder to explain the presence of a nun or a novice. Yet the Borley Nun was seen by multiple eyewitnesses on numerous occasions, over the span of several decades. This included not just members of the Bull family but also their household staff. It is believed that the first reported sightings date back to the 1880s, but that doesn't necessarily mean that earlier apparitions did not take place.

The elusive nun wasn't the only phantom to be reckoned with at Borley. A man in black was also seen inside the rectory on several different occasions, his identity equally as mysterious as that of the nun. The gardens were said to be haunted by a headless man—perhaps the same headless figure who legend insisted drove the phantom coach and horses?

The story of the Borley Nun is that a young nun was having romantic encounters with a monk. The trysts were discovered, and someone bricked her into a wall and left her to starve to death.

Critics of the Borley haunting, many of whom dismiss the case in its entirety, rarely seem to consider motive when they decide that the whole thing was just a hoax. Why would a respected member of the clergy, a bona fide pillar of the community, actively participate in something that, if it were proved to be untrue, would only serve to harm his reputation? By all accounts, the Reverend Harry Bull accepted with equanimity the notion of his home being haunted. During his downtime at the end of the day, he was often to be found sitting in the summer house, keeping a watchful eye on the Nun's Walk, waiting for her to put in an appearance.

Why would Harry Bull have wasted all that time on something he knew to be false? Those who knew him said that the Reverend was completely unfazed by the multitude of ghosts that were said to haunt the rectory. He spoke of having seen them often, particularly the nun, whom he claimed to have encountered in different parts of the grounds.

Whatever else might be said about the Borley haunting, the Bull family believed in its authenticity without a shadow of a doubt. They lived with the ghostly phenomena on a daily basis. Ghosts became almost a part of the fabric at Borley, whether in the form of the ringing of bells intended to summon servants or the appearance of shadowy figures that disappeared into thin air right before their eyes.

Next to Borley Church is a very old graveyard. Rumor has it, though, that there is a mass graveyard where the rectory used to be, and this might explain the spiritual activity.

The reason behind the ghostly goings-on was never satisfactorily explained. The deaths of Henry and Caroline Bull inside the rectory fail to explain the sightings of the phantom nun or the dark man.

Going further back a few centuries, local legend held that plague victims were buried in what would presumably be a mass grave ("plague pit") somewhere on the rectory grounds. This seems to be more a case of hearsay and local folklore than established fact, however, and the claim should be approached with considerable caution.

After being held for more than 60 years by the Bull family, the tenancy of Borley Rectory was taken up by the Reverend Guy Eric Smith and his wife Mabel in 1928.

The forbidding building had been dormant and unoccupied for a year, a vacancy to which its dark reputation had surely contributed.

The Smiths were ignorant of this when they accepted the position at Borley. Their choices of a parish at that time were few and far between, and they were no doubt glad to be settling into a new home. The rectory was a dank and gloomy place, however, and one that was much in need of improvement and maintenance. They would not remain for long.

How much of their discomfiture came from the relatively austere conditions and the ghost stories circulating around the parish, versus from the actual paranormal activity that started up as soon as the Smiths took up occupancy, is something only they could say for sure. However, the Reverend Smith was sufficiently concerned to contact the *Daily Mirror* newspaper in 1929, asking for help with their ghostly problems.

Ghost hunters were few and far between in the 1920s. One of the most prominent was a colorful character that we have already met within these pages: none other than our old friend Harry Price, of Cashen's Gap and Gef the Talking Mongoose fame. Sensing an opportunity, Price visited the rectory in person, ostensibly to conduct a preliminary assessment of the situation.

What Price found—after poking around the rectory itself and Borley in general, asking shrewd questions of the Smiths, the Bull siblings, and various local residents—was the basis for further investigation. The Smiths impressed Price with their earnestness. He judged them both to be credible witnesses, offering compelling testimony concerning the haunting of the rectory. Within the same year, they were gone, leaving the building empty once more in the summer of 1929.

If the haunting had been smoldering up to this point, the arrival of the next tenants poured gasoline on top, blowing it up into a raging inferno. The spotlight fell less on the Reverend Lionel Foyster; much more attention was paid to his wife, Marianne. The 21-year age gap between husband and wife raised eyebrows wherever they went. The Foysters also had an adopted daughter named Adelaide. Their family dynamic was an unusual one, especially for the 1930s. It became more unusual still when, after the Foysters had settled into Borley Rectory,

An 1892 photograph of the Borley Rectory, the same year Rev. Henry Bull died there.

Marianne began an affair with a Canadian lover who moved into the neighboring cottage. The Foysters had interviewed the single father for a job as a potential handyman. He quickly became much more than that, providing the listless Marianne with the excitement she had craved since moving into the dour and lonely old house.

Scribbled writing began appearing on the walls inside the rectory. Some of the messages mentioned Marianne by name, asking for help in the form of mass and prayers.

> On more than one occasion, Marianne saw the apparition of Harry Bull inside the rectory; perhaps he was making good on his promise to express his displeasure at the way things were being run there.

As the Foysters' tenure wore on, the paranormal activity intensified. Bells rang of their own volition. Household items disappeared, sometimes re-appearing elsewhere—and some-times, apparently, gone forever. Disembodied footsteps and knockings became a semi-regular occurrence. Objects such as stones were thrown. The Foysters were never popular with the locals, and some of them blamed the activity on Marianne, as have many of those who are skeptical of the Borley haunting. Even Harry Price, whose most famous case would be Borley, initially took this view. Yet this explanation conveniently ignored the fact that apparently paranormal activity still took place when Marianne was not in residence at Borley, staying with friends out of town. Although she, and potentially her lover, could have faked some of the strange goings-on, it was impossible for them to have faked all of it.

On more than one occasion, Marianne saw the apparition of Harry Bull inside the rectory; perhaps he was making good on his prom-ise to express his displeasure at the way things were being run there. Maybe the former rector disapproved of the adultery being committed under "his" roof by a successor's wife and her lover. Such behavior would hardly sit well with a man of the cloth, particularly when it was being carried out in his former home.

Attempts to exorcise the rectory, in the hope of cleansing it of the haunting, proved to be ineffective.

By October of 1931, the Foysters were growing increasingly perplexed by the haunting. Enter once more the flamboyant Harry Price, who returned to Borley at the invitation of Lionel Foyster. The only stipulation was that Price keep his investigation on the down-low. Price not only agreed but did so in writing; yet anybody who was familiar with the publicity-loving Price could have predicted the outcome nonetheless: Price talked about the case, and even wrote about it in his memoir, albeit with some identifying details changed for publication. He had fallen on hard times and could ill afford a lawsuit. He would not return for several years.

By 1937, the Foysters had since moved out. Never one to let an opportunity pass by, Price rented Borley Rectory lock, stock, and barrel for one year. For a psychic investigator (the commonly used term), it was an invaluable chance to create a ghost lab: a controlled environment that Price would populate with volunteer observers, who would staff the rectory around the clock, living on-site and documenting whatever phenomena took place there. Price intended to write a bestselling book about the yearlong experiment.

Price obtained his volunteers by placing an advertisement in a national newspaper. Application letters flooded in. The psychic investigator winnowed them down to a pool of what he believed to be qualified and suitable applicants and then set about establishing a staffing roster.

Ultimately, although participants recorded having some strange experiences, there was nothing remotely akin to the paranormal activity that Borley Rectory saw during its heyday. When Harry Price and his team vacated the rectory in the summer of 1938, it appeared as if the haunting had all but fizzled out.

In February of the following year, the final tenant of Borley Rectory—one Captain Gregson—accidentally knocked over a lamp, which in turn set fire to the place. By the time firefighters arrived on the scene, it was too late. The building was fully engulfed in flames. Eyewitnesses would later claim that shadowy human forms could be seen in the rectory windows, backlit by the fire; no living people were inside the building at the time.

Fortunately, nobody was hurt, but once the blaze was extinguished, the rectory was a burned-out ghost of its former self. The damage was so great that the structure was declared beyond salvage and repair. It was subsequently demolished. This did not stop claims of phantom lights, footsteps, and other strange noises coming from the demolition site.

TERRIFYINGLY TRUE HAUNTINGS

The rectory burned down on February 27, 1939, when the owner, Captain W. H. Gregson, knocked over an oil lamp. The fire spread quickly, and with the only water available coming from a single well, there was no chance of dousing it.

The legend of the haunted rectory lived on.

The publication of Harry Price's book *The Most Haunted House in England,* along with its sequel, *The End of Borley Rectory,* breathed new life into the story. The reading public was intrigued by this most British of haunted house tales. More than 80 years later, that remains the case. Multiple books and movies have been released, each giving a different take on the strange happenings at the curious rectory in Essex.

Price died of a heart attack in 1948, age 67. His name was to be linked with Borley forever after. It remains his best-known case.

Was the haunting genuine?

In spite of what she told people during her tenancy at Borley, Mabel Smith later changed her tune significantly, claiming she had never believed the rectory to be haunted, let alone been frightened by the paranormal activity there. This reversal helped stoke the fires of controversy.

Paul Tabori and Peter Underwood noted in *The Ghosts of Borley* that, after initially telling multiple people about the strange phenomena taking place in her presence,

> [l]ater (much later) she would provide different versions, completely at variance with her own earlier accounts and with those of others.

Mabel Smith would ultimately declare that the whole affair had been little more than rumors, gossip, and tall tales blown out of all proportion by people such as Harry Price, in the pursuit of publicity. While Price was indeed a shameless publicity hound, this explanation falls far short of explaining the multitude of testimony that was recorded both before and during his association with Borley.

Even if we accept the near certainty that Price exaggerated and sensationalized the ghostly goings-on at the rectory—and some accused him of outright fraud—the fact is that the ghost stories long predated his arrival. The claims also continued after his death, much to the very understandable annoyance of Borley residents. Long after the rectory itself was reduced to rubble, tourists ignored the clearly posted no trespassing signs, wandering the property in search of the ghosts.

Another school of thought proposed that Marianne Foyster was behind much of the allegedly paranormal activity, using it as a convenient cover for the trysts she had with her lover inside the rectory. Admittedly, Mrs. Foyster's personal life was—to put it mildly—something of a train wreck, particularly where her relationships with the opposite sex were concerned. At one point, she was married to two men at the same time.

Following her time at Borley, Marianne lived a mobile life before finally settling in the United States, where she died in 1992. It is possible, perhaps even likely, that she could have been responsible for some of the phenomena reported at Borley, such as the writing that appeared suddenly on the rectory walls; but once again, this fails to account for the ghost stories that surrounded the building before the Foysters moved in, and that continued at the site of its foundation long after the fire had burned itself out.

Prominent British psychic researcher Harry Price wrote about the Borley Rectory ghosts in two of his books: *The Most Haunted House in England* and its sequel, *The End of Borley Rectory.*

Once the rectory was completely demolished, the paranormal spotlight was turned upon the church located across the way. Many of the principals of the Borley story, including members of the Bull family, are buried in its cemetery.

The organ inside the church was said to play all by itself when the building was empty and locked up for the night. Disembodied footsteps had been heard on the footpath in the graveyard on more than one occasion. The phantom nun was sighted in that same graveyard, perhaps having relocated to the church now that there was no rectory for her to haunt. (Although the nun was never seen *inside* the rectory, the majority of those who saw her either lived there, worked there, or were visiting it.) With her audience mostly gone, it would make sense for the ghost to be seen around the more frequently trafficked church.

On December 4, 1975, BBC One (the premier British television channel at the time) aired a documentary film titled *The Ghost Hunters*. It has aged remarkably well, particularly in these days of emotionally charged histrionic ghost-hunting TV, and is well worth watching.

The final segment of three featured Peter Underwood escorting a BBC reporter on an overnight vigil at Borley Church. Before that, it was necessary for Underwood to lay some groundwork. After correcting the reporter on the basic facts ("We're not actually at Borley Rectory, because Borley Rectory stood over there, and is no longer there...."), Underwood gave his interviewer a rundown on the history and ghost-lore of Borley before nailing his colors to the mast and declaring firmly that in his opinion, the rectory really did deserve the sobriquet of "the Most Haunted House in England."

Underwood emphasized that over the period of 1863 to 1935, four rectors, along with their wives, families, and others, all reported seeing, hearing, and feeling strange things while living in, working in, or visiting the rectory. It is hard to argue with the sheer volume of cumulative experiential testimony to which the ghost hunter alludes. One can question and dismiss some of it—but not *all* of it.

In 1975, as now, ghost hunters were amateurs—interested and passionate individuals who made a living working regular jobs

The interior of Borley Church.

and would then spend sleepless nights staking out haunted locations. The next interview took place at a construction site, where one such enthusiast took a break from operating industrial equipment to recount his experiences on the site of the rectory. Geoffrey Croom-Hollingsworth claimed to have sighted the nun early one morning while in the company of a friend. The sighting took place on the former Nun's Walk under the light of a full moon. The figure glided through bushes and railings as though they weren't there. It is difficult not to feel the same amount of disbelief as the skeptical reporter when Croom-Hollingsworth claims the sighting lasted for 9 to 11 minutes. For one thing, even when factoring in the technology standards of the mid-1970s, one is forced to ask why neither observer thought to take a photograph during this extremely long (for a ghost sighting) amount of time.

The apparition, he claimed, was floating approximately a foot above the ground, due to the earth having sunk since the time the ghost was first "produced." Matters escalated when the construction worker's companion threw a brick at the phantom nun. The hurled brick flew straight through her, without meeting resistance or provoking any reaction whatsoever.

If there's even a grain of truth to Croom-Hollingworth's story, then it would appear that the Borley Nun was still active some 36 years after the rectory went up in flames.

Following this encounter with what may or may not have been an apparition on the grounds of the rectory, Croom-Hollingworth and his colleagues turned their attention to the interior of Borley Church in an effort to capture evidence of its ghosts.

Prior to the advent of digital recording technology, ghost hunters used the medium of magnetic tape to record sound (and later video) at haunted locations. Magnetic tape is still used today by many paranormal investigators, as the analog recording mechanism sometimes catches anomalous noises and voices that more modern devices can miss.

In the early 1970s, tape recorders represented the technological state of the art. Croom-Hollingworth and his companions

RUINS OF BORLEY RECTORY, most haunted house in England, provided the photographer who took this picture in 1944 with a puzzling bit of ghost-craft. At instant shutter was snapped a brick (white speck against dark shadow in room at right) rose from the floor, apparently nudged by unseen hands.

A newspaper printed this photo of the rectory in 1944. As the caption states, the white dot appearing in the shadows is a reflection from a brick that suddenly floated up as the photo was being taken.

searched the church to ensure that it was empty, then set a pair of tape machines running, locking them inside the empty building. The result was intriguing, though not spectacular: the tapes recorded what sounded like a door being unlatched and opened. Their attempts to identify the source of the noise were unsuccessful.

Returning one week later, the team again locked their tape recorders inside the empty church. This time, two of the investigators felt as if they were being watched by unseen eyes. Skeptics would rightly point out that this could easily be explained by the power of suggestion. What turned up on the tape, however, could not be dismissed so simply: the sound of a male sighing loudly. It's an impressive catch and one that is challenging to debunk.

More sensory-related phenomena followed. One ghost hunter felt "a presence" pressing itself up against his back. A mysterious knocking sound was heard (and recorded). The interval between raps was precise and regular, but if there was a mechanical source, such as pipes cooling down, the ghost hunters seemed unable to identify it. It should also be noted that more than 50 years before, the Reverend Harry Bull also heard inexplicable knockings inside the church. A case of haunted history repeating itself, perhaps.

On a later visit, yet another sigh was heard—this one deeper in timbre and distinctly more chilling to hear. Much like the first sigh, the second is all but impossible to write off as being a natural part of the environment or the structure settling. The sound clearly came from a human throat. The question then becomes: whose?

After several sessions recording the background noise of an empty church, the trio of ghost hunters spent a memorable night sitting inside the building themselves. The entire group saw pinpoints of light appear in the vicinity of the font. This was followed by an extremely loud clatter. The air began to turn cold. The lights came closer to the ghost hunters and then disappeared.

Were the ghost hunters simply seeing things? The eyes are prone to playing tricks in low light conditions. That would be the simplest explanation, though it would have to be paired with mutual suggestibility in order to make sense for all three to see the same thing at the same time.

Alternatively, the lights could have been some kind of psychic phenomenon. Some psychics would suggest this was the initial stage of a spirit manifestation. It's an intriguing hypothesis, and unfortunately one that remains untested, as they vanished before the ghost hunters could do anything more than simply observe and document their presence.

Today, Borley is a quiet and peaceful place; in many ways, it's the archetypal English village, relatively untouched by the twenty-first century and its ever-increasing urban sprawl. The church still stands, although those who are charged with its upkeep sensibly rebuff the attentions of would-be ghost hunters. Modern-day Harry Prices are no longer welcome, and it is hard to blame the villagers for it.

The rectory may be long since gone to ashes, but a part of it remains—virtually, that is. In 2024, Professor Richard Wiseman and his colleagues at the University of Hertfordshire used digital technology to recreate a virtual reality section of Borley Rectory, the infamous Blue Room. Some considered this to be the most haunted part of the building.

> Today, Borley is a quiet and peaceful place; in many ways, it's the archetypal English village, relatively untouched by the twenty-first century and its ever-increasing urban sprawl.

Wiseman's team used the notes of Harry Price, photographs of the Blue Room, and the floor plans of Borley Rectory in order to get the room interior correct down to the smallest detail. Yet the room exists not just in cyberspace but also in the material world. Its physical component resides in a room at the university. Those who don the VR equipment enter an environment that is interactive. Surfaces can be touched. Furniture can be leaned against or sat upon.

Then come the ghosts. Professor Wiseman and his group are able to interject the Borley phenomena, such as phantom footsteps and disembodied voices, into the virtual experience. They are simulating paranormal activity to order and are using it to populate a test environment that allows them to study its effects on volunteers.

The implications of this experiment are profound. Given sufficient time, effort, and money, further sections of the building could be recreated. It might be possible for future researchers to walk the halls and gardens of a virtual Borley Rectory, sharing the same view that was seen by Harry Price or the Bull family.

Perhaps they will even encounter a virtual nun.

THE R101 AIRSHIP

Hubris: the notion that excessive pride, usually infused with a large bolus of arrogance, often precedes a great disaster. The annals of history are replete with hubristic tragedies, and the British Empire had more than its fair share of them.

Arguably, the poster child was the RMS *Titanic*. Depending upon which source we accept, between 1,503 and 1,517 souls lost their lives when the supposedly unsinkable ocean liner sank beneath the icy Atlantic waters on April 15, 1912. Yet the ship, which one White Star Line employee claimed that not even God Himself could sink, was riddled with design and manufacturing flaws, ranging from incomplete watertight compartments to an inadequate number of lifeboats.

The pride of British maritime engineering struck an iceberg at high speed, resulting in damage to her hull and catastrophic flooding. The *Titanic*'s captain, Edward John Smith, was a highly experienced mariner. By all rights, he should have known better than to push his ship so quickly through waters that were infested with icebergs. Yet visibility was good that night, and Smith had a track record of taking such calculated risks throughout his career. Lookouts were posted atop masts to watch for icebergs, and Smith doubtless felt that the *Titanic* was more than capable of evading any hazards once they were spotted. Indeed, so confident was he that he wasn't even present on the bridge at the time of the collision.

Hundreds of the *Titanic*'s passengers and crew paid for that poor decision with their lives. Smith was one of them, choosing to go down

The RMS *Titanic* (seen here departing Belfast on April 2, 1912) was the pride of the British Empire and was declared unsinkable. So much for hubris.

with his ship in the time-honored tradition of generations of sea captains.

The loss of the *Titanic* delivered a black eye to Britannia's image and constituted a national trauma, the after-echoes of which can still be felt today. At the dock in her departure port of Southampton, the berth in which she was moored—number 44—is still used by cruise liners today. A small memorial plaque serves as a memorial to the tragedy of some 1,500 victims of British hubris.

Just as the age of sail gave way to the age of steam, so did the age of steam transition into the age of flight. Although the British Empire would enter a state of decline after World War II, in the late 1920s, British imperial colonialism still spanned the globe. Up to that point, ships had been the primary method of connecting the capital city of London and the rest of the British Isles with their far-flung overseas territories. Now it was envisioned that vast fleets of airships might be used to convey passengers, merchant goods, and information across those vast distances in significantly shorter transit times than even the fastest oceangoing vessel could accomplish. If war should break out, the airships would be earmarked to deliver soldiers and military supplies quickly to deployment bases around the world.

In 1924, this ambitious plan was codified as the Imperial Airship Scheme. This plan called for two enormous airships, the R100 and R101, to be constructed as the first phase of what was intended to be a national fleet-building program. The sister airships, which would feature different designs and be built by separate manufacturers, would be the precursors for an entirely new generation of vessels if all went according to plan.

The burgeoning airship industry was ramping up production and experimentation throughout the 1920s. Eighteen years after the sinking of the RMS *Titanic,* another tragic disaster would befall the nation. Known as the *Titanic* of the skies, the accidental destruction of the R101 airship is remarkable for many reasons—not least, the ghosts of its crew—who, it was claimed, reached out beyond the grave to explain why it was that the mammoth vessel went down in flames.

After a lengthy design and construction process, both the R100 and R101 took to the skies for trial flights in 1929, undergoing testing

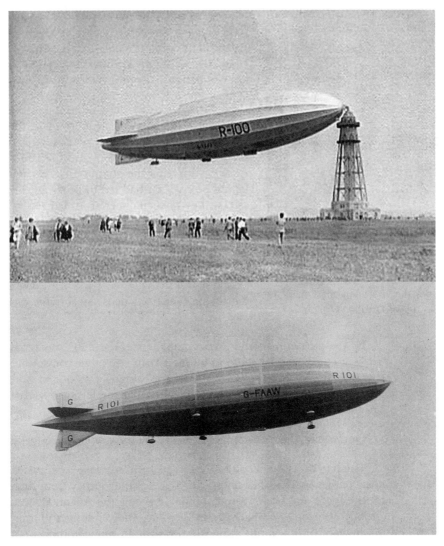

Sister airships R100 (top) and R101 were the first two dirigibles of a planned British fleet.

and air trials. The designers of the mighty dirigibles were all very familiar with the risks associated with airship travel, but some experimental changes were made to the R101 design that had never been incorporated into an airframe before.

Ever since its inception, the fledgling field of air transportation had seen numerous high-profile crashes. Up to that point, it had taken courage (and perhaps even a degree of foolhardiness) to be a passenger

TERRIFYINGLY TRUE HAUNTINGS

After some trial flights the year before, the R101 went on its maiden voyage on October 4, 1930.

or serve as a crew member on board an airship. Floating through the skies in what was essentially a gondola slung underneath a gigantic bag of highly combustible hydrogen gas was definitely not for the faint of heart.

Fully aware of this, those same designers had made every effort to make the R101 not just the latest and greatest airship the world had ever seen but also the safest. After scrutinizing the common causes and failure points that had led to other air disasters, they had engineered a plethora of safety features into the craft. This included less combustible diesel engines instead of the petroleum-based alternatives. The end result, however, was that the R101 was heavier and slower than desired, particularly when the airship's relatively dense steel frame was factored in.

By the time construction was complete and the R101 was ready to fly, it was believed by some to be safer than any other conveyance that was flying through the skies at that time. Others were not so sure; some qualified engineers commented darkly that the R100 and R101 might in fact be death traps.

Once again, there was hubris. Once again, there would be tragedy.

The R101 was the second of the two airships to take to the skies. In the summer of 1930, her sibling, R100, made the journey from England to Canada and back without a hitch, crossing the Atlantic Ocean in order to do so. Later that year, in October, an even longer journey was scheduled to inaugurate the R101: a voyage to Karachi, India.

On paper, the journey seemed straightforward enough, but it was one that had never been made before. In a politically calculated public vote of confidence regarding the airship's safety, included among the passengers was Christopher B. Thomson, the Secretary of State for Air and prime mover behind the airship program. Predictably, the construction process hit roadblocks and underwent multiple delays. Thomson had pushed for the R101 to be put into service as quickly as possible. In order to do so, the testing process had not been as rigorous as it might have been when the first passengers and dignitaries boarded the R101 for its maiden flight to India.

Despite the project's prestige status, it must be borne in mind that the R101 was after all an experimental craft—and the biggest man-made object flying at the time of its launch. The airship was 777 feet from nose to tail and 130 feet wide. The bulk of her cubic footprint consisted of huge, inflatable bladders filled with hydrogen gas, which when inflated would provide the R101 with the lift required to soar.

In order to help change altitude, the airship needed ballast—a substance used to provide it with stability in flight. The R101 was ballasted with water, which could, if necessary, be dumped on the captain's order to trim the airship and level it out.

Much like her spiritual ocean liner forebear, the *Titanic*, the R101 was considered the last word in luxury air travel. Passengers could while away time drinking at the bar or dining on the finest food or simply enjoy watching the landscape passing by below them as they puffed on a cigarette or cigar in the smoking lounge.

Enormous sheds that had been built at their home base in Cardington, Bedfordshire, during World War I were repurposed to house the airship. To most people, the word "shed" conjures up images of small wooden huts used to store tools and gardening equipment. The sheds at

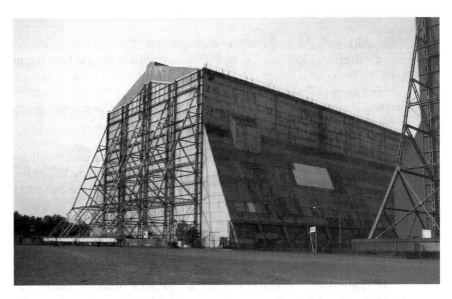

Shed No. 1 at the airfield at Shortstown, Bedfordshire, housed the R101 airship. The empty shell is still there today, a reminder of what could have been a great chapter in air travel history.

TERRIFYINGLY TRUE HAUNTINGS

Cardington couldn't be more different. They were cavernous, constructed from 4,000 tons of steel, stretching to 812 feet long, spanning 180 feet wide, and rising 157 feet high. The doors alone weighed 70 tons.

On the evening of Saturday, October 4, the R101 left her mooring position at Cardington and flew off on her rendezvous with history. Nobody on board suspected how brief that maiden flight was to be or how tragic would be the outcome. Heading southward, the airship passed over the capital and then set out across the English Channel, bound for France. The crew was in a rush to try to get ahead of worsening weather conditions farther along their flight path.

The early morning hours of October 5 found the airship cruising above the French countryside, making a speed of around 30 knots despite there being notable winds aloft. Most of the passengers had retired to their cabins and were asleep in their beds. Shortly after 2 a.m., the R101's nose pitched forward unexpectedly. Fortunately, despite the airship's tail-heaviness, the crew was able to regain normal flight by forcing the nose back up into a neutral position.

This was not the case when the same happened a second time. The airship began to descend again, a descent from which it never recovered. The R101 hit the ground but remained intact, then slowly inched its way forward, dragging against the earth as it went.

Although the airframe was damaged, the R101 had crash-landed relatively intact. However, the hydrogen contained in the gas bags began venting into the atmosphere, where it came into contact with one of the hot engines. Predictably, it ignited. (This became the commonly accepted explanation for the explosion, though it was not conclusively proved and never could be.)

The R101 blew up. The volatile hydrogen gas, along with the diesel fuel for the airship's engines, burned until there was nothing left of the mighty airship but a twisted metal framework and a massive burn scar on the landscape near the village of Allonne.

Forty-eight of the R101's passengers and crew lost their lives in the inferno. Only six crewmen escaped with their lives. One would succumb to his injuries several days afterward. In addition to the death of Lord Thomson, the crash also killed Air Vice Marshall Sir Sefton Brancker, the senior government minister for Civil Aviation. Along with them went all hopes and aspirations for a national airship program in the future. The loss of the R101 was too great a wound to the collective

The R101 crashed and burned in Allonne, Picardie, France, on October 5, 1930. Nothing was left but the frame after the intense fire consumed everything else. Of the 54 people on board, 48 died, including most of the Air Ministry's design team.

psyche of the British public. The R100 was taken out of service and scrapped, along with the remnants of the R101's steel skeleton.

On October 7, the bodies of those who died in the crash were returned to England. The French authorities accorded their remains high honors, with the prime minister of France himself being present. A brace of Royal Navy warships conveyed the coffins across the English Channel, where the British military took over escort duties.

A dedicated train transported them to London. On October 10, before the eyes of a grieving British public, their coffins lay in state in Westminster Hall, each one covered with the national flag as a mark of respect. People queued for hours in order to pay their respects.

On the following day, October 11, the remains were placed back on the train and taken to Bedford. The decision had been made to bury them all together in a mass grave in the churchyard of St. Mary the Virgin Church in Cardington, where their fateful journey had begun and ultimately would conclude. Many of the bodies were so badly burned that they could not be definitively identified. All 48 were laid to rest just a stone's throw from the Cardington sheds with full military honors, including a flypast by fighter planes of the Royal Air Force.

There was, quite understandably, a national clamor to know exactly why the tragedy had happened. It came to light that criticism of the airship's design had been swept under the carpet in the name of expediting the R101's already overdue maiden voyage. The craft was heavy, particularly at the rear, and as a consequence, the crew had found it difficult to gain the lift needed to prevent the final, fatal crash landing.

Most retellings of the R101 story end here, closing the book on what became regarded as a cautionary tale of tragedy. Yet there was more, for the ghosts of the stricken airship would soon begin to speak.

On the afternoon of Tuesday, October 7, while the bodies of the R101 crash victims were being repatriated to Britain, our old friend Harry Price was conducting a séance. The séance was held at his London-based National Laboratory of Psychical Research. Price was assessing the capabilities of the 37-year-old Irish trance medium Eileen Garrett.

Ever since she was a young girl, Garrett had perceived things that others could not, playing with ghostly children in a reminder of the axiom that not all imaginary friends are necessarily imaginary at all. At home one day, she encountered the apparition of her aunt, who was carrying a newborn baby toward her. It was only after the aunt told Eileen that she and the baby had to leave that Eileen learned of her death during labor. Her baby also died.

Irish medium and parapsychologist Eileen Garrett was already well known in the field when she decided to hold séances to contact the victims of the R101 crash.

A sickly youth, Garrett had three children of her own during her first marriage. Her first marriage ended in divorce; her second ended with the death of her husband on the Western Front in World War I. His death was revealed to her in a psychic vision.

Spiritualism exploded across the United Kingdom in the aftermath of the Great War, borne on a tidal wave of grief at the loss of an entire generation of young men in the bloodbaths of trench warfare. Exploring those new horizons convinced Eileen Garrett—and soon, an army of supporters—that she was able to communicate with the dead. Communication was achieved by entering a trance, at which point her "control" would come to the fore. This was a spirit that claimed to be a deceased Arab soldier named Uvani. He facilitated the connection between Eileen and whichever other entities wished to speak through her, much like the moderator of a panel would at a conference.

The intent on that particular Tuesday in October was to attempt connection with the spirit of Sir Arthur Conan Doyle, who had died on July 7. What came through instead was somebody very different.

Eileen Garrett entered a trance state and turned over control to Uvani as usual. In his distinctively slow and halting manner (English was not Uvani's native language), Uvani announced the arrival of a spirit calling itself Irwin.

Using technical terms appropriate to an airship officer, Irwin stated that the R101's "bulk was entirely and absolutely too much for her engine capacity."

Flight Lieutenant H. C. (Herbert Carmichael) Irwin had been the commanding officer of the R101. Speaking through the mouth of Eileen Garrett, H. C. Irwin had an incredible story to tell. As the words spilled out of her, a secretary scribbled away furiously, transcribing the words for posterity. (Price would later publish the account in his book *Leaves from a Psychist's Case Book*.)

Price describes Irwin as being "extremely agitated," completely understandable if one has just died a violent death. Using technical terms appropriate to an airship officer, Irwin stated that the R101's "bulk was entirely and absolutely too much for her engine capacity." Further: "Useful lift too small."

In both assessments, he was correct. The R101 had indeed struggled to attain sufficient lift, something that the design's detractors had already pointed out. Irwin went on to rattle off a laundry list of faults with his doomed airship:

Elevators, the movable control surfaces designed to change the angle at which air flowed over themselves and therefore change the pitch of the airship, had jammed; an oil pipe had gotten plugged; the fabric of the outer skin was too tense, resulting in chafing. If it tore, then the inner gas bags containing the volatile hydrogen would be exposed to the elements.

Due to the R101 being underpowered, it was never able to reach cruising altitude because the airship was too heavy to rise.

The trials that the R101 was run through prior to her maiden voyage were too short, intentionally truncated in order to meet the fast-approaching departure date.

It was a damning list and made absolute sense when one factored in what was known about the R101's flaws. Irwin went on to state that the weather was too poor to safely undertake a long flight and that rain had soaked the fabric of the balloon, adding still more water weight to an already overloaded airframe.

"Nose is down," Irwin went on. "Impossible to rise. Cannot trim. Almost scraped the roofs of Achy. Kept to railway. An enquiry to be held later. It will be found that the superstructure of the envelope contained no resilience and had far too much weight in envelope. The added middle section was entirely wrong. Too heavy. Too much over weighted for the capacity of the engines."

The R101 was indeed nose-heavy, something for which the crew would try to compensate by trimming the airship. "Trimming" is the process of setting the control surfaces, such as the elevators (which Irwin claimed would jam) in such a position that the airship would fly straight and level without any control input from her crew. Pilots trim aircraft all the time. Once it's trimmed correctly, the aircraft can then cruise "hands off" for the most part, flying at a consistent altitude for as long as the air conditions do not radically change. According to Flight Lieutenant Irwin—or the spirit claiming to be him—the R101 could not be trimmed and also refused to rise. That put her in a dangerously unstable state, as demonstrated by the R101 almost hitting the rooftops in Achy, a village located northwest of where the airship finally came down.

Irwin also mentioned "an exorbitant scheme of carbon and hydrogen." This referred to a proposed experiment in which the airship's gas bladders would be filled not with pure hydrogen but rather with a carbon-hydrogen mix. This is what Irwin meant when he said that the airship would get to "no altitude worth speaking about." Although debated, this hadn't happened yet, but it was a piece of information that shouldn't have been known to a member of the public.

The weather had indeed been less than optimal, with rain soaking the envelope as the R101 made for France. Mrs. Garrett was also correct

The memorial to the R101 crash in Allone, France, was unveiled in 1933.

about there having been a middle section added in order to accommodate an additional gas bag. Her reference to the airship having overflown Achy would also not have been common knowledge, as the newspaper reports did not mention the settlement, and it did not appear on many maps, being considered too small to be significant.

Eileen Garrett continued to pour forth a torrent of aviation-specific technical information. This was data that the average person in the street, even if they were well educated, would probably be unaware of. Had the medium set out to defraud Price, she would have had relatively little time to prepare, having to locate technical manuals and absorbing a wealth of complex engineering-related data before regurgitating it while faking a trance state. This would have been no small task, to say the least. Garrett talked about fuel injectors, air screws, and other components of the airship in a knowledgeable manner. Is it reasonable to believe she had spent the last 36 hours taking a—no pun intended—crash course on dirigible design and mechanics, purely in an effort to impress Harry Price?

Could Eileen Garrett simply have read about the crash in the newspapers and prepared her spiel accordingly? It is possible, but unlikely, given the time frame and the depth of information she provided. The R101 went down in the early hours of Sunday morning. Word made it back to England that same day, and it was certainly front-page news in the press all day Monday.

> The terminology used by Mrs. Garrett, such as "disposable lift" and "bore capacity," were directly in accordance with those used by airship crews at the time.

Playing devil's advocate, there was much public discussion regarding the reasons behind the R101 having gone down. Every patron in a pub had an opinion, so some of the information could have been gleaned by picking the brains of her friends and acquaintances but not all of it. Again, the information regarding the proposed hydrogen/carbon mix that was not public knowledge particularly stands out. The terminology used by Mrs. Garrett, such as "disposable lift" and "bore capacity," were directly in accordance with those used by airship crews at the time. A supply officer for the R101, whom Price referred to as "Mr. X" and was actually named William Charlton, read the transcript of the séance and gave his professional opinion that much of what had come through made sense to him.

In short, "Irwin," whether it was truly the ghost of the R101's commanding officer, a figment of Eileen Garrett's subconscious, or a strange form of telepathy, clearly knew its stuff. Whichever was the case, Price for one found the evidence presented via mediumship to be credible, even if he wasn't necessarily convinced that Garrett was speaking with the dead. It should be noted that not everybody was in agreement with him. Some aeronautical professionals were openly critical of the Garrett-"Irwin" communications, alleging that some of their content failed to make a great deal of sense and that not all of the information she provided was as obscure as Price and the experts he consulted made it out to be.

Eileen Garrett's connection with the R101 tragedy was not over yet. After her séance with Harry Price, she undertook similar séances with Major Oliver Villiers of the Air Ministry present. Villiers had known some of those who perished in the R101 disaster and took both a personal and professional interest in the supposed afterlife communications that were being relayed by Eileen Garrett.

Fittingly, one such séance took place on Halloween night of that same year (1930). Once again, a communicator purporting to be Flight Lieutenant Irwin quickly came through via Mrs. Garrett. He announced that "we feel like damned murderers," presumably a reference to allowing the R101 to make her final flight three weeks prior. In death, the commander of the stricken dirigible bitterly regretted not having pushed back against the authorities that had compelled him to captain the maiden flight of a flawed and unready vessel.

Irwin's ghost went on to explain that a broken nose strut had torn a hole in the airship's outer skin, allowing the gusty air to penetrate the interior of the R101. This had contributed to its poor handling characteristics at the time of the crash: "The rush of wind caused the first dive, and then we straightened again, and another gust surging through the hole finished us off."

In future séances, other occupants of the R101 came through. One purported to be the aforementioned Air Vice Marshall Sir Sefton Brancker. Brancker claimed that he and Irwin, along with navigator Ernest Johnston and Major George Scott, the government's assistant director of airship development,, had informed Lord Thomson that the R101 was undergoing technical difficulties that meant the flight should probably be scrubbed. Thomson was having none of it, Brancker said; the senior government minister knew that his reputation was at stake and was hell-bent on getting the airship to India no matter what.

The ghost of Major Scott emerged and backed up Irwin's claim about the damaged strut ripping open the R101's covering. Scott even gave Major Villiers the exact location of the strut, numbering it precisely in accordance with its place on the airship's design blueprint.

Accusations of charlatanry were leveled at Harry Price throughout his career—accusations that were not without merit. Nevertheless, he was not present at the séances that were conducted with Major Villiers, so he could not have influenced their results even if he had wished to do so.

One of the classic motivators behind an intelligent haunting is that of unfinished business. In the case of the R101, assuming that the Garrett communications were legitimate, it is entirely possible that the spirit communicators wanted to confirm the reasons why their airship crashed and make it known that the tragedy was not their fault. Human failure

Officers and crew of the R101 pictured here during flight trials on October 23, 1929, are: (back row, left to right) A. Disley, W. G. W. Short, C. Bottomley, A. Hastings, W. Norcott, A. V. Bell; (third row, left to right) W. Moule, S. T. Blackwell, W. H. King, J. Richardson, H. R. Hudson, S. E. Scott, A. J. Cook, C. Taylor, R. Beake, C. J. Fergusson; (second row, left to right) G. K. Atkins, W. A. Potter, G. W. Hunt, Lt. Commander N. G. Atherstone, H. C. Irwin, E. L. Johnston, M. H. Steff, W. R. Gent, F. Noble; (front row, left to right) H. Rowe, Unknown, Tim the Mascot, H. G. Rampton, H. E. Ford.

had been involved, but most of it had taken place prior to the R101 embarking on her final voyage. The crew had gallantly remained at their posts, wrestling with their controls in a vain attempt to avert disaster. They failed and paid for their efforts with their lives.

To make matters worse, Flight Lieutenant Irwin repeatedly alluded to "them/they," knowing the truth regarding the crash but not allowing it to be told. Not to put too fine a point on it, from beyond the grave, the R101's commander was accusing the British authorities of instituting a cover-up, presumably to protect culpable parties within the government itself. The inquiry into the crash, which was ongoing in parallel with the Garrett séances, was alleged to have been a whitewash.

In addition to wanting the truth to be told, there was another motive. Flight Lieutenant Irwin emphasized that the R100 should never be allowed to make a prolonged flight. It, too, was poorly designed and engineered—another disaster waiting to happen, albeit for slightly different reasons. In this, the spirit got his wish. The R100 was grounded, broken up, and scrapped. Some of the remnants, along with those of

The memorial to the 48 people who died in the R101 crash is located in Cardington, Bedfordshire, England.

the R101, were sold off to the German Zeppelin company—and ended up, it is believed, in the structure of the equally ill-fated Nazi airship *Hindenburg,* which fell from the sky in a blazing fireball over New Jersey on May 6, 1937. Thirty-five of the *Hindenburg's* occupants died, along with one hapless person standing beneath it on the ground.

The curtain was coming down on the age of airships, which reached a fiery end.

One can walk in the graveyard at St. Mary the Virgin and pay respects to the dead of the R101. Inside the church, framed and mounted on the wall, is the British Ensign flag that was flown by the doomed airship. It was salvaged from the wreckage by French rescue workers and stands as a stark reminder almost a century later of the terrible human cost wrought by the tragedy.

The sheds at Cardington that were built to house both the R100 and the R101 still stand today. There's a good chance that you have seen them on the silver screen, as many Hollywood blockbuster movies have been filmed inside them. The R100 shed housed parts of Gotham City for Christopher Nolan's *Dark Knight* series. Two *Star Wars* movies were shot there, as was Marvel's *Black Widow* and a plethora of TV productions.

Perhaps unsurprisingly, the sheds are said to be haunted. Local lore holds that the spirits of some of the restless crew and passengers are responsible for phantom footsteps, disembodied voices, and other strange occurrences that have been reported at Cardington.

We can only hope that someday, they shall finally find peace.

EASTERN AIRLINES FLIGHT 401

Civil aviation progressed from the airship to the propeller-driven aircraft, and ultimately, at the close of World War II, came the jet age. No matter what propelled them, aircraft continued to crash, and sometimes, those crashes resulted in hauntings that are still studied and puzzled over today.

1972 was the deadliest year in civil aviation history. Globally, there were 2,429 deaths as a result of plane crashes and related incidents—a macabre record that remains unbroken today. Over a single 12-month span, no fewer than 55 commercial aircraft underwent fatality crashes.

The Lockheed L-1011 TriStar was a brand-new passenger jet design. Intended to be both luxurious and safe in equal measure, the first TriStar jet left the assembly line in April 1972 and was placed into service that same year. The customer to whom Lockheed delivered that first model was Eastern Airlines.

The TriStar had a futuristic appearance that fit well with the aircraft's high-tech nature. One powerful engine hung beneath each wing, while a third was mounted at the intersection of the vertical stabilizer with the airframe's tail section. It was flown using a highly sophisticated, computer-assisted flight control system that came as close to being a true autopilot as early 1970s technology could deliver.

To say that the autopilot was cutting edge for the time is to understate matters. Eastern Airlines ran a trial flight of its newest, shiniest acquisition in May, shortly after taking ownership of the first airframe. Although the

Eastern Airlines Flight 401 was a new Lockheed L-1011 Tristar 1, touted to be a very safe as well as luxurious aircraft.

airline's top test pilots were in the cockpit, they had very little to actually do. After they started the engines and engaged the automated control system, the L-1011 obediently lined itself up, rumbled down the runway at Dulles International Airport in Dulles, Virginia, and launched into the air. The pilots sat back and relaxed while the TriStar flew itself all the way across the continental United States before landing—again, without any human intervention—at Fort Lauderdale, Florida.

The automatic flight was rightly lauded as a pioneering, brilliant technological achievement. Although it had more than its fair share of mechanical issues, primarily involving the Rolls Royce engines, many pilots nevertheless thought highly of the L-1011. The "set it and forget it" control system, coupled with smooth handling characteristics, meant that the plane could be a dream to fly.

Passengers and cabin crew loved it as well. Although built to accommodate 250 passengers, the TriStar interior was spacious and roomy in comparison to rival airliners. Its kitchen/galley facilities meant that the meals served on board were first-rate, giving customers a superb dining experience that could be enjoyed in relative peace; the L-1011 was also quieter than other jets, making for a less stressful in-flight experience across the board. Latching on to this, the marketing team at Eastern Airlines dubbed it "the Whisperliner." The name stuck.

Before the year was out, however, 101 lives would be lost when an Eastern Airlines TriStar went down in the Florida Everglades.

December 29, 1972, was a Friday. In the United States, as in much of the Western world, it was a busy travel season. Thousands of Americans had flown to visit friends and relatives for the Christmas holidays. Many of them were returning home prior to the beginning of the New Year celebrations.

That night, Eastern Airlines Flight 401 was scheduled to make the New York to Miami run. Totaling the passengers and crew, 176 people were on board the L-1011 when it took off at 9:20 p.m. Eastern, including 13 crew members. 163 were passengers and 13 were crew.

The takeoff and flight went without a hitch. The airliner climbed to cruising altitude and turned south, following the flight plan that had been filed. Food and beverages were served. The atmosphere on board was relaxed and convivial, with not even the slightest hint of the disaster that awaited at the end of the flight.

A little over two hours later, EAL 401 was approaching its destination. A tremor ran through the aircraft as the landing gear came down. Preparing for their imminent descent into Miami International, the flight crew were perturbed to find that the light that indicated the nose landing gear was down and locked had failed to light up.

> **Preparing for their imminent descent into Miami International, the flight crew were perturbed to find that the light that indicated the nose landing gear was down and locked had failed to light up.**

Calmly, Captain Robert "Bob" Loft cycled the landing gear, bringing it back up into its housing and then extending it again.

The indicator light stayed out. Now there was a problem. Was the nose wheel deployed or not?

There was only one way to tell for sure. Somebody had to go down there and look. That duty fell to the second officer/flight engineer, Don Repo, who clambered down into the nose of the aircraft to put eyes on the equipment directly. The problem could simply have been a faulty light bulb, or the gear might really not be down. Repo could only ascertain the truth by peering into a darkened viewport and seeing whether indicator markings were aligned, which would signify that the nose gear was down and locked.

While Repo was checking on the status of the nose gear, the captain and first officer, Albert Stockstill, had his attention set on the indicator light. They were apparently so engrossed that both men missed the audible alarm that warned them that the TriStar was 250 feet either above or below the programmed altitude for that particular part of the flight. This was easy to miss; the sound lasted for just half a second. Neither the captain nor the first officer reacted by increasing power to the engines or altering the pitch of the aircraft in order to arrest what was actually an unplanned descent.

Clearly, the sensible decision was to abandon the landing approach, circle back around, and get back up to a safe altitude until a solution was found. Miami Air Traffic Control granted permission for EAL 401 to do exactly that. The aircraft banked toward the west, taking up a new heading as directed by the air traffic controller. The captain was also told to climb to an altitude of 2,000 feet, which was acknowledged eight minutes before the crash: "Okay, going up to two thousand...."

But unbeknownst to its pilots, the plane was still descending.

At 23:41:40 P.M. the aircraft was down to just 900 feet.

"We did something to the altitude," announced Stockstill.

"What?" Loft replied.

"We're still at two thousand, right?"

"Hey! What's happened here?" Loft exclaimed. It was 23:42:07.

Three seconds later, low-altitude alarms began sounding in the cockpit.

It was too late. The TriStar was in a banking descent, its left wing down. At 23:42:12, the aircraft's wingtip slammed into the swampy Florida Everglades, some 18 miles short of the intended runway. Next came the port side engine, the landing gear, and the fuselage.

EAL 401 broke up on impact, strewing wreckage and bodies across the marshland. The debris field was over a mile in size and included numerous bodies. Some were killed on impact. Others drowned.

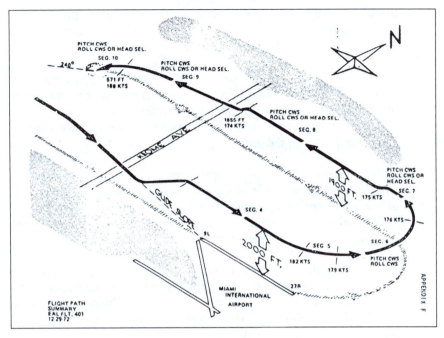

A diagram of the flight path taken by Eastern Airlines 401, including elevation and speeds.

Showing remarkably clear thinking under the circumstances, flight attendant Beverly Raposa called out into the darkness that under no circumstances was anybody to light a match. Aviation fuel had been dumped from the ruptured tanks aboard the wrecked airliner. One match could turn the swamp into a raging inferno, burning the survivors to death.

To raise morale and to help prevent them from slipping into shock, Raposa then began singing Christmas carols with the other survivors.

Ninety-four passengers were killed, as were Loft and Stockstill, along with four members of the cabin crew. Sixty-eight survivors were rescued. Military helicopters flew them to hospitals for treatment. Two of them would die later of wounds sustained in the crash. One of them was Don Repo, who died on New Year's Eve.

The flight crew of Loft, Stockstill, and Repo were all seasoned, experienced aviators. They were well trained and certified to fly the L-1011, so why had the EAL 401 flight ended in disaster?

Following an extensive investigation, it would later be discovered that both of the bulbs in the nose landing gear position indicator had burned out. This had held the attention of the captain and first officer at a time when at least one of them should have been focusing on the flight instruments and on actually flying the aircraft.

The National Transportation Safety Board (NTSB) aircraft accident report concluded that Flight 401 crashed because of "the failure of the flight crew to monitor the flight instruments during the final four minutes of flight, and to detect an unexpected descent soon enough to prevent impact with the ground."

In other words, both the captain and the first officer were so fixated upon the potentially faulty nose gear light that they were heedless of the briefly sounded change-in-altitude alarm. By the time they realized the plane was descending, not gaining or holding altitude, it was too late—the crash was imminent.

Why did the aircraft enter a state of descent when it was supposed to be climbing up to 2,000 feet? It was hypothesized that Captain Loft had accidentally nudged the control yoke, pushing the nose downward slightly. Neither pilot noticed the decrease in pitch, and the autopilot kept it that way right up till the end.

A number of practical safety recommendations were made in the aftermath of the disaster, and it is there that the legacy of EAL 401 should have been rooted. Instead, a series of ghost stories emerged, stories that resulted in a book (*The Ghost of Flight 401* by John G. Fuller) and a subsequent made-for-TV movie starring Ernest Borgnine and Kim Basinger.

INITIAL IMPACT AREA

A photo from the investigation displays the strewn wreckage of the ill-fated Flight 401. A National Transportation Safety Board report blamed human error on the accident.

In the foreword to his book, Fuller claimed to have first learned of the rather unusual haunting while on a Scandinavian flight in 1974. The stories were spreading among crews from multiple different airlines. Six months later, Fuller supposedly heard about it verbatim while traveling on Eastern Airlines when he casually raised the subject with a flight attendant who had experienced it for herself.

According to Fuller, after everything salvageable from the EAL 401 crash site was recovered, some usable parts were installed in other planes of the Eastern Airlines fleet. This is a key point of contention between the author and skeptics, who pointed out that no documentation supporting this claim has ever come to light.

... the apparitions of Bob Loft and Don Repo were sometimes seen. Their purpose seemed to be to warn other flight crews when their aircraft was in some kind of danger....

Regardless, on some of those later L-1011 flights, Fuller claimed, the apparitions of Bob Loft and Don Repo were sometimes seen. Their purpose seemed to be to warn other flight crews when their aircraft was in some kind of danger; the ghosts were acting as something akin to guardian angels, keeping a watchful eye on their peers so that there would be no more tragic accidents in the future.

This fits with the archetype of "ghosts with a mission," something Fuller also wrote about in his book on the R101 haunting (*The Airmen Who Would Not Die*). Each apparition was at first mistaken for a living, breathing, flesh-and-blood person. They were three-dimensional and solid, without even the slightest hint of transparency that cliché associates with ghost sightings. The difference was that one moment the figure was there and the next it was gone; they seemed to pop in and out of reality in a split second.

Don Repo's face reportedly appeared in an oven, staring back at the flight attendant who was operating it. The specter, confirmed by two other employees, warned them to "watch out for fire on this plane" (Fuller, p. 16).

The apparition of Captain Bob Loft was encountered by two flight attendants and the captain of the TriStar aircraft on which they flew, sitting in a passenger seat and staring ahead with a fixed gaze. The ghost studiously ignored both women and the captain when they tried to engage him in conversation before disappearing into thin air right before their eyes. On another occasion, an Eastern Airlines VP chatted with Captain Loft, oblivious to the possibility that he was speaking with a dead man.

Throughout 1973, if the airline employees Fuller claimed to have spoken with were telling the truth, the restless spirits of officers Loft and Repo were popping up regularly; most encounters took place on one specific TriStar, but the pair were also seen on several different Eastern L-1011s, either immediately prior to or during their flights. Captain Loft was encountered sitting in the first-class section on more than one occasion, as pilots often did when traveling on the airline's dime (a practice known as "deadheading"). Not only were they perceived as full-body apparitions, but their faces were sighted peering out of overhead storage bins and the engineer's control panel in the cockpit.

An intriguing encounter documented by Fuller involves an unnamed Eastern pilot who said that Loft's ghost told him: "There will never be another crash of an L-1011. We will not let it happen." Presumably the "we" in question referred to Loft himself and Don Repo, who were keeping a vigilant watch over the safety of the Eastern Airlines fleet.

By the summer of 1974, the ghost sightings, which had spread quickly throughout crews of the Eastern fleet in the aftermath of the crash, had slowed down considerably. Finally, as abruptly as they had begun, the encounters stopped.

The HistoryMiami Museum in Florida has an exhibit dedicated to the disaster and honoring its victims and heroes.

Not everybody found Fuller's book to be credible, however. First and foremost among its detractors was Eastern Airlines itself, which contemplated suing the author for claiming that the company had pressured flight and cabin crews in order to hush up the story, even going so far as to send them for psychiatric evaluation, and potentially endangering their employment. Eastern strenuously denied these allegations.

When push came to shove, Eastern's management decided that the Streisand Effect made such a lawsuit a risky proposition. (The Streisand Effect illustrates that when too much effort is made to minimize or downplay an issue, that effort can backfire and cause the opposite of the desired result by giving the controversy greater prominence in the public eye.) Understandably, taking the case to court in an attempt to prove that their airliners weren't haunted could have given the press a field day with the story—not to mention the fact that it is all but impossible to prove or disprove paranormal activity in the eyes of the law.

The final call was made by Eastern executive and former Apollo 8 astronaut Colonel Frank Borman. Modern-day corporate executives don't get much in the way of respect these days, not least because of the layers of insulation that usually exist between themselves and front-line operations. Not so with Borman, who was awakened by a late-night phone call telling him that EAL 401 had disappeared from radar screens and had probably crashed. After making a quick stop at the Eastern Airlines control center, Borman jumped into

> According to Eastern Airlines, Fuller's book was nothing more than a mishmash of exaggerations, distortions, half truths, and in places outright fiction.

a helicopter and raced to the scene of the crash in order to help supervise rescue and recovery efforts. Speaking about the ghost stories afterward, he dismissed them as being "garbage."

Fuller's sources for *The Ghost of Flight 401* were, he said, primarily Eastern Airlines employees, many of whom spoke to him under condition of anonymity.

For its part, Eastern Airlines claimed to have looked into the ghost stories exhaustively, interviewing a multitude of its employees in an attempt to figure out exactly where the claims originated. They were unable to track down even a single employee who would admit to having run into the ghost of Bob Loft or Don Repo. This would be understandable, if true; the same stigma that has traditionally fallen upon crew members who report encountering UFOs would almost certainly apply to ghost sightings at 30,000 feet as well, particularly during the 1970s. Saying that you saw the apparition of a dead coworker would not be conducive to having good career prospects. Safest just to shut up and not endanger that next paycheck.

According to Eastern Airlines, Fuller's book was nothing more than a mishmash of exaggerations, distortions, half truths, and in places outright fiction. At the heart of it all lay the claim that nonstructural parts from EAL 401 were being used as spares for other TriStars in the Eastern Airlines fleet. According to some sources, this never actually happened; yet others insisted that it did. Whichever is truly the case, this doesn't mean that there was no basis for a haunting—the trauma and tragedy of the crash were all too real, and where one finds a strong surge of emotion, one also tends to find ghosts.

Frank Borman's decision not to sue didn't stop the widow of Captain Loft from launching a suit against John G. Fuller. In 1981, attorneys representing Dorothy Loft alleged that the author had invaded her family's privacy and caused emotional distress by portraying her husband and the father of their children as a phantom. The complaint was ultimately rejected by the court, and hopes of an appeal went nowhere.

The failure of the lawsuit doesn't necessarily reflect on the accuracy of the EAL 401 ghost stories—or the lack thereof. Writing in *From the Captain to the Colonel: An Informal History of Eastern Airlines,* author Robert J. Serling sided with the airline and poured scorn on the claims of a haunting and describes the contents of Fuller's book as being more fictitious than real.

Trudi Smith (front) pictured in 1972. She was one of the crew members who survived the Flight 401 crash.

Any book that is written as a linear narrative requires an ending, a climax of some sorts. *The Ghost of Flight 401* is no different, and it is here that John Fuller went into esoteric mode by using a Ouija board to communicate with what purported to be the spirit of Don Repo. According to Fuller's transcript of the talking board session, the unseen communicator correctly identified Eastern Airlines, the flight number, and the names of his two companions on the flight deck.

After the initial session, the communicator professing to be the dead second officer/flight engineer accurately laid out the reasons for the crash and correctly named members of Donald Repo's family.

A skeptic would point out that Ouija boards can often be influenced by the ideomotor effect, in which sitters subconsciously spell out the answers to their own questions. Additionally, one of the participants was Elizabeth Manzione, an air stewardess and Fuller's research assistant. She would subsequently go on to marry the author, becoming Elizabeth Fuller, and publish an account of her own, titled *My Search for the Ghost of Flight 401.*

After initially meeting him on a flight, Manzione agreed to help the writer with his current project, the book that would become *The Ghost of Flight 401.* Fuller wanted her to discreetly discuss the ghost stories with as many airline personnel as possible to try to figure out the scope and breadth of the haunting.

Over the months that followed, Manzione discovered that the story was widespread among not just Eastern crews and support employees but also those working for other airlines. It should be noted that much of this was hearsay; it was heard secondhand, rather than directly experienced or encountered—

> Proponents of crossing over say that these entities usually fail to move on of their own accord because they become stuck on the material plane after dying under sudden, unexpected, or traumatic circumstances....

the rumor mill, working overtime. Whether they are genuine or not, such stories often take on a life of their own, tales that grow in the telling.

The key question is: just how much of what Manzione was told, and recounted in good faith to John G. Fuller, was truth, and how much was exaggeration—friend of a friend stories?

An oft-debated topic among paranormal enthusiasts is that of "crossing over" ghosts; this is the concept that psychically gifted individuals may be able, in certain instances, to help earthbound spirits transition from this plane of reality to whatever might come next. Proponents of crossing over say that these entities usually fail to move on of their own accord because they become stuck on the material plane after dying under sudden, unexpected, or traumatic circumstances, such as being murdered, being killed in battle, or dying in an air crash. If so, that would explain why so many encounters with the ghosts of Don Repo and Bob Loft were reported by Eastern Airlines personnel. On the reverse side of the coin, however, why weren't there sightings of the deceased passengers, cabin crew, or of the first officer, Albert Stockstill?

Manzione learned that Eastern Airline employees had attempted to perform a "soul rescue" or "deliverance" for the spirit of Don Repo on the L-1011 on which the dead flight engineer's apparition was most often sighted. The intent was to aid him in the process of crossing over. The idea has been around for as long as there have been purported psychics. Some mediums claim to be able to do it; others say they cannot, whereas others maintain that it is not something that can be done under any circumstances, believing that spirits can only cross over when they are ready to do so and not before. As with so many elements of the paranormal, there is no consensus, and much comes down to the beliefs of the individual.

If crossing over is possible, and if it was successfully conducted aboard the L-1011 airliner, then it would offer a reasonable explanation for why Don Repo's ghost suddenly stopped appearing aboard the Tri-Star. No further sightings were reported.

Following the release of both John and Elizabeth Fuller's books on the subject, there was little development on the research front regarding the haunting of EAL 401 for 50 years. In 2022, documentary filmmaker Steve Shippy enlisted the help of psychic medium Cindy Kaza, who was perhaps best known for her work on television shows such as *The Holzer Files* and *The Dead Files,* in an attempt to shed fresh light on the case. The results of Shippy and Kaza's efforts can be seen in the *Shock Docs* TV series episode "Ghosts of Flight 401."

According to Shippy, there have been reports of apparitions, screams, and the chilling sense of being watched in the vicinity of the crash site.

Shippy interviewed survivors of the plane crash, such as Ron Infantino, who had been married for just 20 days when he and his wife Lilly boarded the fateful flight. The couple was returning to Miami from their honeymoon in New York and were preparing to begin their new life together.

On impact, Infantino was hurled into the swamp, where he found himself stark naked, still belted into his seat. The brackish water came up to his chest.

Filmmaker Steve Shippy has asserted that there have been reports of ghostly activity at and near the crash site (pictured).

Ron Infantino survived. Lilly did not. One can only imagine the poor man's feelings in the 50 years that followed that harrowing night.

Shippy also interviewed flight attendant Mercy Ruiz, who had a 22-year career with Eastern Airlines. A fellow flight attendant named Beverly Raposa handed Mercy, who was in a state of deep emotional shock, an 11-month-old baby and instructed her to keep it warm. Mercy Ruiz did as she was told. The child lived but was orphaned in the crash.

"It was negligence," Ruiz told Shippy, speaking of Bob Loft and Albert Stockhill. "They were not paying attention. Unfortunately, it cost them their lives too."

Mercy Ruiz was aware of the ghost stories and found them to be credible.

Shippy also met with Elizabeth Fuller, who reiterated the claim that crashed parts from EAL 401 were distributed among other planes in the Eastern fleet. The author and former flight attendant also emphasized that these were nonstructural components, which would make sense, given the extreme forces subjected to the aircraft when it crashed. The question of whether recovered parts really were dispersed among other TriStars remains a major sticking point in the premise that underpins the case.

Fuller told Shippy that she spoke with Eastern's chief mechanic, who said that "orders from headquarters" led to the repurposed parts being removed from all of the airline's L-1011s, at which point the ghosts of Don Repo and Bob Loft were no longer seen aboard those planes.

Another claim made by both John and Elizabeth Fuller is that pages were torn from official flight logbooks following "unusual incidents" on board. The captain charged with command of an airliner is duty bound to record anything noteworthy in the log, which constitutes a legal document. The Fullers' *Ghost of Flight 401* books allege that a number of these incidents were ripped out and disposed of following ghost sightings aboard Eastern aircraft. Some supporters of these accusations say that the airline's management wanted to sweep claims of a haunting under the rug. Yet falsification of an aircraft log is a crime and could land either the airline or the employee responsible in legal hot water.

Filmmaker Steve Shippy also insisted that salvageable parts from the plane wreck were recycled and reused in other aircraft.

It was "a massive cover-up," Elizabeth Fuller told Shippy, adding that employees lived in fear of losing their jobs if the ghost sightings continued to be reported. She went on to tell the documentarian that in her opinion, some of the spirits of those who died in the crash still haunt the site to this day.

There was only one way to find out.

Shippy and Kaza went into the Everglades and located the site of the EAL 401 crash on December 19, 2022—the 50th anniversary of the tragedy. The concept of anniversary hauntings is a time-honored one among the annals of paranormal research. Sometimes ghostly activity is more prevalent on the exact date of the precipitating incident. Indeed, in some cases, it is the ONLY day or night on which the haunting occurs; for the remaining 364 days of the year, the locations seem to be paranormally inert. Would the same be true with Flight 401?

Their initial excursion took place during the hours of daylight for safety reasons and to scout the scene out. After identifying the specific crash site (Shippy claims that she was not told of the exact location beforehand), Kaza attempted psychometry, attempting to paranormally gather information from the scene via direct physical contact. The medium said she was picking up on a woman screaming.

They returned after dark, keeping a wary eye out for alligators, snakes, and other dangerous critters. The duo used a small group of items that had survived the crash as trigger objects—the term used for any object that may be meaningful when considered in the context of a haunting and could therefore trigger spirits to come forward and interact with paranormal investigators.

While conducting an electronic voice phenomena (EVP) session, attempting to record the voices of the dead, Shippy recorded what he believed was the name "Charles." A passenger named Charles Carmichael died in the crash. He was 73 years old at the time of his death. Also killed was Charles Kuchenbrod, age 42. The air traffic controller who directed EAL 401 on its abortive approach into Miami was also named Charles.

As evidence, the format of EVP is problematic, thanks to an entirely natural phenomenon named pareidolia. The human brain is "wired" to want to make sense out of randomness. We like to see neat and organized patterns where there really are none. Two good examples of this can be seen whenever we look up at the night sky: the Man in the Moon and the constellations.

Nobody really believes that there is a giant face on the surface of the moon, peering right back at us; nor do we believe that Orion the Hunter is up there in the farthest reaches of outer space, brandishing a club or some other weapon. Those are, in reality, random pieces of lunar terrain and scattered stars that falsely appear to form a meaningful pattern. Once a person has seen the so-called Man in the Moon, it is almost impossible to unsee it. The brain wants there to be a familiar pattern there rather than the mishmash of craters, mountains, and dried-up oceans that really compose the surface of that dead world.

How does this relate to electronic voice phenomena? Many recorders that are used to try to capture the voices of the dead will generate staticky pops and hisses when played back. It is among that garbage white noise that, some believe, human voices can be heard, speaking words and sometimes even complete sentences. The problem is, our brains want to make sense out of that noisy chaos and will often superimpose what we think are phrases onto it, it when in reality, those sounds are often no more than the audible equivalent of the Man in the Moon.

In the case of Shippy's EVP, the filmmaker believed that he had captured a complete sentence from the speaker named Charles: "I am the one who died in the plane crash." Listening to the same recording on the television documentary, however, those words are less than clear. Not every viewer is going to find this EVP to be particularly convincing.

Kaza claimed to pick up on several spirits, including the ghost of Don Repo who, she said, felt responsible for having caused the crash. In actuality, Repo was not responsible; the flight engineer was below the cockpit in the so-called hellhole, checking on the status of the nose gear. Responsibility for the crash lay with those who were at the controls.

Shippy interviewed a flight attendant who believes she encountered the spirit of Don Repo in the galley of an Eastern Airlines TriStar; the attendant insisted that the ghostly encounters were widespread and credible. The airline's management worked hard to suppress the stories, she said, because "they didn't want the airline going down."

At the conclusion of his documentary, Shippy and Kaza made the distasteful decision to play aloud the last moments of EAL 401's cockpit flight recorder while both are standing at the crash site. There is a strongly held belief among some that replaying incidents such as the air crash might re-traumatize the spirits that are still active at the location of a tragedy. If a paranormal investigator had a recording of a murder taking place and replayed it at the scene of the crime in the hopes of the spirits hearing it, that practice would be ethically questionable, to say the least. If there are ghosts from the crashed L-1011 still haunting the Everglades, we can only imagine how much emotional pain this experience may have caused them.

> Kaza suggested that a "vortex of spirit energy" may have caused momentary confusion in the cockpit of EAL-401 during its final descent, leading to distraction and, it is implied, the plane crash.

Kaza suggested that a "vortex of spirit energy" may have caused momentary confusion in the cockpit of EAL 401 during its final descent, leading to distraction and, it is implied, the plane crash. Shippy threw in the presence of "Bermuda Triangle energy" as a potential source, attributing the loss of other aircraft in the vicinity over the years to this same cause.

What this hypothesis ignores, however, is the massive volume of flights in the area that have not crashed. Neither the Bermuda Triangle nor the Florida Everglades are considered any more dangerous to overfly than other parts of the world, generally speaking. Nebulously described "paranormal energy" is not needed to explain the crash of EAL 401. As with far too many aviation tragedies, a distracted flight crew and human error were the cause.

The enigmatic haunting associated with EAL 401 is unlikely to ever be solved. On one side lies the account of John G. Fuller and Elizabeth Fuller, chronicling the paranormal experiences of Eastern Airlines employees both in the air and on the ground. Critics have attacked Fuller's reputation as an author, pointing out his penchant for writing paranormal stories such as the previously mentioned *The Airmen Who Would Not Die,* covering the crash of the R101 airship, and *The Ghost of 29 Megacyles,* which examined what Fuller believed may have been a revolutionary new technology that was capable of speaking with the dead.

Both are well-written books, but many reviewers have called into question Fuller's research methods, particularly with the latter title. The "revolutionary technology" that underpins the book does not stand up to close scrutiny, and some investigators believed that Fuller acted in good faith but was conned.

On the other side of the divide was the airline itself, which understandably found the ghost stories to be not only distasteful but also a potential threat to their business. The family of at least one survivor (Bob Loft) found the entire affair sufficiently upsetting to take Fuller to court. Be that as it may, it doesn't mean that the ghost stories weren't real. Clearly, something odd was happening on board subsequent Eastern Airlines flights because the ghost sightings were ubiquitous among personnel from Eastern and other airlines for months before Fuller ever published a word. Was this simply a case of mass delusion—or did the spirits of Don Repo and Bob Loft really haunt those L-1011 airliners, keeping a watchful eye out for potential fires and mechanical failures?

The Ghost of Flight 401 was earnestly researched and written. Aided by his future wife, John G. Fuller did the best job he could, trying to chase down a ghost story as diligently as he could manage. Ultimately, it all comes down to belief.

Elizabeth Fuller, Cindy Kaza, and Steve Shippy stood at the crash site, joined hands, and attempted to perform a mass "soul rescue" to free any earthbound spirits that may have been present at the crash site. Whether this was successful or not, only time will tell.

EASTERN STATE PENITENTIARY

Most dictionaries describe the word "penitent" as *sorrow for one's sins or faults. Being in a state of penitence. Regret for one's wrongdoing.* In other words, to be penitent means that a person acknowledges that they have done wrong, regrets having done so (they repent), and wishes to make amends.

It is from this root that the word "penitentiary" is derived: a place in which wrongdoers can be made to contemplate their crimes and sins and ideally reach a place of repentance. After undergoing a period of incarceration in such a place, the newly chastened individual would then be returned to the world at large, more or less reformed.

Of such hopes was Eastern State Penitentiary born.

Eastern State Penitentiary accepted its first inmates in 1829. They were kept separate from one another for most of the time, left alone with their thoughts and, it was hoped, given sufficient time to contemplate their trespasses and to see the error of their ways. This was how reform was to be achieved—or so the theory went. When taken to the maximum, this method of deliberate isolation was part of the so-called Pennsylvania system of corrections. Many considered it to be barbaric, arguing that forcing inmates to spend so much time alone was tantamount to systematized cruelty. The writer Charles Dickens, author of such classics as *Great Expectations* and *A Christmas Carol*, was a loud and vociferous critic of the system. In Dickens's view, the unnatural quiet and solitary nature of life at Eastern State was soul destroying, capable of crushing the spirit of even the strongest man as the months of a prison sentence dragged out into years.

As time went on and public opposition to the Pennsylvania system mounted, conditions inside the penitentiary began to relax. It was never a particularly nice place in which to serve time, as few prisons tend to be, but neither was it quite the hellhole that it was sometimes made out to be. For rebellious inmates, however, the punishments applied in the name of correction could be extreme. These included being fitted with the dreaded iron gag, a fearsome device that was strapped around the victim's head and was capable of badly lacerating their tongue if they tried to speak, or being suspended from the walls and being doused with buckets of ice-cold water. The hapless recipient of the latter punishment was stark naked at the time, making hypothermia a very real—and dangerous—possibility.

Although the great majority of inmates were male, women also served time at Eastern State. Prisoners worked at a variety of different tasks, as being industrious was one of the virtues that the authorities wished to inculcate in them as part of the reform process. The results of their labor were sold on the open market, with the proceeds then being used to help fund the upkeep of the penitentiary.

Eastern State Penitentiary operated from 1829 until its closing in 1971. Once housing such famous criminals as Willie Sutton and Al Capone, the complex is now a National Historic Landmark.

The latter half of the nineteenth century saw conditions inside the penitentiary grow increasingly crowded until there was no longer the capacity to house a ratio of one prisoner to one cell. Inmates were doubled and even tripled up. Overcrowding ultimately became bad enough that more cell blocks were added in an attempt to keep up with the steadily increasing intake.

As is common with all such institutions, there were deaths at the prison over the years. Some were of natural causes, whereas others were more violent, such as the prisoner who slit his own throat. There were several suicides, often achieved by hanging or self-strangulation, and murders. In 1900, one inmate beat his cellmate to death and cut off his head. Later, shivs, shanks, and other crudely fashioned bladed weapons would become part of the lexicon.

In the twentieth century, Eastern State's history continued to be as colorful as that of any other prison of comparable size. There were riots and fights, but there were also a number of merry Christmases, as photographs currently on display inside the prison show. The Pennsylvania system was a thing of the past. Inmates mixed with one another, for good and for ill. There were escape attempts, some successful, many of them not.

Finally, the penitentiary closed its doors in 1971. It was seen as a relic of a bygone age, no longer suitable to meet the corrections practices of the day. It was also expensive to run. For years, it remained derelict, an eyesore and an unwanted reminder of the past. Yet there were those who saw this as a positive, not a negative. Eastern State Penitentiary had many lessons to teach for those who were willing to listen. Fortunately, this enlightened view prevailed, and a sustained effort was made to preserve the prison based on its value as a historical site. This is why, at the time of writing, it is possible for visitors to pay a small admission fee and experience the place for themselves.

Stepping foot inside the monolithic walls of Eastern State Penitentiary today, it is easy to see how the prison achieved and maintained such a fearsome reputation. The place is huge and sprawling. It has the look of a medieval fortress, complete with crenellated towers and high walls—a stronghold capable of withstanding a siege indefinitely. If a person wearing a step counter were to walk all the way around the building, they would cover about a mile just by keeping to the outer walls. Eastern State Penitentiary is huge.

When seen from the air, the prison is laid out in the style of a British Union Jack flag. In the center is a hub, from which seven spokes—

The design of Eastern State Penitentiary with its seven wings radiating out of a center like the spokes of a wagon wheel was considered revolutionary at the time, and a number of later prisons used it for a model.

the cell blocks—extend outward, each of them being accessible from that central point. In addition to the cells, separate structures provide housing for those who worked at the prison. There was also space constructed for support functions such as storage, food preparation, administration, and medical care, to name just a handful. A major penal institution is akin to a small town. Needs as diverse as dental care, library services, and record keeping must all be met and maintained. Inmates had to be able to eat and to exercise. Much of that food was grown on-site, and the open spaces used for recreation are still there.

Accompanied by some fellow paranormal investigators, I visited the penitentiary on a warm summer day and was surprised at how cold and gloomy the interior was. Stepping across the threshold from the outside into the prison itself really does feel like entering another world. Fortunately, Eastern State is a museum piece today. It allows current and future generations to experience something of what the harsh conditions would have been like when it was still a functioning penal facility.

Ghost stories have swirled around the place for years, but those who administer the active museum today tend to downplay them. They prefer to emphasize the role Eastern State plays in keeping history alive rather than focus on the tales of phantom footsteps and shadowy figures that are said by many to prowl its long-abandoned cell blocks.

An employee named Gary Johnson suffered a terrifying experience while inside Cell Block #4 one day. Johnson, a locksmith by trade, was working on the door to one of the cells when he was suddenly struck by the feeling that he wasn't alone. He was all alone on the block at the time—at least, he had no flesh-and-blood company in that part of the prison. But the locksmith just couldn't shake off the feeling that somebody was watching him. This intuition was confirmed when Johnson saw a black, shadowy figure dart across the cell block and disappear into the darkness.

A photo of one of the wing corridors at the penitentiary during the author's visit there. Tourists can still visit Eastern, including during the annual Haunted House Halloween that the prison hosts.

Gary Johnson also claimed to undergo what was tantamount to a physical assault, being pinned down by an invisible force that rendered him completely unable to move.

An eerily similar sight to the shadow figure seen by Gary Johnson was captured on camera by the cast of TV's *Ghost Hunters* when they investigated the prison in 2004. The presence of a swirling, black mass, flitting quickly like a dark cloud blown on the wind, was never satisfactorily explained.

Sightings of shadow figures and apparitions are ubiquitous at Eastern State Penitentiary. They have been seen in the cells, sitting or standing in absolute silence; presumably, these are the ghosts of inmates who have long since been paroled, not just from prison but from life itself. The figures of phantom prison guards are also reported, sometimes standing atop the observation towers as though keeping a watchful eye on their charges in the yard below.

Animal ghosts have been a well-documented phenomenon for many years, particularly when it comes to man's best friend. Eastern State Penitentiary is said to have its own phantom pooch, a dog named Pep, who got something of a "ruff" deal in life and ended up being sent to the clink for it—at least, according to legend. The truth is slightly different.

In August of 1924, a glossy, black retriever was sent to Eastern State Pen by the governor of Pennsylvania, Gifford Pinchot. The prison warden duly accepted the governor's offer of a free dog (what choice did he have, after all?), and the 18-month-old bundle of four-legged

Inmate C-2559, so the story goes, was a black Labrador named Pep, who was incarcerated in 1924 for killing a cat. In actuality, Pep belonged to Governor Gifford Pinchot, who donated his own pet as a way to boost morale among the prisoners.

energy arrived before the prison gates that same month. The morale at Eastern State was low at that time, with the cells full and tempers flaring. The addition of a dog may have seemed like a small thing to some, but it would have brightened many inmates' dark days considerably.

Then, as now, prison guards had a difficult job, one that was both dangerous and perpetually stressful. Maintaining a sense of humor in such a bleak and dreary place was a survival mechanism, with jokes serving as a much-needed safety valve. This is probably why Pep's entry in the Eastern State Pen arrival logbook has the hapless pup being booked in on a charge of murder, with a life sentence being listed as his term of incarceration. They even went so far as to have Pep pose for a mug shot. Corrections officer humor at its finest.

Except the tale grew in the telling, as such tales are wont to do. By the time the story reached the newspapers, Pep was falsely accused of having murdered in cold blood the Pinchot family cat. If ever a prisoner was framed for murder, it was Pep. There was a public outcry, with protests and stern letters deluging Governor Pinchot's mailbox. In an effort to clear the matter up, he and his wife made a public statement declaring Pep's innocence and explaining that the only reason he was being sent to Eastern State was in order to improve morale.

To his credit, in the style of good boys everywhere, Pep was unfazed by his change of circumstance. By all accounts, he lived a happy life within the walls of Eastern State Pen, bringing a little extra joy into the lives of those who had precious little of it. After spending a couple of years as king of the hill there, Pep was "paroled" for good behavior and transferred to another facility in Pennsylvania, where he spent the rest of his days beloved by all, inmates and officers alike.

According to legend, Pep's ghost is still seen padding his way throughout the prison. In life, he could roam wherever he felt like going. However, he is far from the only dog to have lived at the penitentiary, and he only spent two years there. He did not die at Eastern State, so I find it far more likely that the phantom dog that has been reported could be one of the numerous guard dogs that were employed by the corrections officers to keep the prisoners in line. Pep is simply the best known of many dogs to have called the prison home; to this day, his mug shot greets visitors who come to tour Eastern State.

If Pep is the most famous animal associated with the penitentiary, then its most famous—or perhaps that should be infamous—human inmate was none other than Alphonse Capone, the Chicago crime lord who was made famous for his clash with U.S. Treasury agent Eliot Ness and his cadre of "Untouchables."

Visitors flock to Eastern State for many reasons. Some come for its history. Some come for the ghosts. Virtually all of them want to see the cell that Capone occupied before they leave. Nearly 80 years after his death, the legendary gangster has lost none of his fascination or macabre interest.

As a man, Al Capone was ambitious, brutal, and cold-blooded to the core. Crossing Capone, whether intentionally or by accident, was a surefire way to get badly hurt or to wind up dead. The mobster left a slew of maimed men and dead bodies in his wake as he climbed the ladder of organized crime.

Worming away in Capone's brain throughout much of his adult life was the ticking time bomb named syphilis. This incurable sexually transmitted disease came from an unprotected romantic interlude when Capone was a young man. Among the many effects syphilis has on the human body is to render the victim prone to violent outbursts and rages. From his earliest days, Al Capone was temperamental, given to bouts of anger that alarmed those around him. The influence of syphilis served to magnify those temper tantrums, sometimes to homicidal levels.

Aping the name of Ness's crimefighting squad, Capone liked to think of himself as being untouchable. He was not. Capone's legend grew too big, too fast, drawing national headlines and disapproval from the highest levels—the White House. In 1931, Herbert Hoover, the president of the United States, charged his law enforcement agencies with taking Capone down by whatever means necessary. In Hoover's view, the reputation for violence that Chicago had attained was largely due to Capone's gangster activities. He wanted it stopped and wanted an example to be made of the crime lord who sat at the center of organized crime in the city like a spider in his web.

Capone was responsible for numerous murders and thousands of ruined lives because of the prostitution rings he oversaw and the

Al Capone's cell at Eastern (top) versus a typical cell. Even though he was in prison, the gangster boss managed to get special treatment!

various criminal rackets he masterminded. In a turn of events that very few saw coming, Capone's violent endeavors weren't what finally brought him down. He fell afoul of an implacable force that was even more powerful than he and his army of heavily armed thugs: the Bureau of Internal Revenue, which had Capone in its sights as the target of an extensive investigation.

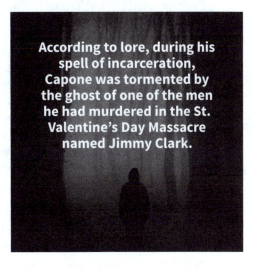

According to lore, during his spell of incarceration, Capone was tormented by the ghost of one of the men he had murdered in the St. Valentine's Day Massacre named Jimmy Clark.

Once the investigative dust had settled, Capone was hit with 22 charges of tax evasion. In his arrogance, the mobster simply hadn't filed taxes for much of his income, and his bookkeepers weren't particularly effective at hiding the illicit money once the federal investigators started poking around in Capone's business affairs.

Capone had better lawyers than he did accountants. The prosecutors could only make five of the charges stick, but those five proved to be more than sufficient to ruin him. Capone was sentenced to 11 years in prison. He served his sentence in multiple prisons, but none of them were Eastern State.

Capone had done time at Eastern State in May of 1929, a couple of years before his biggest, best-known trial would put him behind bars for a long stretch. He was arrested in Philadelphia for the crime of carrying a concealed weapon. The courts put him away for a year; he spent just over half of that at Eastern State. He lived like a king in a cell that was lavishly furnished as befitted his status as a wealthy and feared criminal kingpin. He even had his own personal radio to help while away the hours and received stellar treatment from the prison guards.

According to lore, during his spell of incarceration, Capone was tormented by the ghost of one of the men he had murdered in the St. Valentine's Day Massacre named Jimmy Clark. Capone had the cell all to himself, but allegedly, he would cry out that he was being tormented by Jimmy's specter. Some nights, the gangster could be heard talking to Jimmy when he was all alone in the cell. Capone was, by some accounts, absolutely terrified of the man, shrieking and crying helplessly during some of the worst episodes.

Whenever anybody went to check on him, nobody was present in the cell but Al Capone.

The situation worsened when Capone was sent down to the Atlanta Penitentiary, then to Alcatraz, for his 11-year stretch, and there are those who believed that Jimmy was a vengeful spirit who wanted payback for his murder. On the other hand, it's certainly possible that "Jimmy" was a symptom of Capone's ever-worsening syphilis, which was rotting his brain and causing a plethora of unpleasant effects as it did so.

Al Capone never completed his 11-year sentence. The authorities released him in 1939, judging him to be so mentally deficient that he was no longer capable of running even a small criminal enterprise. The powerful crime lord was gone forever, reduced to an almost childlike state at times. His mental faculties continued to degrade, even as Capone wasted away in what passed for retirement.

Herbert Hoover had gotten his wish. Al Capone was a broken man in almost every sense of the term. He continued talking to invisible people or, sometimes, just to himself. He died on January 25, 1947, the victim of a plethora of diseases. He was 48 years old.

His ghost still gets around, apparently. Capone's afterlife is said to be every bit as varied and interesting as his physical life was. He has been reported to haunt such locations as Alcatraz; the Old Baraboo Inn (Wisconsin); and Bachelors Grove Cemetery in Illinois, to name just three. Eastern State Penitentiary is one of the few places Capone spent time that he is not said to haunt.

Shown here in 1930, Al Capone went from major crime boss to mental child in the span of a decade.

Those who own or oversee some haunted locations make no bones about their willingness to cash in on their ghosts. Not Eastern State Penitentiary. In 2013, tour guide Ben Bookman told NPR's Laurel Dalrymple: "Most people making TV shows come in looking for ghosts. That's not the story we tell. Inmates were real people. These were people's lives. Seventy thousand people spent time here. We're not going to glorify it, and we're not going to make fun of it."

This is an entirely understandable, even admirable, position to take. Yet it does not invalidate the scores—if not hundreds—of accounts of paranormal activity that are attached to Eastern State.

Many prisons have their ghost stories. It would be remarkable if Eastern State were to be an exception. Contrary to popular misconception, Eastern State Penitentiary was not equipped with a gas chamber or with an electric chair. No executions were ever carried out there. As previously stated, the deaths that took place at the prison were either of natural causes, such as disease, illness, or simply advanced age, or homicides, with one inmate turning on another.

As has often been stated, where one finds strong emotion, one also tends to find ghosts. Inside the walls of Eastern State Penitentiary, the emotions ran strong for more than 140 years. Much of that emotion was negative: hopelessness, despair, bitterness, resentment, and anger. Yet there was also a wealth of positive emotion associated with the place. Oral histories speak of not only the guards but also some of the inmates being deeply upset when word of the penitentiary's closure was officially announced. For them, there was genuine affection for Philadelphia's gothic house of correction.

Walking those once teeming but now empty halls today, the visitor to Eastern State Penitentiary is struck with a definite sense of not being alone. Who can say how many unseen eyes are upon them—and why they still linger in that dark and haunted place?

SHEPTON MALLET PRISON

Shepton Mallet Prison—known to those who worked there and who served time there simply as "the Mallet"—is the United Kingdom's oldest prison. Many believe that it is also the most haunted, although competition is fierce. There are a number of other penal institutions that could make similar claims, such as Cornwall's Bodmin Jail.

The prison is named after the town that houses and supports it. Although the prison itself, more properly known as HMP (Her Majesty's Prison) Shepton Mallet, has long since closed its doors and ceased to function as an actual prison, the name of the town and the name of the prison are inextricably linked in the public consciousness.

In many ways, Shepton Mallet bears a strong resemblance to Philadelphia's Eastern State Penitentiary. Both are huge and imposing behemoths, with walls so high they appear unclimbable. Yet the Mallet came from humbler beginnings, as there was once a smaller gaol on the site of what would later become a sprawling giant beast of a prison. To lend some perspective, the original location actually hosted executions for the crime of witchcraft during the mid-1600s—more than a century before the birth of the United States.

Gaol life was miserable and brutal by equal measure. The place was a cesspool, a melting pot where hardened criminals such as murderers and rapists were thrown in with those who were incarcerated for relatively minor crimes such as theft and trespassing. Female prisoners would have constituted easy prey for the more predatory male offenders. Even children were not safe from being banged around in the gaol.

Shepton Mallet Prison in Somerset, England, opened in 1625 and remained an active prison until 1930, when it was closed but reopened in 1939 as a military prison for the British and Americans. It returned to civilian use in 1966 and closed again in 2013. Today, it is a tourist attraction.

Sanitation was somewhere between poor and nonexistent. Disease was rampant. Guards were corrupt. There was no effort toward rehabilitation. The purpose of the gaol was to keep the convicted separate from the outside world. Few members of the public or the authorities cared what went on behind the walls so long as the prisoners remained out of sight and by extension out of mind.

The 1800s saw Shepton Mallet's footprint grow bigger. Crime was on the rise, primarily because poverty and social unrest were too. All of those newly sentenced prisoners needed to be housed somewhere, and the government's solution was to expand prisons like the Mallet and to cram prisoners in like sardines inside a can until the prison was almost fit to burst.

Public opinion was very clear on the subject of prisoners being idle. It was unpopular to have inmates sitting around doing nothing. The idea of work was introduced to the Mallet, with treadmills and rope picking being just two of the methods by which inmates could work off their debt to society. Rope picking—unpicking old ropes—was a particularly onerous and unpleasant task, one that could leave the picker's fingers swollen and bleeding at the end of a work session.

In short, for much of the prison's early life, conditions were harsh, and intentionally so. Capital punishment was a lawful occurrence under British law, and those executions tended to take place at prisons. The preferred method of execution was hanging, and indeed, the position of executioner was a viable career choice for adult males of good standing.

The Mallet hosted seven executions during the time period of the late nineteenth to the early twentieth century. Rather than bury them in the consecrated ground of churchyards or cemeteries, the law dictated that those who were put to death at the behest of the court should be buried inside the walls of the prison at which the sentence was carried out. In the case of Shepton Mallet, the bodies of those convicted to die were placed in graves very close to one of the inner walls, lined up in a row alongside one another.

Their graves are unmarked to this day, and countless visitors to the Mallet have walked past and even over them without having any idea that they were there.

1939 brought the declaration of war against Germany. Even the most highly regarded armies have their bad apples, and the British authorities determined that there was a need for a dedicated military prison. The Mallet fit the bill nicely. Soldiers, sailors, airmen, and marines from the British armed forces were incarcerated there in the early stages of the war. Some found it preferable to fighting. Others brought their penchant for violence inside along with them and turned it on their fellow inmates. Hardened gangsters the Kray twins (Ronnie and Reggie) served some time at the Mallet after having been incarcerated in the historic Tower of London.

A sign placed near the wall where prisoners were executed by firing squad can be found in the prison yard.

At the height of winter, the night of December 14, 1940, was bitterly cold. Three British soldiers fatally asphyxiated in Cell

#142. Autopsies revealed that all three had succumbed to carbon monoxide poisoning. Fortunately, their fourth cellmate survived, although he was rendered critically ill. Carbon monoxide is a colorless, odorless, and tasteless gas that kills by displacing oxygen from hemoglobin. Many victims die in their sleep, unaware of the gas leak that means they will never wake up again. In order to combat the cold, prisoner cells were heated with gas burners. The military prison guards could set the intensity level of the burners from outside each cell but hadn't taken the necessary safety precautions before doing so. Cell #142 lacked the proper ventilation needed to prevent the accumulation of poisonous gas, and three men paid for that complacency with their lives.

There were reprimands and disciplinary action, but one can only wonder if the dead men would have thought that to be adequate recompense for what amounted to criminal negligence on the part of the guards.

The United States entered the war in December 1941 and quickly formed an alliance with Britain. From the outset, it was clear that the British Isles would serve as a jumping-off point for the invasion of Nazi-occupied Europe. Thus an increasing number of American service personnel—most of them male—flooded the country.

After some initial suspicions, much of the British public ultimately welcomed them with open arms. The vast majority of American soldiers behaved impeccably—at least, as impeccably as high-spirited military men can. Inevitably, a very small number turned to crime, the most serious offenders committing acts of rape and murder among the civilian population.

By 1942, Shepton Mallet had been turned over to the U.S. military authorities to serve as a penal facility. Those personnel who committed relatively minor infractions served their sentences under conditions of hard but fair discipline and were either returned to their units or discharged. The hardened, irredeemable offenders were subject to execution, a process for which the prison used its dedicated hanging chamber.

A British hangman was employed to perform the deed itself under the supervision of American officers. There were 18 executions of U.S. servicemen before the war ended in 1945. Sixteen were carried out by hanging. The remaining two were death by firing squad and took place in the prison yard.

Rather than bury them within the walls of the Mallet, as the British authorities had done with their civilian dead, the U.S. Department of

Defense had the bodies of their executed criminals shipped to France and interred in the so-called plot of shame in the Oise-Aisne U.S. military cemetery. Its official designation is Plot E.

The executed men all wore their service uniforms, but all identifying markers such as signs of rank or unit patches were cut away first, signifying their dishonorable rejection by the army and the nation they were sworn to serve. Even in death, their names go unremembered. Each grave marker is numbered but bears no identity of the man buried there. There isn't even a U.S. flag flying over the plot, as there is with every other U.S. military cemetery in the world.

Some 80 percent of the men buried in Plot E are black. Historians looking back upon their cases have raised the disturbing questions of just how much of a role racism played in their convictions.

Yet things may not be quite that simple. Some 80 percent of the men buried in Plot E are black. Historians looking back upon their cases have raised the disturbing questions of just how much of a role racism played in their convictions. Was every man truly guilty of the crime he was said to have committed, or were there any miscarriages of justice carried out by a military legal system that was demonstrably biased against non-Caucasians?

Perhaps some of the ghostly activity that has taken place at the prison since the end of the Second World War may be attributable to these lost souls, men who were convicted of vile crimes and ended their lives under conditions of shame and ignominy.

Be that as it may, it is an undeniably striking contrast that the U.S. military put more prisoners to death at Shepton Mallet in a span of three years than the British government did in three centuries.

At the conclusion of the war, Shepton Mallet was returned to British hands and became a civilian prison once more. It remained such until its closure in 2013.

Throughout that time, the ghosts continued to walk the prison's grounds and cell blocks. Arguably, the most famous apparition is the one known as the Lady in White, which is admittedly one of the classic archetypes of ghost lore, particularly in a country as richly vested in history as Britain.

Prison guards (or correction officers, in modern parlance) tend to be hardy, no-nonsense individuals, given to common sense rather than flights of fancy, doing a job in which any inmate one passes might be packing a shiv and a grudge makes one pragmatic and hyper-aware of one's environment. It isn't a career field well suited to daydreamers or the overly imaginative. Such men and women also don't lack courage. A plentiful supply is needed just to set foot on a cell block wearing the uniform of the hated "screw," in prison terminology.

All of this makes it even stranger that a number of hardened prison guards lived in fear of the Lady in White, some of them even refusing to patrol the prison alone after nightfall. Others claimed that parts of Shepton Mallet were prone to supernatural cold spots, which would come and go whenever the ghostly woman was nearby. One guard claimed to have been physically attacked by an invisible entity, making one of the few instances in the history of corrections when a prison officer was more afraid of assault by the dead than by the living inmates he was guarding.

Such was the hubbub caused by the phantom Lady in White that an investigation was ordered by the Home Office. Disappointingly, the official finding of the British government did not find in favor of there being ghosts haunting the prison. To have done so would have opened a huge can of worms, one that no self-conscious civil servant would have wanted anything to do with whatsoever.

The claims were documented by the respected ghost hunter Peter Underwood, however, and remain an indelible part of HMP Shepton Mallet's history. They were foremost in my mind when I spent four nights at the prison in 2022, researching my book about the haunting, *Spirits Behind Bars*.

Signage in the prison's B Wing shows the cell where the TV miniseries *Des* was filmed.

Since its closure in 2013, the prison has been part living history museum, much like its American counterpart Eastern State Penitentiary, and part popular filming location for such movie productions as *Paddington 2* and the BBC television drama *Des*. The latter featured the actor David Tennant portraying the serial killer Dennis Nilsen, the "Muswell Hill Murderer," who killed a dozen young men between 1978 and 1983. Although Nilsen never actually spent time imprisoned at Shepton Mallet, the cell that was used as a filming location has been left just as it appeared on screen and sealed off from public access.

Psychic medium and fellow author M. J. Dickson was sentenced to accompany me on what proved to be a very paranormally active four-night incarceration at the Mallet.

After parking our vehicles within the prison walls, one member of our investigative team was nonplussed when his new car suddenly decided to take on a life of its own. The trunk unlatched itself and started raising and lowering itself while its driver stood by and watched. There was little else he could do. The trunk didn't respond to his increasingly irritated jabbing at the key fob. Finally, the car went silent and went back to behaving normally. It had never done anything like that prior to driving into the yard at HMP Shepton Mallet, nor has it acted up again since.

There was not only torrential rain, thunder, and lightning during the investigation but also the much-talked-about blood moon, which some believe holds a mystical significance. There was disappointment that the Lady in White failed to put in an appearance, not least because her identity still remains unknown. What would a woman in a long, white dress even be doing in a high-security prison? Nobody seems sure of the answer, and nobody purporting to be her tried to communicate with the paranormal investigators via Ouija board, EVP, or any of the other tools and techniques we employed.

That's not to say that the Mallet didn't keep our team busy. On several occasions, investigators heard footsteps in different parts of the prison. Sometimes they would be the sort of furtive shuffling sound that implied a stealthy, sneaking movement pattern; at other times they were loud, clear, and crisp. In one instance, I was standing outside in the parking lot and heard the confident tread of footsteps coming toward us from just a few feet ahead. So bold were they that I actually

Suicide nets were strung across the cell block to break the fall of any potential jumpers.

thought an intruder had broken into the prison or had snuck in somehow and was coming to do us some harm. I rushed forward to confront them. The footsteps instantly stopped. There was, of course, nobody there. Not a fox, a cat, a rat, or even a mouse scuttling by, though there was no way any animal could come close to making a tread that heavy.

Shadow figures abounded, particularly on the cell blocks. The blocks are dimly lit, with a few pools of light breaking up the much greater areas of darkness. Much of the investigation took place over-night, as the prison was open for public visitation during the day. The eyes like to play tricks after dark, particularly as the night wears on and they begin to grow tired. Yet, more than once, different investigators were absolutely convinced that the group was being stalked by a tall, shadowy figure. It was seen atop one of the elevated landings, just stand-ing there and watching. Somehow, that behavior seemed more sinister than if it had been moving. Investigators took flashlights and went after it, but the figure was long gone when they arrived. For the sake of thor-oughness, they went from cell to cell, clearing the entire floor. Whoever the team saw, it had not been a flesh-and-blood person. Perhaps a long-dead occupant of one of the cells had come out to observe the night's proceedings. Or maybe a guard was still making his rounds, years after the Mallet had discharged its last-ever prisoner.

Normally, when investigating a haunted location, it is standard practice for paranormal researchers to focus on the hot spots. Not so with a place as large as Shepton Mallet, which could have easily swal-lowed up a team of a hundred people. Based on interviews with staff, there were so many potential hot spots that they had to be whittled down to a selected few. The execution chamber was one of them. In-stalled by the American military, the room has a distinctively off-putting atmosphere. Not only is the trapdoor used by the hangman still present, but so is the condemned man's cell, in which he spent his last night on Earth and got to eat his final meal prior to execution.

More deaths occurred in this part of the Mallet than in any other, and on the day of a hanging, the relatively small chamber was packed with military officers who had the duty of observing the proceedings and witnessing the process of justice being carried out. It was a surpris-ingly lengthy process. U.S. military law required that the senior officer present read out all of the charges of which the condemned man had been found guilty. He also got to soapbox, saying whatever he deemed appropriate before the executioner tightened the noose around the con-vict's neck, placed a hood over his head, and positioned him properly over the trapdoor. British civilian executions were much less formal and

Inside the execution chamber, this trapdoor shows where condemned soldiers stood before they plummeted to their deaths.

took a fraction of the time. Finally, when there was no more left to say, the lever was pulled, the trapdoor swung open, and the prisoner plummeted down until the rope snapped taut, hopefully breaking his neck.

Executioners were professional and diligent men. They took pride in their work, calculating the exact length of rope needed to achieve a quick and clean death. Although the crimes of which the condemned were convicted had been brutal and savage, the method of their execution was relatively humane. One was certainly less likely to suffer a painful and protracted demise than with a death by firing squad, which ran the risk of the shooters' aim being off—unintentionally or, in some cases, deliberately.

A lot can be gleaned during a paranormal investigation by simply sitting quietly and allowing events to unfold. When this was done within the execution chamber at HMP Shepton Mallet, footsteps would be heard coming from the corridor outside or the vicinity of the condemned prisoner's quarters. Voice recordings captured a belligerent male voice barking out the words "Get back!" The recorder was sitting atop the trapdoor at the time, and whoever had spoken those words must have been very close to it—perhaps a warning or remonstration for the investigators to stay away from the gallows?

Based on the harsh, commanding tone, it seemed likely that the invisible speaker was a prison officer. It was a voice that brooked no argument, one that seemed used to being obeyed. The man spoke for a second time just a few minutes later on the recording, booming, "What's that?" It seemed to be a reaction to something one of the paranormal investigators had said shortly beforehand.

Out on one of the cell blocks, an angry male voice left us an EVP that made his feelings clear in no uncertain terms: "F*** you" was the succinct message, delivered in a threatening manner that sent the investigators' hackles up. Disembodied words are one thing, but they're more alarming when backed up by physical phenomena. A loud boom came from the uppermost floor of the deserted cell block. It was clearly the sound of a heavy cell door slamming shut with some force.

Somebody was apparently not happy that a paranormal investigation was taking place. Whoever it was seemed to follow our investigators as they walked away from the cell block and back to the operations center, according to our medium, M.J., who sensed an aggressive male presence trailing her every step of the way—a truly disconcerting experience to have in a prison with a violent history like that of Shepton Mallet.

At the time of writing, the prison continues to conduct educational tours and paranormal events for the public. School visits give children an eye-opening glimpse into life behind bars and allow educators to segue into related subjects such as women's suffrage—suffragettes were once imprisoned there as a consequence of campaigning for women's rights. As a living museum, HMP Shepton Mallet represents all of British twentieth century society in a microcosm.

But beware: as paranormal investigators who dare to experience the Mallet after dark sometimes learn, it isn't always the most welcoming of places—especially when the ghosts come out to play.

GETTYSBURG BATTLEFIELD

A haunting can be caused by many things. At the heart of many can be found a single common factor: strong, powerful emotion. The more intense that emotion is, the more active the paranormal activity associated with the haunting tends to be.

It's said by some that love is the most powerful emotion in the world. That may or may not be true. Certainly, there are countless examples of places that are haunted by the spirit of somebody who loved them very much. When somebody loves a place with all their heart, it is sometimes possible for a piece of them to remain behind after their death. Many is the haunted house in which the resident ghost is that of a former resident, one who likes to keep a protective eye on the place toward which they felt so much affection during their physical lifetime.

When it comes to the realm of hauntings, however, intense trauma seems to be more powerful than love. Key components of such cases are the extremely strong sensations of pain and fear. Pain can be an emotion in addition to being a physical sensation. Fear generates a palpable energy all its own, as anybody who has ever been truly terrified out of their wits can attest.

During wartime, hundreds of thousands, if not millions, of people may live in a state of constant anxiety and fear. Those who are fighting must wrestle daily with the ever-present possibility that they could be wounded, maimed, or killed at any time.

Then there are the loved ones that the servicemen and women leave behind. Kept in the dark because of operational security, the families and friends of deployed military personnel live in their own personal hell during wartime, particularly when the first flag-draped coffins start to come home.

Ever since the time of antiquity, war and ghosts have been linked, engaged in a symbiotic relationship that has generated claims of haunting after haunting. The towns of Lexington and Concord, scene of the infamous "shot heard 'round the world" that kicked off the American War of Independence and ultimately led to the birth of the United States, have their own ghost stories. The North Bridge at Concord, the scene of early fighting between British redcoats and local militiamen, was reputed to be haunted long after the last soldier departed the area. Farmers avoided it after dark, unwilling to chance an encounter with the unquiet dead who were killed in the battle.

> Ever since the time of antiquity, war and ghosts have been linked, engaged in a symbiotic relationship that has generated claims of haunting after haunting.

Death and war walk hand in hand. It is estimated that the War of Independence cost the Patriots somewhere between 25,000 and 26,000 lives (not counting the civilian population). About a quarter of those soldiers were killed on the battlefield itself, whereas the lion's share died of injury and illness. Disease ran rampant throughout both armies, particularly when they were deployed in the field. Prisoners of war were kept under harsh conditions and given minimal food, with little access to hygiene or medical care. Small wonder that disease exacted a much greater toll than the volley fire of massed British musketry.

Historians believe that the British lost a comparable number of men themselves.

As costly in lives as the war for control of the North American continent was, its grand death toll—known informally as "the butcher's bill"—paled by comparison to the American Civil War. Almost one hundred years later, this war ushered in armed conflict on an industrialized scale. Beginning in 1861, vast armies equipped with the latest in weaponry were mobilized and hurled against one another. Although more skillful commanders attempted to use maneuver to their advantage, seeking to turn a flank or exploit the enemy's weaknesses, many Civil War battles were little more than brutal slugfests.

Take, for example, the Battle of Antietam. Fought on September 17, 1862, this engagement became the single bloodiest day in all of American history. With an estimated 23,000 casualties, its cost almost equaled the loss of Patriot lives during the entire War of Independence *on a single day.*

The American Battlefield Trust estimates that around 620,000 soldiers were killed during the Civil War—more than ten times the butcher's bill of the War of Independence. There were few parts of the country that the Civil War did not touch. Men and boys of all ages died painful deaths on lonely battlefields spread out across both eastern and western theaters of war.

One consequence was a sudden upsurge in the popularity of Spiritualism, which had begun in 1849 in Hydesville, New York. The infamous Fox Sisters claimed to be able to communicate with the spirits of the dead. As the death toll mounted during the years 1861–1865, so too did the desire of widows and bereaved families everywhere to reconnect with their departed loved ones. They sought assurance that although their husband or son may have bled out on the ground of a Civil War battlefield somewhere, his soul was prospering in the heavenly realms.

No less an authority than President Abraham Lincoln convened séances in the White House. It may be that the burden of sending so many Union soldiers out to die in his name was a heavy one for the former lawyer from Illinois. If so, it would be hard to blame him for seeking solace in the hope that their spirits had not been snuffed out forever.

Today, 160 years after the guns finally fell silent, many Civil War battlefields and the population centers that surround them still reverberate with the after-echoes of those bloody days. Entire books have been written about the hauntings associated with these sites. The foremost of them all must surely be Gettysburg.

Would it surprise you to learn that none other than President Abraham Lincoln believed that séances were effective and that he held them in the White House?

The name is synonymous with carnage. Over the span of four days in the summer of 1863, the Union Army of the Potomac under General George Meade clashed with the Confederate Army of Northern Virginia, commanded by General Robert E. Lee. Over that relatively short span of time, the armies sustained a combined casualty count of approximately 52,000 men killed, wounded, captured, or missing. That's comparable to the casualties suffered by the U.S. military during its eight-year involvement in the Vietnam War.

Although no formal survey has been conducted, it's likely that more ghostly activity is reported at Gettysburg and in its general vicinity than at any other battlefield of the American Civil War. The National Park Service dislikes discussing the possibility of ghosts and hauntings, taking the not unreasonable view that the focus should not be diverted from the sacrifice made by the men who fought, bled, and died on that most hallowed of ground. It's a valid point. Yet countless books have been written about the battle of Gettysburg, covering almost as many aspects of the campaign as can possibly be imagined.

Former park ranger and licensed battlefield guide Mark Nesbitt has spent decades collecting tales of ghostly goings-on in and around the battlefield, chronicling them in his *Ghosts of Gettysburg* series of books. Few people know the paranormal side of Gettysburg as well as Mark does, and his books are required reading for those with a fascination for Civil War ghost lore.

A Confederate cannon used to defend Pickett's position remains on the old battlefield. Many believe that the land where so many died on both sides is heavily haunted.

In the summer of 1863, only around 2,000 people lived in Gettysburg. A large part of the town's strategic value was due to its location: the key fact that it sat at the crossroads of 10 different roads. Moving grand armies meant implementing massive supply chains and required significant logistical support. Horse-drawn carts and wagons needed roads in order to move supplies. Columns of troops made much better time marching on those same roads than they did trudging across fields. With hindsight, it was inevitable that the two armies would meet at a place where so many roads intersected.

Moving 160,000 men into position to fight took time. On July 1, the first day of the battle, Confederate forces coming in from the north and west of Gettysburg slammed into a relatively thin screen of dismounted Union cavalrymen who were commanded by General John Buford. The Confederates were under orders from Robert E. Lee to under no circumstances bring on a major engagement—orders that they duly ignored by getting into a dustup with the horse soldiers in blue. Buford knew good ground when he saw it. He dug in his heels and called for infantry support, holding on for dear life until reinforcements arrived under General John Reynolds.

Reynolds was the first general to die in a battle that would go on to kill eight more. He was shot in the head while commanding his troops from horseback, a prime target for Confederate marksmanship. Falling from the saddle, John Reynolds was dead before he hit the ground.

On the afternoon of that first day, pushed to breaking point by the unyielding Confederate sledgehammer, the Union defensive lines finally broke. Their brigades withdrew, retreating back through the town of Gettysburg, harried by the Confederates every step of the way until the retreat became a veritable rout.

It was a running battle. There were islands of Union resistance, heroic last stands that cost the defenders dearly. One such desperate battle took place at John Kuhn's brickyard, where a lone Union brigade attempted to hold its ground against Confederate forces that significantly outnumbered them. Formed in line on a sloping stretch of ground, the Union soldiers fought valiantly but were quickly overwhelmed by superior numbers and firepower.

A sergeant of the 154th New York Volunteer Infantry, Amos Humiston, was fatally shot but managed to somehow make his way out of the brickyard before he finally collapsed and died. Although there don't appear to have been any sightings of Sergeant Humiston's ghost, his death would lead to one of the darker hauntings associated with the battle.

Kuhn's Brickyard, where Sgt. Amos Humiston was mortally wounded trying to hold up the Confederate advance.

His body was discovered in the aftermath of the battle and, like many of the fallen, remained unidentified at first. The only clue to his identity was an ambrotype that the dead man clutched in his cold, stiff fingers. It depicted an image of three children—children who were now tragically orphaned.

Tribute to Amos Humiston and his children, close to the spot where his body was found clutching a picture of the three children. This led to the establishment of Gettysburg's Orphanage, which would become one of its most haunted buildings.

Newspapers were contacted and the ambrotype was reproduced and widely distributed. A national search was conducted in an effort to identify the children and, by extension, extension their dead father. Finally, Amos's widow, Philinda, recognized the picture and learned that her husband was dead in a manner that must have come as a complete shock.

The three Humiston children were far from the only ones who lost their fathers during the battle. All major Civil War battles created orphans, a ghastly byproduct of the human toll that was wrought. In Gettysburg, there was clearly a need for a facility in which the children of fallen soldiers could be cared for: an orphanage. The National Soldiers' Orphans' Homestead was duly established, opening its doors on November 20, 1866.

It was only fitting that the first matron was Philinda Humiston. She was by all accounts a kindly woman, somebody who put her heart into caring for the orphans who were placed in her charge. Her own children (Fred, Alice, and Frank) lived at the homestead with her, and for the earliest part of its existence, the orphanage was a relatively warm and happy place.

That changed for the worse when Philinda Humiston moved on in 1869. Her replacement the following year was a cruel and malicious woman named Rosa Carmichael. Although the Gettysburg story has few actual villains, this evil individual certainly qualifies. Appointed to a position of absolute power over the most vulnerable members of the community, Rosa Carmichael launched a reign of terror, inflicting both physical and emotional abuse upon her young and vulnerable charges.

Dark rumors began to circulate concerning what was happening behind the closed doors at the homestead. It was claimed that Rosa Carmichael employed older boys as enforcers, having them beat the younger children whenever they broke one of her countless rules—or whenever the whim took her. Although it was never proved, some even said that children had been known to disappear, never to be seen again. If this was true, then it can only be hoped that they escaped rather than meeting some darker end at the hands of Rosa and her lieutenants.

Although not all of the claims were substantiated, further investigation revealed the presence of what amounted to a dungeon in the basement of the homestead. Iron manacles were used to bind children to the cold walls, where they might be left for hours or days in pitch-black, sometimes near-freezing conditions. Some prisoners of war received better treatment from their captors than the orphans of Gettysburg did from their supposed benefactor.

Once these abuses came to light in 1877, there was a public outcry. The people of Gettysburg were outraged. Rosa Carmichael was tried and found guilty of assault, for which she paid a fine of just $20 (about $600 today). Rather than stay and attempt to brazen it out, she skipped town and vanished. Little is known of her life either before or after her sadistic tenure at the National Soldiers' Orphans' Homestead, but she had done irreparable harm to its reputation. The orphanage was closed down in the aftermath of the scandal.

It was claimed that Rosa Carmichael employed older boys as enforcers, having them beat the younger children whenever they broke one of her countless rules—or whenever the whim took her.

The building spent much of its time as a museum and today is a draw for paranormal enthusiasts who come to investigate claims of ghostly children that are said to still haunt it. Much of the paranormal activity takes place below stairs, and it has become traditional for visitors to leave toys and games as gifts for the phantom kids. On the several occasions I investigated the orphanage in person, teddy bears, dolls, and toy cars were everywhere in the basement. According to our host, they are regularly moved around when the building is empty.

The voices and laughter of children are sometimes heard, speaking and giggling out of thin air. Disembodied footsteps run across the floorboards, perhaps a lingering after-echo of bygone days in which kids played games within the walls of the homestead—or perhaps fled in fear from an imminent beating or worse. Having heard those footsteps for myself while sitting on the ground floor at the rear of the building, I can personally confirm that this auditory phenomenon is very real.

Electrical disturbances also plague the homestead. My fellow paranormal investigators and I noted that the lights seemed to take

The orphanage as it stands today, with an inset photo of how it looked in Grant's day.

on a life of their own, switching themselves off and on with nobody even close to the switches. Were the spirits of the former orphanage having fun with us, or could this simply have been attributed to aging wiring?

According to author and psychic Sam Baltrusis, who accompanied me on an overnight investigation, the spirit of Rosa Carmichael was an active presence at the orphanage. There's a popular misconception that a person must die at a given location in order to haunt it; case after case has proved that to be untrue. Although historians have no idea what happened to Rosa after she was all but driven out of Gettysburg as the target of public outrage, it is entirely possible that she returned after her death for reasons best known only to herself.

After tuning in psychically to her presence, Baltrusis claimed that her motivation for haunting the building was that she was sick and tired of her character being maligned for so many years. Rosa's ghost felt as if she had been unfairly treated, the psychic noted, before adding his own intuition that not all of the facts of the case have been discovered yet. If this is true, then it may be that Rosa Carmichael has been tarred with a blacker brush than she deserved. Until new information emerges, however, her reputation shall remain stained, particularly among the people of Gettysburg.

> When it comes to the realm of ghosts and hauntings, it is a long-held truism that one has a tendency to find whatever one goes looking for.

Despite the many peaceful and happy years that the homestead spent as a museum, it is primarily because of the phantom children and their alleged tormentor that people come to visit the orphanage today. Could it be that this focus on the darkness attracts darker energies? When it comes to the realm of ghosts and hauntings, it is a long-held truism that one has a tendency to find whatever one goes looking for. In other words, search for the darkness, and you just might find it.

After prowling the hallways, Baltrusis said that there may be human remains that lie undiscovered either beneath the homestead itself or in its immediate vicinity. Although some have speculated that there may be the bodies of soldiers that were placed in temporary graves and then forgotten or misplaced, a more chilling possibility exists: if the stories regarding disappearing children contain any truth, might they have ended up in unmarked graves close to the site of their death?

As the first day of fighting drew to a close, the Union forces had all but lost the town of Gettysburg. They had been driven out to the periphery and clung to a defensive position on Cemetery Hill.

The Confederates didn't have it all their own way. They occupied buildings on the outskirts of Gettysburg and settled in to exchange harassing fire with the Union troops clustered on Cemetery Hill. On July 2, fire went back and forth between the two sides.

One of the oldest buildings in town, the Sweney House provided an excellent tactical advantage to the grey-jacketed soldiers who used its attic to take potshots at their enemies at the far end of Baltimore Street. The Union soldiers returned fire, blistering the exterior brick wall that faced Cemetery Hill with so many gunshots that around 150 pockmarks can still be seen there today.

July 2, 1863, was a hot day. With minimal airflow inside the enclosed, poorly ventilated space, the conditions inside the cramped attic would have been sweltering. As soldiers were hit, they were most likely carried downstairs to the cellar to receive medical attention. In addition to being a temporary refuge for the wounded and dying, not to mention storage for the bodies of those who were killed, the cellar of the Sweney House provided a place for the civilian residents to shelter. As the streets of Gettysburg became a hornet's nest above their heads, the people of the town sheltered in their own cellars, warned by the military not to come out until the shooting stopped. That would not happen for three days.

The Farnsworth House exterior as seen from Baltimore Street. Captain Elon Farnsworth (inset) commanded Brigade 1, Division 3, of the Cavalry Corps.

The Sweney House still stands today, though it now bears the name of Elon Farnsworth, a captain in the U.S. Cavalry Corps who died in a near-suicidal charge against Confederate defenses on the final day of the battle. Thousands of visitors flock to the Farnsworth House Inn each year. It is a place where one can find good food and drink, a friendly atmosphere, and, most importantly of all, a chance to connect with the history of Gettysburg. It is possible to tour the attic and the cellar, along with other parts of the house.

As part of the research process for my book on the haunting of the Farnsworth House, I spent several days and nights with full access to the property. Along with a small group of paranormal researchers, I investigated late into the night and spent the early morning hours sleeping in some of the most haunted rooms.

Interviewing the staff and owners, it seemed that everybody had a story of at least one ghostly encounter to share. Some had heard their names being called when nobody else was present. Others had been touched by unseen hands. Many had heard the sound of disembodied footsteps or phantom knocks and raps on the walls and doors. A few had even seen shadow figures and apparitions inside the Farnsworth House.

On their advice, I focused much of my time and attention on the attic and the cellar. From a purely pragmatic point of view, these were the two places in which the majority of deaths inside the house occurred. Aggressive voices came through the spirit box in the attic, filled with the sort of anger and profanity that would befit the rough and ready demeanor of soldiers at war.

For several nights, I slept in the most haunted bedroom in the house, the Sara Black Room. Numerous visitors have reported lying in

The Sara Black Room, directly beneath the attic. Visitors are disturbed in the night by heavy footsteps, thuds, and dragging noises from above them.

the big four-poster bed and having invisible hands tug the sheets and comforter off them in the middle of the night. Alas, nothing of that nature happened to me. Nor did I hear the heavy thuds, pounding footsteps, and dragging sounds coming from the attic directly above, which are other commonly reported phenomena in that room. It has been hypothesized that these are after-echoes of the Confederate soldiers who hunkered down in the attic during the battle and that the dragging sounds were made as they moved comrades who had been wounded to a safer place.

Part of the Sara Black Room also plays a role in the haunting. According to local lore, a young boy named Jeremy was hit by a speeding horse and carriage on Baltimore Street. Brought into the house to be cared for, he died in what is now the en suite bathroom. Records on this are sparse, but staff at the Farnsworth House attribute much of the playful paranormal activity to Jeremy's mischievous but well-meaning ghost. He's a trickster, a spirit who delights in waking people up with a start or moving things around in the middle of the night.

Jeremy the ghost boy has become such a fixture at the Farnsworth that he has a room named after him. It is filled with toys such as dolls, brightly colored balls, and wooden blocks. Jeremy's ghost seems to be heard rather than seen, but the same is not true of his grieving father, whose dour and morose spirit has been sighted walking throughout the house or sitting in a bedside chair in the nearby McFarlane Room. While sleeping in that particular room, I wondered whether this was the shadow figure that had been captured on a trail cam video taken by two guests at the Farnsworth House. I interviewed them and found both to be credible eyewitnesses who had no explanation for how a dark human shape seemed to run *through* their four-poster bed when the room was empty and locked.

Right next to Sara's room is the bathroom in which a young boy named Jeremy is said to have died after being hit by a speeding horse and buggy in the street. Jeremy's mischievous ghost haunts the Farnsworth House to this day.

The cellar is home to a haunted artifact, a tall mirror; some believe it has a spirit attached to it, and others think it serves as a kind of conduit between the material world and the spirit realm. Several photographs taken of this mirror show phantom "extras"—figures, faces, or body parts that were not visible when the picture was taken. It requires little imagination to sit in the pitch-black cellar and conjure up the sense of what it must have felt like in 1863 to hear the constant roar of muskets and rifles coming from up above. This would have been coupled with the screams and moans of the wounded, along with the stench of death, decay, and human waste, as the cellar had nothing in the way of sanitation.

Sitting on a bench in the cellar one afternoon, I was jabbed sharply in the small of the back by what felt like a fingertip. Whipping around to demand an explanation, I found nobody sitting behind me within arm's length. Plainly, someone had wanted to make their presence known. One of the long-dead casualties of the battle, perhaps—or the playful Jeremy, up to his usual antics? I never found out.

It's widely known that the only civilian fatality of the battle was 20-year-old Miss Virginia "Jennie" Wade. Born and raised in Gettysburg, on the third day of the battle (July 3), Jennie was at her sister's home, located at the far end of Baltimore Street. The house still stands, sitting between the Sweney (Farnsworth) House and Cemetery Hill. This essentially put it in a no-man's-land between the Union and Confederate forces, caught in the middle of crossfire between the two opposing sides.

The Jennie Wade House exterior with statue of Jennie Wade.

Jennie's sister, Georgia, had given birth the week prior, and Jennie was spending some time helping her out while Georgia took care of the baby.

Unlike other residents of Gettysburg, Jennie had not taken shelter in the cellar when death came calling for her. That fateful morning found her preparing bread in the kitchen of the small home. The house was built of sturdy brick, but the doors were wooden and would not stop bullets.

In general, both sides took pains to avoid targeting civilians wherever possible, but nothing could be done about stray rounds. One such projectile penetrated not one but two doors and hit Jennie in the chest. Her body was taken into the custody of Union soldiers before finally being given a temporary burial in the yard of the house.

(Some believe—though it is impossible to prove—that the shot that killed her was fired by a Confederate soldier from the attic window of the Sweney House.)

Although she never owned it, what's come to be known as the Jennie Wade House has a firm reputation for being haunted. It is located directly across the street from the orphanage and looks out onto Cemetery Hill. Amorphous, black clouds have been seen inside the house, particularly in the cellar, where some accounts hold that Jennie's body rested for a short period before her brief interment outside. She now rests in the Evergreen Cemetery on the opposite side of the road, and an American flag flies perpetually over her grave—an honor accorded to very few women.

The author explores the dungeon in the cellar of the orphanage, where children were manacled to the wall for hours, sometimes days, on end.

Just who haunts the house that bears her name is unclear. It's easy to leap to the conclusion that the ghost of Jennie Wade would be responsible for the phantom footsteps and the eerie light phenomena that have been reported inside the house. Some visitors believe they have seen her apparition there. Yet it should also be borne in mind that not only were many Union soldiers killed on Cemetery Hill, which directly abuts what is now the parking lot, but many of the dead also rest in the nearby cemeteries for civilians and soldiers alike. Some psychics have claimed that the spirits of the orphanage sometimes cross the street to visit the Jennie Wade House and vice versa.

A case, perhaps, of "Am ghost, will travel."

Walking the streets of Gettysburg and the battlefield that surrounds it on all sides, one feels a connection with the past that can be difficult to describe. There is an almost indefinable but very real sense that the veil between the world of the living and that of the dead is thinner in that place than it is almost anywhere else. Much as is the case in Tombstone, Arizona, re-enactors walk the streets, and one is forced to wonder whether some of them are not what they appear to be. It is tempting to reach out and touch the Union or Confederate soldiers one passes, just to make sure that they are living, breathing flesh and blood rather than the apparitions of a bygone age. The same is true of the ladies in flowing gowns and period-appropriate dresses who frequent the sidewalks and hostelries of Gettysburg. If some of them should turn out to be ghosts, how would we really be able to tell?

In this author's opinion, both the licensed tour guides and the historical re-enactors are the lifeblood of the entire Gettysburg experience. Each of them works to keep the history and spirit (no pun intended) of Gettysburg alive in their own unique way. Guides roam the field and tell the story of what unfolded in that summer of 1863 over and over again, their brains chock-full of facts and figures, down to the most minute detail. The re-enactors fire weapons, ranging from pistols all the way up to cannons, to give visitors a more visceral experience of the sound and fury that once enveloped the battlefield. They sleep outdoors under canvas, sometimes permitted to pitch their tents upon some of America's most hallowed and sacred ground.

On the first day of the battle, there were around 15,000 casualties. The second, which saw Lee's Confederates launching costly attacks against both the left and right flanks of Meade's army, resulted in 20,000 more. It resulted in little more than a stalemate, with the Confederacy inflicting (and sustaining) heavy losses for no appreciable strategic gain.

Re-enactments of the Battle of Gettysburg are extremely popular with tourists and Civil War buffs, with thousands of volunteers gathering each year to recreate the tragic chapter in American history.

The third and final day, July 3, found Lee throwing what remained of his bloodied and weary forces against the only point of the Union line he had not yet hammered hardest: its center. His reasoning made sense. Meade had to be weak *somewhere*. If the boys in blue had been strong on both the left and the right flanks, then it stood to reason that the weak spot had to be in the middle.

Unbeknownst to Lee, General Meade had spent the hours of darkness from the night of July 2 into the early morning of July 3 reinforcing his center. Against the advice of his trusty "old war horse" and second-in-command James Longstreet, Lee ordered an all-or-nothing assault. It was preceded by a massive artillery bombardment, one so ferocious that it shook buildings and shattered windows for miles around. Although the Confederate gunners knew their stuff, they had limited ammunition supplies remaining, and the barrage did little to soften up the Union center in advance of the infantry attack.

Led by generals Pickett, Pettigrew, and Trimble, the fateful attack has nevertheless gone down in the history books as "Pickett's Charge." Twelve thousand five hundred combat effectives formed ranks and marched across open fields, straight into the mouth of the Union cannons, rifles, and muskets located on Cemetery Ridge. Predictably, it was a slaughter.

Pickett was an aggressive officer, but even he had balked at what he had been asked to do. His division was shredded in the assault, as were those of his peers. Coming under increasingly heavy fire as they neared the Union position, the Confederate ranks were blasted apart as flying lead tore bloody swaths through them. There was no questioning the courage of the attackers, some of whom actually reached the Union lines, but the attack faltered in the face of implacable resistance.

Half an hour after it had begun, 6,500 casualties had been sustained—more than half of the Confederate force. The survivors limped their way back to the starting point, demoralized and bitter, straggling their way past the bodies of their dead comrades and accompanied by the screams of those who had suffered grievous wounds.

Pickett's Charge is known as the "high watermark of the Confederacy." Although the war would continue for two more years, the South never had a realistic chance of winning afterward. The best of Lee's fighting force was broken—many would say wasted—on that stretch of ground outside Gettysburg.

Walking the Charge today, one gets a sense of how terrifying it must have been to march straight into the muzzles of those Union cannons. Accompanied by a fellow investigator, I did so just after the battlefield had opened to the public early one spring morning. We were both stunned to hear the distinctive sound of cannon fire, perhaps a residual echo of the bombardment that had preceded Pickett's doomed attempt to breach the Union defenses. It felt like a genuine privilege to experience. Unfortunately, nobody was around to hear it other than one of my trusted colleagues, but accounts of hearing small arms fire and cannon fire are surprisingly common. Sometimes this can be explained by the presence of re-enactors practicing their craft; at other times, it is more likely evidence of the residual haunting that permeates so much of the Gettysburg battlefield.

Venturing out onto the battlefield after dark is not permitted, and this rule should be respected by all visitors. However, it is allowed on occasion under very specific circumstances. I was fortunate enough to lodge for several nights at one of the historic farms located on the battlefield itself, within close proximity to Devil's Den and the infamous Slaughter Pen. It was from this location on July 2 that Confederate soldiers serving under General John Bell Hood formed up to launch a desperate, and ultimately unsuccessful, assault on Little Round Top—the hill upon which

Devil's Den, a heavily defended Confederate position on the second afternoon of the battle.

Little Round Top as seen from Devil's Den. The Confederates came close to seizing the hill on the second day, but they were narrowly beaten back by troops of the 20th Maine Regiment.

the extreme left flank of the Union battle line was anchored. Hood was severely wounded in the arm, and his attack was repulsed.

The farmhouse was peaceful and retained much of the feel of the 1860s. Nothing of a ghostly nature happened within its walls during our stay, as far as I am aware, but a very curious thing happened outside. A fellow paranormal investigator set up cameras, complete with microphones, to cover the battlefield surrounding the farm while we slept throughout the night. At around 4:30 a.m., on the part of the field over which the Confederate attack once advanced, one of the mics recorded the crisp, clear sounds of a bugle call.

Such calls were used by commanding officers to coordinate battlefield troop movements and to relay orders such as attack and retreat. They were also used for more mundane purposes while an army was encamped, such as wake up, assemble, call to breakfast, and so on. The camera picked up nothing visually, and there were no re-enactors on that section of the battlefield. Even if there had been, it's unlikely they would have been up and about at that time, let alone blasting out calls on a bugle. This was likely another residual phenomenon, the brief opening of a window into that fateful summer of 1863, a window that quickly slammed shut again.

When Civil War enthusiasts talk about the third day at Gettysburg, Pickett's Charge tends to get much of the attention. That's understandable, but other things were also happening elsewhere. About 10 miles to the southwest, a regiment of Union cavalry—the "Fighting Sixth"— was dispatched on a mission to interdict a Confederate wagon train carrying supplies.

Unbeknownst to the Union troopers, a much larger force of Confederate cavalry was also roaming the area. It would be a gross mismatch: a single regiment of 400 versus an entire Confederate brigade, backed by an artillery battery. Named after the closest town, the Battle of Fairfield was a resounding defeat for the Union. After a strong start in which the dismounted Union horse soldiers gave the attacking Confederates a bloody nose, the men of the Sixth Cavalry were ultimately overwhelmed and were badly beaten.

Houses in Fairfield and on the roads that surrounded it were pressed into service as makeshift field hospitals. There were numerous casualties, men who had been shot or lacerated with the razor-sharp blades of cavalry sabers. Some died, and it's said that they were buried in temporary graves located in and around the town.

One of those houses had been built in 1757, with new parts being added to the structure in later years. It went by the name of the Fairfield Inn. I had heard about its haunting through two fellow paranormal investigators from Texas, the Klinge Brothers. They had investigated the Fairfield Inn for their TV series *Ghost Lab* and had caught on camera a very impressive shadow figure, peering back at them from one of the mirrors on the second floor, in the original part of the property.

The Klinges tried to identify the mysterious shadow spirit and received an EVP that clearly said the name "Private John

The mirror in which Private John Riley's shadow figure was captured by the Klinge Brothers.

Riley." Historical research would go on to prove that there had indeed been a soldier present at the battle with that name, and his final disposition remains unknown. Could this have been the shadow figure who had obligingly put in an appearance on Barry Klinge's camera?

Much like the Farnsworth House, the staff and owners of the Fairfield Inn all seemed to have experienced something ghostly. The bartender noted that glasses were never quite safe whenever his back was turned. They had a habit of spontaneously flying off the shelf or falling to the ground, even when nobody was within touching distance. Somewhat disconcerting was the discovery of a broom that was standing vertically upright in the hallway one day, perfectly still and unwavering. How it had gotten there and why it didn't fall to the ground were never explained.

One employee was roaming the second floor when she encountered a black, amorphous mass traveling across the upstairs landing. As described, it sounded similar to the dark cloud that had been reported at Eastern State Penitentiary. She didn't wait long enough to find out, bolting back to the office and slamming the door shut behind her.

The Fairfield home has been converted to an inn.

I interviewed a law enforcement officer and his significant other, both of whom had been staying in the master bedroom in the oldest part of the building. They watched in astonishment as a drawer slowly slid out of a piece of bedroom furniture, apparently pulled out by invisible hands.

One has to be careful when accepting such experiences, however believable, at face value. I discovered this while staying at the Fairfield when a cabinet door popped itself open in my room one night. At first, I was flabbergasted, but after a few moments of research, I soon discovered that stepping on a very specific part of the aged floorboards sent a vibration along the board up to the dresser, which in turn triggered the door's release. Being close to 270 years old, the Fairfield Inn has developed considerable structural tilt over those centuries. Large sections of the flooring lean at an odd angle. Floors bow, and the staircase is warped. The structure behaves in unpredictable ways when pressure is applied to it.

Although we heard none of the disembodied voices and even growls that have been reported by customers, my team and I heard footsteps walking through those empty hallways. These were sometimes followed by loud thumps, as though an invisible somebody was punching or kicking a part of the building.

In the early hours of the morning, a little before 5 A.M., only another investigator and I were present at the inn. We each had our own rooms; she was at the front of the building, and I was at the rear. She awoke engulfed in a cold chill, feeling as if, in her own words, she had been "put in a meat locker." She finally managed to get back to sleep after pulling the covers up to her ears in a last-ditch effort to get warm.

At the very same time, I was awakened by the sound of a loud thud. It was the sound of the heavy, counterweighted wooden front door being slammed shut. I thought nothing of it at the time, believing that a staff member had come in early to start their shift. Only later that day would I learn that we were the only two living people in the building.

All of the doors were closed and locked when I checked on them. Intriguingly,

Main staircase at the Fairfield Inn, where phantom footsteps are often heard.

my colleague had been closer to the front door than I was, yet she had heard nothing. The digital voice recorders that we had set out and left running overnight picked up the sound quite clearly. Based on the fact that the front door remained secure, we had to assume that the sound was another residual auditory phenomenon, a type of paranormal recording that I had heard and she had not. Checking the video security cameras confirmed that we had gotten no living company until much later in the morning.

During the Battle of Fairfield and the aftermath of the Battle of Gettysburg, the Fairfield Inn had seen its share of casualties. It had served as an ad hoc field hospital and had no doubt been the scene of numerous amputations and other gruesome surgeries as the physicians struggled to save as many limbs and lives as possible. The Army of Northern Virginia passed through Fairfield on its July 4 retreat from Gettysburg. A recalcitrant George Meade refused to pursue, something that drove President Abraham Lincoln into apoplexy; had Meade done so, the Civil War might have ended there and then.

The parlor, where it is said General Robert E. Lee may have stopped to refresh himself after retreating from the battlefield.

Robert E. Lee stopped to eat at the inn as his bedraggled army filed past along the Fairfield Road outside. We can only speculate as to what was on his mind, but more battles—both victories and defeats—awaited him on the long and bloody journey to his ultimate surrender at Appomattox Courthouse.

Many of those battlefields would come with ghost stories of their own, but few if any can hold a candle to Gettysburg. When all is said and done, it has a serious claim to be the most haunted town in the United States and, without question, one of the most important.

THE STANLEY HOTEL

In a busy hotel bar, the smartly dressed bartender accepts an order for bourbon on the rocks from his busiest customer. Pouring the drink with finesse, he slides it across the countertop toward the eager patron, who accepts it with the barely disguised excitement of an alcoholic who has just fallen off the wagon. Hard.

The patron fishes a bill out of his wallet but is rebuffed.

"No charge to you, Mr. Torrance," demurs the bartender equably. His client is puzzled.

"No charge?" Jack Torrance frowns, not understanding.

"Your money's no good here."

The scene is an absolutely classic moment of the silver screen. As crafted by cinematic auteur Stanley Kubrick, it introduces the audience to the next stage in the descent of Jack Torrance (as played by Jack Nicholson) into madness, horror, and, ultimately, death. Played by actor Joe Turkel, Lloyd the bartender is a ghost, as is everybody else surrounding him in the bar. The Overlook Hotel is an evil place, haunted by malicious ghosts and overseen by a terrifying supernatural force that wants to possess and corrupt the soul of Jack's young son, Danny.

The movie is, of course, *The Shining*.

Tens of thousands of tourists travel through the city of Boulder, Colorado, each year and drive the long, winding canyon up to the moun-

Opened to the public in 1909, the Stanley Hotel in Estes Park, Colorado, was built by Freelan Oscar Stanley, founder of the Stanley Motor Carriage Company, for use by vacationing Easterners and also those suffering from tuberculosis. Said to be haunted, the remote setting outside of Rocky Mountain National Park inspired Stephen King's classic horror novel *The Shining*.

tain town of Estes Park. Some are heading up to Rocky Mountain National Park to appreciate the great outdoors, but many of them are on a pilgrimage: they're in search of the hotel that inspired Kubrick's classic movie, which was itself an adaptation of horror maestro Stephen King's novel of the same name.

I spent several years giving tours at the Stanley Hotel. During the daytime, I talked primarily about the history of the hotel, its place in popular culture, and how it came to be. At night, the clientele was much more interested in hearing ghost stories. When I took the job, I was both curious and somewhat apprehensive regarding the claims of paranormal activity at the hotel. Many called the Stanley the most haunted hotel in the United States. How much of that was true, and how much was simply a marketing ploy designed to sell tickets?

The answer proved to be a pleasant surprise. I do not claim to speak for the ownership of the hotel, nor have I ever been in a position to do so, but I quickly learned that the upper echelons had a much greater interest in the history of the Stanley and its importance as a cultural icon than in the ghost stories. In terms of philosophy, it's fair to say that the emphasis was on sharing the history of the hotel rather than the haunting.

Although Stephen King helped put the Stanley on the map and keep it there, it is also fair to say that *The Shining* has given the public a somewhat distorted view of the hotel. Although in my experience it certainly has its ghosts (one does not need to look very far to find a staff member who has had a brush with the uncanny), they tend to be of the pleasant variety, by and large. Nobody has ever smashed their way through doors with a fire ax at the hotel, to the best of my knowledge. But there are grains of truth scattered throughout King's story, as we shall see.

An inventor, architect, and businessman, Freelan Oscar Stanley is best remembered as cofounder, with his brother, of the Stanley Motor Carriage Company, but his fortune actually came from making photographic plates.

The Stanley Hotel was built in 1909 by Freelan Oscar Stanley, who (with his twin brother, Francis Edgar) founded the Stanley Motor Carriage Company. F. O., as he preferred to be called, and his wife, Flora, first came to Estes Park in an attempt to mitigate the symptoms of F. O.'s pulmonary tuberculosis. Many physicians directed their TB patients to Colorado's mountain communities in the early 1900s, as the fresh air and clean water were believed to be highly beneficial. They certainly were for F. O., whose symptoms completely resolved during his first summer in the mountains.

The Stanleys built their own home in Estes Park and would spend each summer enjoying the good life there, but there was little to nothing in the way of social life to be found in what would one day become the gateway to Rocky Mountain National Park. The only way for Mr. and Mrs. Stanley to enjoy a social scene was to create one for themselves, and that is exactly what they did, spending two years constructing a grand hotel on a hillside overlooking the town.

Getting up to Estes Park in the early 1900s was an adventure in itself, and the Stanleys solved this issue by sending their famous Stanley Steamer cars down to the closest railway station to pick up guests and shuttle them up to the hotel. It was not at all unusual for families to spend the entire summer at the Stanley. One entire floor—the third—was set aside as a dormitory for children and the nannies who looked after them. The sounds of laughter and kids playing there was an everyday occurrence, and they still echo around the third floor of the Stanley today. More than one hotel guest has complained about the noise of boisterous children running up and down the hallway outside their third-floor room, only to be told that there were currently no children staying in the hotel.

A good friend related an experience that his friend had at the Stanley when he was staying on the third floor after a social function. The man is an Army Special Forces operator and as such is always hyper-aware of his environment. He made sure to lock and secure his room before going to bed, only to wake up in the middle of the night to find his door ajar and a young boy peering mischievously around it. After making direct eye contact with him, the child slowly retreated. Nonplussed (what on Earth was a child doing in his room so late at night, and how had the door gotten unlocked?), the man got out of bed and went to the door, poking his head out into the hallway. It was totally deserted.

If its reputation is to be believed, the most haunted room at the Stanley is 217. The story behind it goes back to the summer of 1911, when an acetylene gas explosion blasted a chambermaid through the

Front lobby of the hotel, decked out for Christmas. The brown color scheme was painted on by the set decorators for the miniseries *The Shining*. The hotel owner liked it enough to keep it that way.

floor of Room 217 (then the hotel's presidential suite) and into the ballroom below. The chambermaid's name is believed to have been Elizabeth Wilson, although there are multiple contradictory newspaper accounts that give different variations on that name and change various elements of the story. The explosion was very real, however, and as staff at the hotel today have settled on calling her "Miss Wilson," so shall I.

Miss Wilson did not die in the explosion, and after a hospital stay she returned to work at the hotel, where she remained for many years. She is said to haunt Room 217 to this day, however, and seems to strongly disapprove of unmarried couples sharing a bed in there (an unseen force is said to push them apart) or of rowdy guests who fail to show the proper respect to HER hotel. During the filming of *Dumb and Dumber,* portions of which were shot at the Stanley, actor Jim Carrey was assigned the room and checked out less than three hours later without giving any reasons why. One is forced to wonder whether he had an encounter with the spirit of Miss Wilson or simply didn't like the atmosphere of the place.

Stephen King, then an up-and-coming horror writer and not yet the literary icon he would become, visited the Stanley in September 1974. He and his wife, Tabitha, were the only guests at the hotel, which was due to close down for the winter, and were allowed to choose any room they wanted. Of course, they plumped for Room 217.

Although King has never claimed to have had a ghostly experience in Room 217, he did admit to having a brain-bender of a nightmare in which a fire hose outside the room somehow came alive and chased his three-year-old son, Joe—now an accomplished author of horror in his own right—through the hallways of the Stanley. This, in conjunction with a late-night drink and a ghost story or two in the company of a bartender named Lloyd Grady (or so the story goes), served as more than enough inspiration for Mr. King to formulate the concept of what would one day grow into *The Shining.*

Some visitors are disappointed to learn that Stanley Kubrick's movie adaptation of the same name was never actually shot at the hotel (Kubrick famously refused to travel overseas and almost always preferred to shoot on soundstages and location close to his home in the English countryside). But the TV miniseries version was. For several weeks, that cast and crew lodged in the Stanley while simultaneously using it as their version of the Overlook Hotel. According to the DVD commentary, many people had ghostly experiences during their stay, and the Stanley's reputation for being haunted was well deserved.

The hotel's concert hall is said to be the most haunted room at the Stanley.

The hotel's concert hall, which is modeled on the architectural style of the Boston Symphony Hall, is also extremely active. Said variously to be haunted by the spirits of three children, a former maintenance worker named Paul, and a man named Eddie (who seems to confine himself to the balcony area and loves to mess around with the lights), the concert hall was my favorite place to visit during the years I gave tours. Many paranormal enthusiasts feel the same way, and that part of the Stanley grounds is a firm favorite with most of those who cross its threshold. After all, it isn't everywhere that allows you to literally walk in the footsteps of the great Harry Houdini, who trod the boards at the Stanley Concert Hall and is one of the few ghosts who *hasn't* been said to make an appearance there. Given Houdini's notoriously skeptical outlook on the afterlife, that makes complete sense.

A love of music permeates the hotel to this day. Flora Stanley had such a love for melodies that she maintained a music room at the front of the hotel, one that has breathtaking views of the Rocky Mountains—particularly at sunrise and sunset. Her ghost has been seen in that same room, usually in proximity to the Steinway piano she loved so much during her lifetime. The piano is sometimes heard playing with nobody at the keys.

Although it's hardly a ghost factory, as some proclaim it to be, visitors, guests, and employees at the Stanley continue to report strange occurrences. Not all of them are easy to debunk, such as the lady on a late-night tour who photographed a shadowy woman's figure floating in the air behind her while in the basement of the concert hall. During my time at the hotel, members of the tour department were meticulous about trying to find rational explanations for the many eerie things that occurred there.

One summer evening, I took a typical group of customers into the concert hall. We were all sitting on the balcony, 20 guests and myself, and I was talking about the history of the hotel. Suddenly, loud and heavy footsteps could be heard pounding across the wooden floor one story beneath us. We all craned our heads to look over the balcony,

Haunted though it may be, there is no question that the handsome interior of the Stanley Hotel is worthy of appreciation.

fully expecting to find that a boisterous guest had let himself in and was clowning around.

Of course, nobody was there. I thought fast. The concert hall has a basement, so it would be easy to fake something like this if you went down there and hammered on the ceiling with a broom handle or something similar. Taking two of the customers with me, I went down to the basement and checked the exits. They were all securely locked. Then we went methodically from room to room, searching high and low for any signs of a flesh-and-blood prankster. There was none. Yet we all knew what we had heard: 21 of us had witnessed those footsteps. That many people don't hallucinate the same thing at the same time. To this day, I have no rational answer for what happened. Whether this was an intelligent greeting, one of the concert hall spirits making their presence known, or simply a residual remnant of days long past remains a mystery to this day.

Opinions may be divided on whether the Stanley is a great haunted hotel, but it is undeniably a great hotel in its own right. I am and will always remain deeply fond of this grand old dame of the Rockies, having made some very happy memories of my time there. If you should find yourself in Colorado with a little time on your hands, I highly recommend paying the grand old lady of the Rockies a visit for yourself.

Please tell the ghosts that Richard sent you.

THE SALLIE HOUSE

From the eerie delights of the Stanley Hotel in Colorado, we now move eastward toward the American Midwest, as we turn our attention to a haunting of a much darker character.

It seems as though one can hardly move in the paranormal field these days without encountering a "dark," "negative," "evil," or "demonic" haunting. In the experience of this author, many of the locations that are so labeled do not deserve that fearsome appellation. But there are some notable exceptions, and one of them is the notorious Sallie House (also sometimes known as Sallie's House).

The case first came to light in the 1990s, thanks to the intervention of what remains to this day one of the very best examples of paranormal reality television: a show called *Sightings*. Hosted by the urbane Tim White, a respected broadcaster and a general in the U.S. Air Force Reserves, *Sightings* was a show that covered ghosts, hauntings, UFOs, cryptids, and other strange phenomena. Lacking much of the sensationalism that plagues contemporary para-tainment, *Sightings* told it like it was and was always willing to showcase a spooky mystery.

It was from *Sightings* that the American public first learned about the psychic medium Peter James and his extraordinary experiences aboard the haunted ocean liner RMS *Queen Mary*—particularly its eerie swimming pool, which was said to be haunted by the ghost of a little girl who had drowned in it. An equally extraordinary Peter James case was known to viewers simply as "the Heartland Haunting"; it was so called because it took place in an unspecified town in the Heartland,

The Sallie House (back view inset) in Atchison, Kansas, is the residence of the ghost of Sallie, which has made the home an attraction for curious tourists.

that part of the United States that is associated with old-fashioned (in a good way) values and a rural lifestyle. The *Sightings* production team kept the specific location of the town a closely guarded secret, as they also did with the identity of the family afflicted by one of the most violent poltergeist outbreaks on record.

The town, viewers would later learn, was the community of Atchison, Kansas. Atchison is perhaps best known for being the birthplace of the legendary aviator Amelia Earhart, whose aircraft disappeared without a trace in 1937 while she was trying to circumnavigate the globe.

A young married couple named Debra and Tony Pickman were excited to move into their new home and had no inkling whatsoever of the paranormal nightmare that was about to engulf them.

During the process of researching this book, I was fortunate enough to meet Debra in person. I was impressed with her integrity and her willingness to discuss the haunting that she and her family endured without exaggeration or hyperbole. After multiple in-person interviews that lasted for many hours and a phone interview with her husband, Tony, I found them both to be credible witnesses, good people who had suffered a period of terror and torment that sounds more like a horror movie than something out of real life. (Indeed, a made-for-TV movie starring Beau Bridges and Miguel Ferrer, *Sightings: Heartland Ghost,* offered a heavily fictionalized version of the Sallie House haunting.)

So, why call it "the Sallie House"? The first inkling that something wasn't quite right in their new home came when the Pickmans discovered toys apparently moving of their own accord in the nursery, a small room at the top of the staircase. From these strange but modest beginnings, the paranormal activity quickly started to ramp up until both Debra and Tony had no choice but to accept the fact that they had moved into an extremely haunted house. Even worse, things turned violent, and it soon became apparent that Tony was the focus of a malicious entity that had no qualms whatsoever about hurting him.

Scratches began to appear on his body, long, irregular, and often deep enough to draw blood. A visiting sensitive claimed that the Pickmans were being tormented by the spirit of a little girl named Sallie, who by all accounts had quite the mean streak. This was further supported when Peter James visited the house to film an episode of *Sightings* and claimed to have seen the apparition of a little girl standing in an upstairs window, silently staring down at him.

The *Sightings* film crew documented scratches and welts appearing on Tony's body right in front of their eyes and returned to the Sallie House again and again to cover the remarkable paranormal activity that was taking place there.

One aspect of the haunting that does not seem to bear close scrutiny is its backstory. The tale goes that Sallie, who was said to have been somewhere between five and nine years old, was brought to the front door of the house back when it was the home of a physician. She was suffering from a ruptured appendix and was in imminent danger of dying. Recognizing this, the doctor placed Sallie on his table and performed surgery on her abdomen—without anesthetic. The poor

The second-floor nursery seemed to be ground zero for paranormal activity in the Sallie House. The first sign of the haunting was when the toys began to move of their own accord.

little girl died anyway during the procedure, suffering immense pain as she did so.

It's a tragic, moving, and also somewhat terrifying story, and yet I have not been able to find even a shred of evidence to support it. I could not locate any children named Sallie buried anywhere in Atchison nor find a record of one having lived or died in the town. In her autobiographical book *The Sallie House Haunting,* Debra Pickman notes that there was a Sallie Hall who died in Atchison, but she was 34 years old. She adds that researchers for *Sightings* believed they may have identified a 5-year-old named Sallie, who died alongside her mother in some kind of vehicular accident. Sadly, there is no documentary proof, other than the researchers' recollections.

Whatever the truth may be, the story of a vengeful young Sallie still persists despite the fact that nobody seems to be entirely sure of its origin, and to this day, it is repeated by some people as though it is the unvarnished truth. As a writer and researcher, I am very much open to receiving and reviewing evidence to back up Sallie's origin story, but at the moment, I regard it as being equally likely to be folklore as fact. Unless records should happen to surface to support the case, the jury will remain out.

This means that the true root cause of the Sallie House haunting is murky at best, and I suspect that we will never be 100 percent clear on what exactly lies behind it all. Although the Pickmans appear to be the first tenants of the house to experience significant paranormal activity there, there are also claims that the child of a former occupant played with an "imaginary friend"—one who just happened to be a little girl. Many paranormal investigators hold the view that imaginary friends are not always imaginary.

There has been no shortage of visitors and paranormal investigators who believe that the haunting is a malevolent one and that "Sallie" is not actually the spirit of a little girl at all. One possibility that makes a great deal of sense to me is the thought-form hypothesis. This holds that the story of Sallie has been told so many times, to so many people, that it has quite literally taken on a life of its own. A thought-form arises when large amounts of concentrated thought are brought into focus on one single idea. In other words, each person who has heard or told the story of Sallie's gruesome death inside the house has unwittingly contributed to the creation of a sort of "simulated Sallie"—they may have created a ghost of their own, the result of directed thought and mental energy on a prolonged, mass scale.

While this hypothesis goes some way to explain why the Sallie House is still paranormally active to this day, it fails to account for one critical piece of the puzzle: where did the entity originally come from? The Pickmans heard no accounts of their house being haunted when they first moved in. Whatever was responsible for the violent activity that plagued them, it was unlikely to have been a thought-form unless it happened to have been created in secret and very deliberately by somebody who used to live in the house before them.

This ball sometimes hurls itself down the staircase as though an invisible child is playing catch with it.

Be it a ghost, a thought-form, or even a demon as some have claimed, whatever lies at the heart of the Sallie House haunting still tends to behave aggressively on occasion. One friend I've known for many years refuses to go back after, he claims, suffering spontaneous burns on his legs while down in the basement. Another paranormal investigator I spoke to was shaken when she hit a deer just a few minutes after leaving the house, totaling her car in the process. Fortunately, she was not seriously injured.

During my 2021 investigation of the Sallie House, Debra Pickman was initially reluctant to step foot back inside the house that had caused her and her husband so much torment. We conducted the initial part of our interview on the front porch. After a while had passed, she kindly agreed to go in and relate some of her experiences to me in person.

As soon as one enters the house via the front door, one is confronted with the staircase that leads up to the second floor. She and Tony frequently heard footsteps running up and down that staircase at night, footsteps that seemed childlike in nature.

"There's someone or something at the top of the stairs," Debra observed, relating how the figure of what appeared to be a military serviceman had once appeared on a photograph taken of the upstairs landing. The figure was wearing a brimmed hat and was carrying what looked like a saber.

On more than one occasion, Debra would feel the swoosh of an invisible *something* rushing past her on the staircase as she was going up

Steps leading down to the cellar, where occult rituals are said to have been carried out.

or down. It was almost as if a kid had ducked past her, though nothing was ever visible.

I'm self-admittedly about as un-psychic as it is possible to get, but I told her that the house felt very warm and pleasant to me. Debra replied that it did not feel particularly bad to her as she approached it from the street that afternoon but that there had been times—particularly at the height of the haunting—when the negative energies had been virtually palpable, practically "oozing out the front door." On some of those days, Tony was physically attacked by the entity haunting the house.

The violence he sustained reached frightening levels at times, and while some tried to dismiss the whole thing as being self-inflicted, this ignores the fact that Tony was carefully monitored by the crew of *Sightings* and kept under continuous observation as scratches appeared on his skin in front of the camera's unblinking eye. There is also no readily apparent motive for either Debra or Tony to have faked anything. By the time all was said and done, neither of them could wait to get out of that house and start over somewhere new.

It seems that everybody has an opinion on what it is that haunts (or doesn't haunt) the Sallie House. Simply writing the whole thing off isn't an option, at least not to anybody maintaining a balanced approach to the subject. The haunting is a complex case. Even today, there are people who spend nights in that house—sometimes completely and utterly alone—and have literally nothing whatsoever happen to them. Others leave before sunrise, terrified by the paranormal activity that's taking place.

One medium who accompanied me to the house on a balmy afternoon visit could only stand to be inside for a few minutes before coming under what he said was a sustained psychic assault. He ended up checking into a hotel in Atchison rather than spend another minute inside the Sallie House, yet I spent that same night sleeping completely peacefully there.

I've always maintained a healthy degree of skepticism toward the idea of certain houses or objects being "cursed." However, one of my several visits to the Sallie House prompted me to reassess that point of view. I left the house in the wee small hours of the morning, heading west on the interstate toward my home in Colorado. Along with my fellow investigators, I had made a point of doing some light work and cleansing prior to leaving, purely as a protective measure. Less than an hour outside of Atchison, at around 3:00, I totally lost control of my vehicle, a pickup truck. I was driving at 70 MPH, cruise control set, pondering the events of that night's paranormal investigation. Without a warning, I was suddenly fighting to stay on the road.

The truck skidded, making a teeth-grinding groaning sound, but I was able to regain control and pull over to the side of the road. Getting out to inspect it, I saw that the rear driver's side tire was completely shredded. Flaps of rubber hung in tatters from the bare wheel. There was almost nothing of the actual tire left—it had suffered a catastrophic failure. Now, these things happen, but these were new tires with less than 5,000 miles on them and had very little in the way of wear and tear.

I called a friend who was a trusted psychic medium. She reached out to try to "read" the situation, and not only did she tell me that I was being followed around by some sort of tall, thin, negative shadow entity but added that the accident I had was an attempt by the Sallie House to prevent me from leaving. To this day, I'm still not sure what to believe about that, but I'm a man who likes to hedge his bets: the first thing I did when I pulled into my driveway at home was to spend 10 minutes getting the most thorough sage-down I've ever had in my entire life.

From an experiential point of view, the Sallie House has rarely disappointed me. To counterbalance the quiet nights I've spent there, others have offered up a whole host of tales of strange activities. REM pods repeatedly went crazy, without obvious explanation. Lights have switched themselves on and off. Doors opened and closed themselves. Footsteps were heard walking around the empty second floor. Estes Method EVP sessions yielded some truly knockout responses to our questions. Perhaps most memorably, a fellow investigator named Rob jumped halfway out of his skin when he felt a small, child-sized hand press against the small of his back—underneath his T-shirt.

The author takes a break during his Sallie House investigation.

I still don't know what haunts the anonymous-looking house in Atchison, but I do know that no matter what the naysayers claim, it *is* haunted. Furthermore, while they can sometimes be playful and at other times be so quiet as to be practically inert, whatever spirit or spirits can be found within its walls are not necessarily going to play nicely with others.

Should you ever decide to find out for yourself, I advise you to be cautious just in case.

ALCATRAZ ISLAND

The official name was the United States Penitentiary, Alcatraz, but to those who were incarcerated there, the craggy island located in the middle of San Francisco Bay had a number of less formal monikers: some called it "The Rock," and to others, it became "Devil's Island" and "Hellcatraz."

Just like many of the prisoners who ended up serving time there, Alcatraz had made a fearsome reputation for itself. Part of that reputation stemmed from the unforgiving regime that was enforced upon the inmates; another part was the legend that the prison was all but impossible to escape from. This was an assertion that would be tested repeatedly over the years, sometimes with disastrous results for those who tried.

Alcatraz began its life as a defensive installation, not as a prison. The island occupied a commanding position in the bay, and to a military eye, it was apparent that any cannons placed there would make life very difficult for any hostile naval invasion force that tried to anchor nearby. It was also a natural place for a lighthouse, guiding mariners home through the sometimes foggy waters of the California coastline. The U.S. military surveyed the island in 1855, and soon thereafter, construction began on what would become Fort Alcatraz.

The island was ringed with fortifications. Its teeth came in the form of heavy gun batteries. The Civil War came and went. Fort Alcatraz was manned but never engaged in hostilities. In fact, its greater purpose was the incarceration of military prisoners and civilians who were deemed a threat to the Union cause. In a particularly shameful episode,

Alcatraz Island was initially used by the U.S. military. The location in the bay was quite strategic. This model shows how Military Point Alcatraz looked in the 1860s.

Native Americans were imprisoned there for failing to obey the regulations imposed upon them by the U.S. government. Living conditions were squalid, with inmates sleeping cheek by jowl in communal cells, sweltering in the summer heat and freezing in the winter cold.

As the nineteenth century gave way to the twentieth, conditions at Alcatraz had improved significantly—though hard work was still the order of the day. The military liked its prisoners to work. They were made to engage in various forms of manual labor. Although other forms of work were available to some inmates, the most common was the mind-numbing, strength-sapping practice of turning big rocks into smaller rocks for hours each day. Alcatraz was run efficiently, and thanks to the in-house educational system, a prisoner had a greater chance of making something of himself there than he would have had in a civilian penitentiary.

1934 saw Alcatraz change hands, transferring from the stewardship of the U.S. Army to that of the federal government. Organized crime was rampant throughout the country, and a depressed economy led some people to acts of desperation. American correctional facilities were bursting at the seams with inmates, and there was a need for increased cell capacity. Although it was relatively small in size, its island status meant that Alcatraz fit the bill perfectly for housing some of the "most troublesome prisoners." In fact, this is putting it mildly. When the government set out its plans for the new facility at Alcatraz, it planned for the prison to house the very worst of the worst, men of whom it wanted to make an example, thereby serving as a deterrent to other would-be criminals. Gangsters were at the top of this list, as the government declared war on the Mob.

A new system of security features was designed and implemented prior to the arrival of the first civilian prisoners, including complete overhauls of the cells. The new system involved several safety features designed to protect the prison guards, such as the capacity to open and close cell doors singly or in groups by the equivalent of "remote control"— a special unlocking mechanism.

In case things got really out of hand, the guards would also have heavy firepower in the form of machine guns.

The military prisoners had been relatively well behaved, all things considered. Nobody was foolish enough to expect the same standard of behavior from the hardened criminals who would soon call Alcatraz home. A number of gun galleries were installed, both within the prison buildings and in watch towers around the island, so that guards armed with rifles would be able to surveil their colleagues who were in direct contact with the inmates. In case things got *really* out of hand, the guards would also have heavy firepower in the form of machine guns. If things ever got truly out of control with the 250-plus prisoners that were being held on the island, the guards were capable of turning it into a slaughterhouse.

Fortunately, that never happened, but it came close on several occasions. One would think that the worst thing about serving time on Alcatraz would be the company one had to keep—being constantly surrounded by some of the country's meanest murderers, mobsters, and thugs would be enough to make even the hardiest man paranoid. Yet surprisingly, what seemed to bother inmates the most wasn't the rigid prison regime or the potential for violence to explode at any time from the inmates—it was the silence. By order of the prison warden, a condition of

TERRIFYINGLY TRUE HAUNTINGS

perpetual silence was enforced upon the convicts, which was found to be so psychologically stressful that some men simply snapped and took to self-harm in a desperate attempt to get transferred off the island.

When it became clear that the imposition of silence was having a corrosive effect on morale, the order was rescinded. To those who endured it, along with a proportion of the American public when they read about it in the newspapers, the condition of silence was considered to be cruel in the extreme.

Of all the high-profile inmates of Alcatraz, undoubtedly the most notorious was our old friend Al Capone. The crime lord was one of the earliest civilian residents of Alcatraz, as was reflected by his inmate number: #83. Although he wasn't the security or escape risk that many of his peers were, Capone's transfer to Alcatraz reflected the desires of both the president and FBI director J. Edgar Hoover to see him publicly humbled and served up as an example of what happened when one criminal bucked the system so blatantly.

Unlike his cell at Eastern State Penitentiary, the cell at Alcatraz (pictured) was not specially appointed for Al Capone.

Sending Capone to The Rock was as much a publicity stunt as it was a legitimate prisoner transfer. Indeed, his celebrity status meant that there was more risk *to* Capone on Alcatraz than there was from him. He was not well regarded and narrowly avoided being stabbed to death by an inmate named Jimmy Lucas.

For Capone, life on Alcatraz was very different from his experience at other prisons, such as Eastern State Penitentiary and Atlanta. He quickly found that the prison staff, from the warden himself on down to the guards, could not be bribed, bought, or intimidated into doing whatever it was that Capone wanted. The luxuries and special treatment he was once able to buy at those other institutions were a thing of the past once he stepped off the boat onto Alcatraz Island.

Al Capone's time on Alcatraz passed, but it passed like a kidney stone. Sometimes he was akin to a model prisoner, performing his chores diligently and flying under the radar. Then, out of nowhere, he was found getting into fights and scrapes. Much of this can be attributed to the syphilis that was slowly eating away at his mental faculties. Toward the end of his days on The Rock, he spent an increasing amount of time in the prison hospital, where the doctors did their best to alleviate the symptoms of his illness.

Coming to Alcatraz meant a major fall in status for the mobster, with Capone going from a feted crime lord to a menial laborer who performed moderately strenuous duties around the prison. Although the media was initially fascinated by how Capone was dealing with life behind bars at America's toughest penitentiary, the warden and his staff were careful to insulate Capone from as much external attention as they could.

Capone left Alcatraz in January 1939, having spent the best part of four years on the island, and was sent to the Terminal Island Correctional Institution in Los Angeles. He was released from that prison in November 1939.

The mandate of silence was revoked during Capone's tenure at Alcatraz. Although he couldn't play any musical instruments at the time of his arrest, he learned to play the banjo while serving his sentence on Alcatraz. While he wasn't the most talented player, Capone was able to hold a tune as part of the prison inmate band, the imaginatively named "Rock Islanders."

Long after Alcatraz was shut down as an operational corrections facility, the strains of banjo music were reported, echoing through the

Known as "The Rock," Alcatraz Island and its federal penitentiary have a reputation of being nearly impossible to escape.

still and empty cell blocks. It seems to originate from the shower room, where Capone would often practice with the instrument.

Whether this is an intelligent haunting or a residual one is impossible to say for sure, but I lean toward the latter explanation. As we saw in the chapter dedicated to Eastern State Penitentiary, Al Capone has a rather busy afterlife. Why he would want to drop in and visit his least favorite prison just to play the banjo is difficult to say, and it seems more likely that what park rangers and visitors are hearing are the paranormally recorded sounds of Capone practicing the instrument back in his earthly lifetime.

During its lifetime as a federal prison, the only way onto and off of the island was by boat. There was nowhere for an aircraft to land. Any civilian or unidentified boat coming within 200 feet of the island needed to present a permit or risk being fired upon by the ever-vigilant guards, who manned the towers around the clock.

The waters of San Francisco Bay were rough and choppy, with riptides that could drag a swimmer under and drown him. They were also shark infested. So, even if a wannabe escapee could slip out of the prison, escape the roving eyes of the guards in the towers, and make his way into the water successfully, there was significant risk in trying to swim one's way out of Alcatraz.

Yet, despite Alcatraz's supposed invulnerability to escape, there were still those who thought it worth a try. In 1936, an inmate named Joe Bowers tried to go over the barbed wire and dive into the bay. He ignored warning shots fired from a guard tower. Bowers was shot in the chest, and his body fell 75 feet into the waters of San Francisco Bay. Between the fall and the gunshot trauma, he did not survive.

On the very foggy night of December 16 the following year, inmates Ralph Roe and Theodore Cole sawed through their cell bars and wriggled through the window. Hightailing it to the edge of the island, they jumped into the bay. To this day, it is unknown whether they swam to safety, drowned, or were eaten by sharks. The official verdict was that the frigid bay waters had claimed both their lives, but no bodies were ever recovered.

Over the years, the inmates of Alcatraz brutalized themselves and one another. Several murders and suicides took place there. Sometimes, the prisoners turned on their captors.

The bloodiest phase in the prison's history began on May 2, 1946, and was not resolved for two more days. It resulted in multiple deaths,

The cell house walls were heavily damaged by mortar fire launched by the U.S. Marines trying to quell the prisoner violence within.

TERRIFYINGLY TRUE HAUNTINGS

even more injuries, and prolonged siege and was given the title "The Battle of Alcatraz."

Six prisoners were involved in the attempt, which began with beating a guard unconscious in order to steal his keys. Their next step was to gain access to weapons supplies and arm themselves, then release fellow prisoners and start taking guards as hostages. The goal was to use them as leverage, bartering their lives in exchange for a boat that would transport them away from the island.

Of course, it was never going to be that simple.

The nine hostages had been corralled in Cells #403 and #404. Frustrated by the lack of apparent progress, one of the mutineers, an inmate named Joseph Cretzer, emptied his purloined pistol into the cell, shooting the helpless prison guards at close range.

The warden ordered his guards to storm the prison. The assault was met with strong resistance. A blizzard of gunfire was exchanged between the attackers and the defenders, neither of whom wanted to give up ground to the other. The guards had help in the form of the U.S. Marines, who provided them with demolitions and even mortar support.

Once the dust settled on May 4, 14 guards were wounded; three of the ringleaders were dead, killed in the counterattack; two prison guards had also been killed. The remaining three prisoners survived. Two of them were executed in the gas chamber at San Quentin Prison, convicted in the deaths of the guards. The third prisoner was sentenced to an extra 99 years' incarceration.

After-echoes of the battle are said to still reverberate through the prison in the form of footsteps, disembodied screams, and inexplicable loud noises on the empty cell block. Sightings of the three dead conspirators have also been reported. Considering the extreme stress and violence associated with the two-day incident, it is not surprising that something lingers all these years later. Like much of the paranormal activity reported from Alcatraz, it seems to be residual in nature—which is probably for the best.

Vying with Al Capone for the title of most notorious prisoner is Robert Stroud, the so-called Birdman of Alcatraz. Most people know of Stroud from the 1962 movie *Birdman of Alcatraz,* in which he was played to fine effect by the actor Burt Lancaster. As is so often the case with fictionalized retellings of actual events, the version of Robert Stroud's story that made it to the silver screen relied heavily on artistic license.

Stroud was a cold-blooded killer, having murdered a bartender named Charlie Dahmer by repeatedly shooting him with a pistol. The killing took place in 1909, when Stroud was 18 years old. After being sent to prison for manslaughter, he later stabbed an inmate who he thought had sold him out to the jailers.

Seven years later, Stroud upped the ante even further by stabbing a prison guard named Andrew Turner to death. This effectively sealed his fate. Robert Stroud would never regain his freedom and was fortunate to escape with his life. The judge presiding over Stroud's murder trial sentenced him to death by hanging. It was only after a tireless public relations campaign led by his mother

Convicted murderer Robert Stroud was known as "The Birdman of Alcatraz" because he had become quite the amateur expert on ornithology and wrote two books about canaries.

that the murderer was granted clemency by President Woodrow Wilson. The sentence of execution was downgraded to one of life imprisonment.

Much of that sentence was served in solitary confinement, and Stroud spent considerable time drawing and reading. Since his initial prison sentence at Fort Leavenworth in Kansas, he had a particular fascination with birds and made it his business to study them in detail. He even wrote and self-published a book, *Stroud's Digest on the Diseases of Birds*.

Stroud had come to Alcatraz in the winter of 1942. In 1955, author Thomas E. Gaddis published a biography of Stroud's life, the eponymous *Birdman of Alcatraz*. This pushed a narrative of Robert Stroud being a kind and gentle soul rather than someone coldly responsible for the brutal assaults and killings he had committed. He was a troublesome prisoner despite spending much of his time alone. Stroud resented not being permitted to keep birds in his cell, as he had been allowed to do in Kansas.

It's surreal to think that Robert Stroud's life was the focus of both a best-selling book and a successful Hollywood movie, and yet he was denied access to both of them. In contrast to the sensitive and joyful portrayal by Burt Lancaster, the real Stroud was a deeply unhappy man. He tried to take his own life several times while incarcerated in Alcatraz, unsuccessfully.

The Birdman did make it off the island alive in the end. After 17 years as an inmate of Alcatraz, in 1959 he was transferred to a facility in Missouri, where he was no longer confined to solitary. His final days were relatively happy ones. On the night of November 20, 1963, 73-year-old Robert Stroud went to sleep. He never woke up.

Gaunt and dour, the Birdman was a distinctive figure. There are multiple claims of his apparition being sighted at Alcatraz, usually within the vicinity of his old cell. Much like the sound of Al Capone's banjo, it seems likely that the apparition of Robert Stroud is residual, as his time spent at Alcatraz was far from happy. In another parallel with Capone, this period also saw a marked diminishment in Stroud's faculties. It is said that Stroud heard voices talking to him in his cell, a believable claim that could reasonably be explained by his steadily worsening mental illness.

Alcatraz was decommissioned as a penitentiary in 1963 after being deemed too expensive to remain in operation. After occupation by in-

Once a place of despair and violence, Alcatraz is now a federally protected bird sanctuary with an estimated 30,000 nesting seabirds, including cormorants, gulls, and herons. Also, salamanders, deer mice, seals, and other animals find a home here.

digenous activists and a period of dereliction, custodianship of the island was taken over by the National Park Service. Public visits have been permitted since 1973, and ghostly occurrences continue to be reported from The Rock.

In 2024, a team of climate researchers took up residency on Alcatraz Island for three weeks, sleeping in the cells on D Block. Their purpose was to study the effects of global warming upon the island itself. While they were there, the scientists also learned some unanticipated lessons about the paranormal.

According to a June 16, 2024, article by Molly McCrea ("Alcatraz Island Climate Researchers Have Haunting Experience Staying in Prison Cells"), one member of the team experienced the sound of a crowd of people walking around inside the empty prison. Everybody else was asleep at the time.

Then came the sound of piano music. In a long-abandoned penitentiary. In the middle of the night.

Could it possibly be that not *every* occupant left The Rock on the last boat out?

HAUNTED HIGH SEAS

Despite the fact that the twenty-first century is currently in its third decade, with more scientific knowledge at the fingertips of the average human being than at any other time in history, superstitious practices are still alive and well. We walk around ladders rather than risk going under them. Some people throw salt over their shoulder in order to ward off bad luck or evil spirits, depending on which version of the superstition they subscribe to.

Triskaidekaphobia is the irrational fear of the number 13. Rather than attempting to apply reason or logic, the owners of tall buildings refuse to have a floor designated the 13th. Many airliners skip the 13th row of seats for the same reason, and you won't be able to catch a flight from Gate 13 because it usually doesn't exist. Check into a hotel, and the chances are that there'll be no Room 13. The same applies to hospital rooms and patient bays.

Some people laugh at superstitions such as this, shrugging them off and paying no mind. Others take them very seriously indeed. Two of the most superstitious vocations in the world are those of actor and sailor. Of the two, the latter seems to be leading in the superstition stakes.

This mindset dates back to the days of the ancient mariners. Sailing the world's oceans has always been a dangerous profession and remains so to this day despite the advent of modern technologies and training. Even a relatively small stroke of misfortune could mean death.

Those who crewed sailing ships made a habit of carefully placing a coin beneath the mast before leaving harbor. The rationale was simple, if macabre: should the ship sink, the coins would pay the ferryman of legend to transport the souls of its crew across the river of death.

The least likely day of the week for such a voyage to begin was Friday. Sailors have long believed it to be the unluckiest of days on which to sail; Friday the 13th would have been a double no-no. It was also considered unlucky to rename a ship or boat once it had been christened; the presence of a woman at sea was regarded as being even worse luck, as were redheads; and bananas were the equivalent of kryptonite to a sea voyage. This innocent-seeming fruit brought lurking death in the days after it was first discovered because bunches of them often contained stowaways in the form of venomous spiders.

Early mariners believed wholeheartedly in sea monsters, the great dragons of the deep, and in the danger of sailing so far that one could fall off the edge of the world.

Considering all this, it should come as no surprise that they were absolute believers in ghosts. Stories of haunted ships, not to mention the apparitions of ships, are almost as old as the seafaring profession. These tales span the entire globe, as indeed do the oceans themselves.

The greatest of all oceanic ghost stories has to be that of the doomed ship the *Flying Dutchman*. The first examples of the story date

An 1860s painting by Charles Temple Dix portraying the *Flying Dutchman,* the ghost ship that is doomed to sail the seas for eternity without rest.

back hundreds of years, to the seventeenth century, and likely began as tall tales shared among Dutch sailors over a bottle of grog. The Dutch East India company was both powerful and influential, competing with its British equivalent for commercial maritime supremacy. The legend not only spread like wildfire but spun off into multiple different variations.

According to one version of the myth, the *Flying Dutchman*'s obstinate captain, a man named Vanderdecken, was trying to sail around the notoriously treacherous Cape of Good Hope, always without success. Swearing that he would keep trying until the end of the world, he and his crew were cursed by the Devil into doing exactly that: sailing the seas for all eternity.

Some versions hold that the phantom brigantine can only sail into port once every seven years, allowing the captain to search for the only avenue of breaking the curse: to find a woman who would be faithful to him until her dying day. Another version has the captain playing either cards or dice with the Devil, wagering his soul on the game—with predictably bad results for Vanderdecken and his crew.

Yet another variant has the captain recognizing the futility of his Sisyphean quest to round the Cape and outright selling his soul to Satan in exchange for safe passage around it.

As dark poetry, it's a peerless legend. There is, however, no evidence that it was ever based on a real ship.

Now firmly ingrained into the fabric of sailing culture, the story of the *Dutchman* has made fodder for poetry, opera, paintings, literature, and even Hollywood blockbuster movies, as any fan of Disney's *Pirates of the Caribbean* film series knows.

The truly strange thing is that actual sightings of the phantom sailing ship have been reported for centuries. Can these be put down to hallucinations, mirages, the effects of too much rum, or even simply the ramblings of sailors with overly active imaginations?

Possibly. On the other hand, it could also be the case that so many salty sea dogs told the story of the *Dutchman* over and over again that the tale literally took on a life of its own. In other words, it became a thought-form, also known as an egregore. This can occur when enough collected thought accumulates after being concentrated on a single focus. The titular Sallie of Sallie House fame may well be an egregore, for example. The same may also be true of the Black Monk of Pontefract and potentially other hauntings.

Disney recreated the *Flying Dutchman* for display at its private Castaway Cay, a small island where its cruise ships stop.

The tale of the cursed ghost ship likely grew in the telling as it spread from tavern to tavern and from ship to ship. British and French sailors heard it and passed it on. Before long, spooky stories of the *Flying Dutchman* were being told everywhere, and sightings of the ship began to crop up not just in the seas surrounding the Cape of Good Hope but rippling out farther across the ocean.

The *Dutchman* is said to glow with an eerie, ethereal light, reflecting its supernatural origins. No matter how rough the seas or how harsh the weather, the ship glides onward as though unaffected by the material world. Giving the legend an even more macabre twist was the claim that those who encountered the phantom ship were doomed to die.

Arguably, the most credible eyewitness to encounter the ghost was a youth who would one day become the monarch King George V, the man who would rule Britain from 1910 to 1936 and the grandfather of Queen Elizabeth II. He was not a man given to flights of fancy. Sent to sea as a midshipman serving in the Royal Navy, George was a junior officer aboard the frigate the HMS *Inconstant*. In 1881, the warship was cruising in Australian waters, voyaging from Melbourne to Sydney—far from South Africa and the Cape of Good Hope, the *Dutchman*'s traditional sailing grounds.

Young George was standing watch in the early morning hours of July 11 when suddenly the lookout sighted another vessel sailing in close proximity to *Inconstant*'s port bow.

The ghostly brigantine glowed with an incandescent red light; it serenely crossed the frigate's bows, giving not the slightest acknowledgment of the Royal Navy ship's presence. The midshipman and 12 of his shipmates reportedly saw the *Dutchman* quite clearly, according to the *Inconstant*'s logbook, an official document into which the sighting was dutifully entered.

As quickly as she had emerged from the darkness, the phantom disappeared, never to be seen by the sailors again.

Adding some weight to the claims of the *Flying Dutchman* being an ill omen for those who saw her was the report that the lookout who first sighted the ghost ship slipped and fell from the topmast six hours afterward. He was killed instantly and given the traditional seaman's burial at sea later that afternoon.

The primary source regarding this brush with the *Flying Dutchman* is an 1886 book titled *The Cruise of Her Majesty's Ship "Bacchante," 1879–*

In this nineteenth-century illustration, one can see the effect of the Fata Morgana mirage in which certain weather conditions can reflect light to generate a ghostly image above the horizon. Some posit that this is one possible explanation behind ghost ship tales.

1882, published by MacMillan & Co. of London. The book was compiled from the private letters and journals of Prince George of Wales and his brother, Prince Albert Victor, who was also present on the HMS *Inconstant* at the time of the sighting.

Did the crew of the HMS *Inconstant* really encounter the world's most famous phantom ship in the dark, predawn hours of July 11, 1881, or were they fooled by a mirage or some form of temporary mass delusion? While it's tempting to dismiss the whole thing out of hand as being nothing more than a tall story, the fact that the ghost sighting made it into the ship's log suggests that the officers and enlisted men truly believed what they were seeing. Additionally, two other warships, the HMS *Tourmaline* and the HMS *Cleopatra*, both signaled the *Inconstant* to inquire whether she had also seen the strange, red glow.

In the nineteenth century, Britannia ruled the waves. Britain's Royal Navy was the preeminent maritime power, the backbone of the British Empire. Frigates were the backbone of the Royal Navy; smaller and faster than the heavy ships of the line but larger than the nimbler yet lightly armed sloops and cutters, this class of ship struck a good balance between speed and firepower. There was a constant demand for trained seamen to crew them. Much of this at-sea education took place on training frigates such as the HMS *Eurydice*.

In 1877, after 34 years of front-line service, the *Eurydice* was beginning to show her age. Rather than send her to the wreckers yard, it was determined that the worn-out ship still had it in her to serve as a floating schoolroom. Sailors learned new skills of the trade, or honed existing ones, all under the watchful eye of instructors. In March 1878, she was returning from a training cruise in the West Indies and had made it most of the way home when disaster struck in the waters off the Isle of Wight.

A sudden onset of bad weather caused the frigate to heel over onto her side. Unfortunately, the officer of the watch had made a fatal error: the gun ports had been left open in order to let fresh air enter the musty belowdecks environment and make conditions more tolerable for the sailors. Water poured in through the open gun ports, swiftly filling the ship's hull and weighing her down. By the time the weather had brightened again, the *Eurydice* had sunk, taking all but two members of her crew down to the ocean depths with her.

More than 300 officers and enlisted men (the precise number is unclear) had gone to a watery grave. Standing on a nearby headland watching her go down was a 3-year-old boy named Winston Spencer Churchill, the future prime minister of Britain.

An 1871 painting of the *Eurydice* by William Howard Yorke. Commissioned in 1843, the ship was lost in an 1877 storm off the Isle of Wight, and all but two of the crew perished.

The navy was eventually able to recover the sunken frigate, but so great was the structural damage that she was considered unfit to perform even the role of a training frigate. Her once stout timbers were broken up and used to refit other vessels.

It seems fair to say that the *Eurydice* was, in the end, an unlucky ship, though her decades of service to the Royal Navy make that debatable. Yet her story does not end with the frigate's scrapping in 1878. The HMS *Eurydice* had a strange afterlife.

The nautical term "ghost ship" describes a physical vessel that is found sailing the ocean without any crew members on board. The best example of a ghost ship is the *Mary Celeste,* a brigantine that was discovered on the high seas in 1872, six years before the *Eurydice* met her demise. The *Mary Celeste* was believed to be an unlucky ship, and the fact that her entire company vanished without a trace would seem to bear that out. She was sailing from New York to Genoa when it seems likely that the crew abandoned her for some unknown reason; one of the ship's boats was absent, so clearly, *somebody* had abandoned ship. Yet none of the personal possessions were gone.

Even today, ghost ships can be found drifting along on the ocean currents. Some of them are abandoned rusting hulks that have been adrift for years; others are surprisingly new and in good condition. None of them are ghosts *of* ships. After the *Eurydice*'s sinking, more than one ship's company claimed to have spotted her at sea in the same area in which she sank.

The phantom frigate almost collided with a Royal Navy submarine during the 1930s. It was only through the quick reactions and evasive action taken by the sub's experienced captain, Commander Frank Lipscomb, that the collision was averted—or was it? The vessel was an antiquated 30-masted frigate that fit the description of the HMS *Eurydice* and that promptly vanished in the middle of open water with nowhere for it to go but beneath the waves—or into thin air.

Other mariners have sighted the phantom frigate over the years. Her appearance is always the same, even down to the open gun ports along her sides.

Perhaps the best-known sighting took place in 1998, when Prince Edward Windsor encountered the ship while making a documentary film off the coast of the Isle of Wight—and caught her on camera. Tantalizingly, the film was damaged, rendering only a very brief clip usable. If this really was the ghost of the stricken frigate, then that would make Prince Edward Windsor the second member of the British Royal Family to experience a close encounter with a phantom ship just like his great-grandfather King George V was said to have done with the *Flying Dutchman* 117 years prior.

It would appear that more than 150 years after her destruction, the ghost of the HMS *Eurydice* is still patrolling British waters and may be doomed to do so for all eternity.

If so, she isn't alone.

From haunting ships to *haunted ships*....

Even years or decades after they have sailed into port and have been moored for the last time, it's surprising how many ships seem to have a resident ghost or two still aboard. This is particularly common with warships, especially those vessels that have either seen active combat duty or been involved with some kind of traumatic incident.

One of the most haunted warships in the world is the USS *Hornet*. Designated CV-12, this aircraft carrier has a long, storied history—and ghostly encounters to match.

The *Hornet* steamed into World War II's Pacific Theater in the summer of 1943. She and the rest of the U.S. Navy had their work cut out for them, pushing the Japanese military backward across the ocean in a series of island-hopping missions that would culminate in an assault on the enemy home islands, or so it was believed. In reality, the invasion of Japan would be rendered moot by the Japanese surrender in the aftermath of two atomic bomb detonations. But the carrier saw plenty of combat prior to that.

The USS *Hornet* (CV-12) was launched in 1943 and took the name of the *Hornet* (CV-8) that had sunk the previous year during the Battle of the Santa Cruz Islands.

Aircraft operating from the *Hornet's* flight deck flew missions against Japanese-held islands, the names of which came to be written in blood in the histories of World War II: Tinian, Guam, Iwo Jima, and Okinawa. Her air wings supported amphibious and ground assaults by U.S. Army and Marine Corps units, and the *Hornet's* fighters also intercepted Japanese bombers and their fighter escorts.

Immediately before the war's end, the carrier launched bombing raids on the Japanese homeland itself before sustaining damage in a typhoon to such a degree that she required extensive repair. By the time the USS *Hornet* was ready for sea once more, victory had already been declared on September 2, 1945. She would see further war service more than 20 years later when the Vietnam War broke out.

In addition to her service under fire, the *Hornet* also performed rescues at sea, including the recovery of the Apollo 11 astronauts Neil Armstrong, Buzz Aldrin, and Michael Collins after their return from the moon.

The USS *Hornet* was decommissioned on June 26, 1970, and the *Essex-class* aircraft carrier was turned into a floating museum, permanently moored in Alameda, California. Not only can members of the public visit her there, taking a bow-to-stern tour of one of the ships that turned the tide in America's favor during World War II, but it is even possible to spend a night aboard her.

She has made so much history during her operational lifetime that it would be remarkable if ghosts weren't encountered aboard the *Hornet*. Although she wasn't badly damaged by enemy action during any of her combat tours (the weather at sea was a different story), there were deaths from both accidental causes and suicide down through the years. The apparitions of former crew members have been sighted aboard the ship, still on duty decades after the carrier's final decommissioning was completed. This includes a sailor sporting a set of "dress whites," the distinctive U.S. Navy uniform.

Electrical and mechanical phenomena abound on the ship, including the classic flickering lights despite there being no issues with the wiring, toilets (or heads, as sailors call them) flushing of their own accord, and hatches (doors) opening and closing of their own volition. Disembodied voices and footsteps have been reported on numerous occasions. In the long-empty hangar bays, where aircraft were brought belowdecks for maintenance, repair, and re-arming, the sounds of sailors working on phantom planes has been heard.

> **Some claim that the *Hornet* is the U.S. Navy's most haunted ship. It is a claim that is impossible to definitively prove and equally difficult to dispute.**

Some claim that the *Hornet* is the U.S. Navy's most haunted ship. It is a claim that is impossible to definitively prove and equally difficult to dispute. The ship's nickname, "Gray Ghost," was supposedly earned because the Japanese Navy erroneously believed this stealthy aircraft carrier had been sunk on no fewer than three occasions. Even after having spent 55 years tied up, she continues to earn that title, albeit for an entirely different reason.

From the Gray Ghost we move to the Sea Witch, more formally known as the USS *Salem* (CA-139). Named after the town made infamous by the witch trials of 1692–1693, construction on the heavy cruiser was completed in 1947. She was built in the naval shipyard at Quincy, Massachusetts; fittingly, it is here that she can still be found today.

The *Salem* was completed too late to see service in World War II. Thus, she never fought in a single combat action, but that's not to say that the ship didn't experience trauma in a different form. Her sick bay saw several deaths, and in August 1953 she made full steam to aid earthquake victims on the Ionian Islands of Greece. Casualties were estimated at approximately 800. The *Salem*'s crew provided food, water, and medical care to the survivors as part of the disaster relief

As a heavy cruiser, the USS *Salem* now makes for an impressive feature display at the U.S. Naval Shipbuilding Museum in Quincy, Massachusetts.

effort. There were just three doctors serving aboard the battle cruiser at the time.

One ship's officer compared the devastation that was inflicted upon the Greek settlements to that which had been inflicted at Hiroshima and Nagasaki by atomic weaponry. Navy corpsmen treated injured victims at hastily rigged first aid stations. The relief effort was emotionally traumatizing for every member of the ship's company.

The USS *Salem* reached the end of her operational life span in 1959. Much like the *Hornet*, after a lengthy period spent in mothballs, she was saved from the wreckers yard and preserved as a floating maritime museum—the only heavy cruiser of her kind in the entire world. Walking her decks today is like stepping back in time, as I learned when resident paranormal investigator Don DeCristofaro invited me and a team of fellow researchers aboard the Sea Witch to experience her for ourselves.

She is, in many ways, a time capsule. Her custodians have taken excellent care of the ship. Wandering throughout the ship and then climbing up to the bridge with its commanding views of the main deck and the heavy gun turrets that take pride of place, it was easy to picture what the mighty warship would have felt like when she was the flagship of the U.S. Sixth Fleet.

It appears that members of the ship's crew still walk her decks, both above the waterline and below. Shadow figures have been encountered throughout the ship, and it has been hypothesized that in addition to being former sailors, noncommissioned officers, and officers of the *Salem*'s complement, some may be the spirits of those who lost their lives during the 1953 earthquake; they were restless souls who remain attached to the ship, some of whom died aboard as doctors fought to save their lives.

The *Salem* is also known for its electronic voice phenomena, which range from friendly and welcoming to the much more sinister cry of *"Get out!"* Not every spectral sailor, or civilian companion, is eager for the company of outsiders.

Don and his colleagues have reached an understanding with the spirits aboard the ship with a mutual respect and, in some cases, affection existing between the living and the dead.

EPILOGUE: HAUNTED HOSTELRIES

From cursed families living in haunted mansions to abandoned hospitals and rectories, by way of supernatural talking animals, witches in the backwoods, angry poltergeists, and tragic air disasters …

… across blood-soaked battlefields and haunted hotels to phantom ships and ships crewed by phantoms …

… from prisons to ghost towns of the wild, wild West to thought-forms and child egregores …

… we have finally come full circle. We began this journey with pubs and inns on a dark winter's night, telling fireside ghost stories. It is with a handful of those same haunted hostelries that we will now bring matters to a close.

Many drinking establishments have their ghosts. Some are the result of violent death—bar fights gone bad, accidental deaths, and in some cases, outright murder and execution. Other spirits linger for different reasons, haunting places in which they were happy during their earthly lives.

One of the places that has a strong claim to the title of the oldest inn in Wales is the Skirrid Mountain Inn, which can be found in the historic Welsh village of Llanvihangel Crucorney. Historians believe that there has been an inn on this site for about a thousand years. It was the center of village life for generation upon generation. Births were celebrated there, as were weddings. Deaths were mourned and lives com-

Also known simply as the Skirrid Inn, the Skirrid Mountain Inn is located in the Welsh village of Llanvihangel Crucorney. Local legend is that it served as a meeting place for rebels against King Henry IV as well as a court of law where executions were conducted on the spot.

memorated at their ending, the dead toasted with ale and wished Godspeed on their journey into the next life.

Except maybe not all of them chose to leave the inn. Many ghosts are said to haunt the Skirrid, a word that means "shaking" or "trembling." Skirrid Mountain, which watches over the inn and gave the place its name, supposedly got that name because lightning struck it while Jesus Christ was dying on the cross.

Look up at the painted sign that hangs over the inn's door today, and you the visitor will see the legend immortalized there.

Taking pride of place in the bar is the Pwcca cup. That's not a typo; it's Welsh for "Devil's cup." Sitting in a special alcove, the cup has traditionally been filled with ale at night and left outside the Skirrid Inn as an offering to the Dark One and his minions, a bribe in exchange for them to bypass the Skirrid and find somewhere else to unleash their torments. Legend has it that the cup would always turn up empty the next morning, which could mean either that the forces of evil were quite partial to a pint of Welsh beer or that there were some rather drunk foxes and badgers staggering around the village for generations, until the practice of leaving the Pwcca cup out was finally discontinued. Fortunately, Satan still seems to be leaving the Skirrid Inn in peace. Hopefully, he will continue to do so.

Many who crossed over the Skirrid Inn's threshold year after year, some of them from their late teens all the way until they died of old age, are buried in the church graveyard just a short distance uphill. In life, many stumbled past the cemetery on their way home after an evening's revelry; now their remains lie there, some at rest and some very much not.

Some are friendlier than others.

One of the most disturbing stories associated with the Skirrid involves a guest who was strangled by an unseen force that felt like a hangman's noose slowly and inexorably tightening around his neck. This may be connected with the most infamous "guest" associated with the inn.

Seventeenth-century judge George Jeffreys ran a mean courtroom. With a penchant for sentencing those who were found guilty to dance at the end of a rope, he earned the nickname of "the Hanging Judge."

This appellation also derived from his presiding over the so-called Bloody Assizes in 1685, a plot to depose King James II from the throne and replace him with a monarch more to the plotters' liking. The coup attempt failed. The king's reaction was a predictable one: dozens were hanged, many of them by order of Jeffreys. Others died of illness in jail due to the horrific conditions. Those who survived temporary imprisonment and also escaped the hangman's noose were often deported, where death frequently found them anyway due to tropical illnesses and other maladies of life in a hostile land.

According to legend, the second floor of the Skirrid once served as the courtroom of the Hanging Judge. Sentence was passed on the accused by Jeffreys and then, if that

Those found guilty at the inn were hung right there from a noose tied to the staircase banister.

sentence was death, the guilty were supposedly hanged inside the inn, the noose tied off from a banister atop the master staircase. The soon-to-be-executed victim was taken, with their hands bound, to the top of the stairs and pushed off, plunging to their death at the bottom.

It's a macabre story and one that has been told for many years, but there isn't much in the way of proof to back it up. Nobody is entirely sure of where the legend originated, but it makes little practical sense. Why run the risk of damaging the ornately carved wooden staircase or of having the victim's falling body accidentally hit one of the sides on its downward fall, thereby botching the execution? It would be far sounder to construct temporary gallows in the back garden of the inn, where there is plenty of open space for a crowd to gather. Public executions were commonplace in the seventeenth century. Not only were they a form of public entertainment, but it was an opportunity for justice to be carried out in full view of all and sundry. The more witnesses that came to view it, the more value an execution carried as a potential deterrent.

> In addition to obtaining several very clear EVP recordings, the highlight of our investigation was a rather strange video capture. A shadow figure was recorded walking across the dining room and then back again.

Equally difficult to pin down is evidence to confirm the presence of the Hanging Judge at the Skirrid Inn during his lifetime; yet ghost stories persist, with claims that either Jeffreys himself—or alternatively his personal executioner, the Hangman—haunts the place. The latter is said to be a monstrous character, cruel and sadistic, a description that does seem more than a little stereotypical. Encounters with the Hangman take place on the staircase, where visitors sometimes report being overwhelmed with fear or experiencing a sudden cold chill even on the warmest of days as if an invisible energy were passing through them.

I was fortunate enough to spend several nights investigating the Skirrid, staying in what's said to be the most haunted part of the aged building: Room 1.

Investigating the pub was challenging until late at night due to the sheer amount of noise contamination from the main bar downstairs. Yet once the last customer had gone home for the night, the doors were locked and we had the Skirrid Inn all to ourselves. The place took on an entirely different character when all was dark and quiet. One felt as if there were eyes watching from the shadows. Suggestion, perhaps, or possibly the presence of one of the inn's many reported ghosts.

Several times, my fellow researchers and I saw shadow figures throughout the inn. Most often, the sightings took place on the upper landing, where hangings were said to have taken place. In addition to obtaining several very clear EVP recordings, the highlight of our investigation was a rather strange video capture. A shadow figure was recorded walking across the dining room and then back again. Nobody was present in that part of the inn at the time, and we were unable to find a non-paranormal explanation for the shadowy movement.

Stranger things were to come. After the window of Room 3 opened by itself, the hot tap in the bathroom of Room 1, which I had left running at full blast in order to heat up the water prior to shaving, suddenly closed itself off. Despite careful examination of the tap and subsequent experimentation, I was never able to figure out how it had managed to shut itself down.

The Skirrid Inn has many layers of history, is steeped in rich tradition, and has been deeply beloved by generation upon generation of villagers. Whether the stories concerning the Hanging Judge and his malevolent cohort are true or not, it is impossible to deny that *something* ghostly happens in that place on a very consistent basis.

High up on the lonely, windswept moors of Cornwall stands the infamous Jamaica Inn. Given international renown by the novel of the same name, written by Daphne du Maurier in 1936, the inn became even more well known when Alfred Hitchcock directed a film adaptation in 1939.

I had the great honor of scribbling down a few lines of prose while sitting at Daphne du Maurier's own personal writing desk.

The inn dates back to the mid-eighteenth century, approximately 1760, and was used as a stop on the coach trail that ran across the country. Smugglers operated in the area, plying the coastlines of Cornwall, and much of the contraband liquor passed through the Jamaica Inn on its way north.

Today, Jamaica Inn remains as well known as ever it was. A constant stream of visitors crosses the threshold into the bar, drawn as much by the spectral stories as by the great hospitality.

Built in 1750, the Jamaica Inn was long associated as a stopping point for smugglers as they passed through Cornwall's Bodwin Moor. So famous for smuggling was it that Daphne du Maurier made it the setting of her 1936 novel, *Jamaica Inn*.

Many of the original rooms are said to be haunted. My wife, Laura, was lying alone in the four-poster bed in Room 5 when she felt invisible fingers stroke her ankle. There have been many reports over the years of similar leg-touching taking place in Rooms 3 and 4. A second time, after she was feeling distressed and anxious, she felt a reassuring pat on her shoulder. The room is said to be haunted by a little girl named Hannah. Numerous residents of Room 5 have left tokens of appreciation for the child's spirit, primarily toys and handwritten messages.

In that same room, an earlier guest got the shock of his life when he emerged from the bathroom to find wet footprints in the carpet, circling his bed. They were the size of a child's feet. He checked out soon afterward in rather a hurry. Some even claim to have seen Hannah's apparition standing by the side of the bed, though I slept undisturbed during my stay in Room 5.

Cornwall's association with *Poldark*, the well-known TV series and the novels on which it is based, has been well publicized. The Jamaica Inn gift shop carries the books, shelving them alongside the works of Daphne du Maurier. Even the word "Poldark" conjures up images of people in period clothing, and the inn has a ghost who looks as if he has stepped out from that shadowy world into our own.

A mysterious male apparition, wearing an old-fashioned tricorn hat, has been reported numerous times over the years. He haunts the oldest part of the inn and has been spotted in more than one of the guest rooms, lurking silently, observing the occupant as they lie in bed. Once he has been seen, the man in the hat disappears into thin air. Nobody knows his identity, but this enigmatic phantom is a mainstay of Jamaica Inn ghost lore.

One of the stranger stories relating to the inn dates back to the mid-1800s, when one of the patrons at the bar put down his drink half-finished and walked outside into the night after somebody called for him. He was never seen alive again. The next day, his dead body was found on the moor. Despite the suspicious circumstances, the crime— if indeed it was a crime—was never solved. The man's restless spirit has been given the name Jack. His ghost has been reported both inside the inn and sitting in the courtyard outside, facing the road.

Most of the original rooms overlook the front courtyard. Guests often report being awakened by the sound of horses' hooves on the stones outside, most likely a residual audible phenomenon from the days when it was an active coaching inn. Similar in nature is the sound of a baby crying, which many people have reported hearing over the years. This always seems to happen in the oldest part of the structure.

During our stay, Laura also received an unexplained scratch on her forehead while poking around in the attic space above the former stable block. She felt the distinct touch of a hand on her forearm in the smugglers museum when nobody was within touching distance of her in what is now the on-site museum.

It was an eventful stay in other ways. A fellow investigator was awakened early one morning by the frightening sensation of her entire bed shaking. Yes, she was alone at the time! She was staying in one of the older rooms, which perhaps increases the likelihood of having a ghostly experience.

Like most haunted hostelries, the Jamaica Inn not only accepts the presence of its ghosts, it actively embraces them. I encourage you, dear reader, to do the same. No matter where you may live, and no matter to where you may travel, it is likely that there is a haunted location nearby. Some are open to the public, and many of them welcome visitors at appropriate times and under certain conditions.

Epilogue: Haunted Hostelries

If you have enjoyed this journey into the realm of great hauntings, perhaps it is time to take the next step. It is a fine thing to sit around a fire and tell ghost stories; it is even better to experience them for yourself.

Be respectful …

Stay safe …

… but above all, be curious.

I'll see you in the darkness.

PHOTO SOURCES

Alamy stock photos: p. 124.

Authenticated History of the Bell Witch, 1894, reproduction, Rare Book Reprints, 1961.

Bibliothèque Nationale de France: p. 121.

Brad06 (Wikicommons): p. 88.

Chris6d (Wikicommons): p. 212.

EmbraerSkyPilot (Wikicommons): p. 222.

Richard Estep: pp. 2, 4, 6, 8, 9 (top and bottom), 30, 32, 34, 35, 36 (top), 38, 40, 59, 61, 62, 63, 65, 68, 72, 74, 76, 78, 79, 80 (top and bottom), 100, 106, 146, 149, 159, 162, 163, 165, 170, 171, 172, 176, 177, 178, 179, 180, 183, 184, 185, 186, 187, 188, 192, 194, 196, 197, 200, 201, 203, 204, 205.

Federal Bureau of Investigation (Chicago bureau): p. 154.

Foxearth.org.uk: p. 98.

Geograph Project (geograph.org.uk): pp. 115, 125, 158, 232, 233, 236.

Mike Graham: p. 148.

The Haunting of Cashen's Gap: A Modern "Miracle" Investigated, 1936: pp. 14, 15, 16, 18.

Heritage Auction Gallery: p. 56 (left).

William Hope: p. 105.

JustPere (Wikicommons): p. 134.

Lazlo911 (Wikicommons): p. 174.

Lexington50 (Wikicommons): p. 208.

Library of Contress: pp. 113 (top), 174 (inset).

Life Magazine: p. 107.

Manchester Daily Dispatch: p. 20.

Mead Art Museum: p. 169.

Museo Britannico del Soprannaturale: p. 104.

Mx. Granger (Wikicommons): p. 44.

National Museums NI: p. 112.

National Transportation Safety Board: pp. 131, 132, 138, 139.

Jon Proctor: p. 128.

The Province and the States: A History of the Province of Louisiana Under France and Spain, and of the Territories and States of the United States Formed Therefrom, Volume VII, 1904: p. 3.

Dietmar Rabich: p. 216.

Royal Museums Greenwich: p. 225.

SDASM Archives: p. 136.

Shutterstock: pp. 24, 25, 27, 36 (bottom), 45, 48, 50, 52, 99, 181.

Photo Sources

Gage Skidmore: p. 51.

Sswonk (Wikicommons): p. 229.

Brian Stansberry: p. 95.

Thesab (Wikicommons): p. 152 (top and bottom).

Tres calcetrines (Wikicommons): p. 210.

United Kingdom Government: pp. 114, 117.

U.S. Department of Justice: p. 213.

U.S. federal government: p. 215.

U.S. Navy: p. 227.

Victor A. Chapman collection, SkyeWaye: p. 113 (bottom).

Www78 (Wikicommons): p. 84.

Public domain: pp. 56 (right), 57 (top and bottom). 85, 87, 92, 101, 118, 150, 193, 220, 223.

FURTHER READING

Bell, Richard Williams, and M. Todd Cathey. *Our Family Trouble: The Story of the Bell Witch of Tennessee.* M. Todd Cathey, 2013.

Byers, Shannon Bradley. *Paranormal Fakelore, Nevermore: Real Histories of Haunted Locations.* Lilburn, GA: Paranormal Genealogist Publishing, 2017.

Du Maurier, Daphne. *Jamaica Inn.* London: Pan Books, 1979.

Estep, Richard. *Blood, Death and Fears: The Haunting of Old South Pittsburg Hospital.* Privately printed, 2022.

————. *The Fairfield Haunting: On the Gettysburg Ghost Trail.* Privately printed, 2018.

————. *The Farnsworth House Haunting: On the Gettysburg Ghost Trail.* Privately printed, 2019.

————. *Spirits Behind Bars.* Privately printed, 2019.

Estep, Richard, Bill Bungay, and Katrina Weidman. *The Black Monk of Pontefract: The World's Most Violent and Relentless Poltergeist.* Privately printed, 2019.

Fitzhugh, Pat. *The Bell Witch: The Full Account.* Nashville, TN: Armand Press, 2009.

Fuller, Elizabeth. *My Search for the Ghost of Flight 401.* Cork: BookBaby, 2014.

Fuller, John G. *The Ghost of Flight 401.* Boston, MA: Putnam, 1976.

Fuller, John G., and Darrell Sweet. *The Airmen Who Would Not Die.* Manassas, VA: Berkley,1980.

Gaddis, Thomas E. *Birdman of Alcatraz.* Mattituck, NY: Amereon, 1965.

Gwynne, S. C., and Nicholas Boulton. *His Majesty's Airship: The Life and Tragic Death of the World's Largest Flying Machine.* New York: Simon & Schuster, 2023.

Ingram, M. *An Authenticated History of the Famous Bell Witch.* Privately printed, 2019.

Owen, Iris M., and Margaret Sparrow. *Conjuring Up Philip.* Toronto: Colombo & Co, 2000.

O'Connor, Sean. *The Haunting of Borley Rectory: The Story of a Ghost Story.* London: Simon & Schuster, 2023.

Further Reading

Pickering, James H. *Mr. Stanley of Estes Park.* Edited by Susan S. Davis. Kingfield, ME, and Estes Park, CO: Stanley Museum, 2000.

Pickman, Debra. *The Sallie House Haunting: A True Story.* Woodbury, MN: Llewellyn, 2010.

Playfair, Guy Lyon. *This House Is Haunted: The True Story of a Poltergeist.* New York: Stein & Day, 1984.

Pohl, Lynn. *Waverly Hills Sanatorium: A History.* Charleston, SC: The History Press, 2022.

Price, Harry. *The End of Borley Rectory.* London: George G. Harrop, 1946.

———. *Leaves from a Psychist's Case-Book.* London: Gollancz, 1933.

Price, Harry, and R. S. Lambert. *The Haunting of Cashen's Gap: A Modern "Miracle" Investigated.* London: Methuen, 1936.

Taylor, Troy. *Season of the Witch: The True Story of the Bell Witch of Tennessee.* Jacksonville, IL: American Hauntings Ink, 2013.

———. *Suicide & Spirits: The True Story of the Rise and Fall of the Lemp Empire.* Jacksonville, IL: American Hauntings Ink, 2019.

Underwood, Peter, and Paul Tabori. *The Ghosts of Borley; Annals of the Haunted Rectory.* Newton Abbot, England: David & Charles, 1973.

Willin, Melvyn. *The Enfield Poltergeist Tapes: One of the Most Disturbing Cases in History. What Really Happened?* White Crow Books, 2019.

Wilson, Colin. *Poltergeist: A Classic Study in Destructive Hauntings,* Woodbury, MN: Llewellyn Publications, 2009.

INDEX

Note: (ill.) indicates photos and illustrations

Index

Playfair, Guy Lyon, 46–47, 49, 50–51
Pohl, Lynn, 34
poltergeists
    Bell Witch, 83–96, 84 (ill.), 85 (ill.), 87 (ill.), 88 (ill.), 92 (ill.), 94 (ill.), 95 (ill.)
    Black Monk, 71–81, 72 (ill.), 74 (ill.), 76 (ill.), 78 (ill.), 79 (ill.), 80 (ill.)
    Enfield (UK) poltergeist, 43–53, 44 (ill.)
Potter, W. A., 124 (ill.)
Price, Harry
    animal ghosts, 14, 16–17, 18, 20
    Borley Rectory, 100, 102, 103, 104, 105, 105 (ill.), 109
    R101 airship, 118, 122, 123, 124
Pritchard, Diane, 73, 76, 78, 85
Pritchard, Jean, 73–78, 79
Pritchard, Joe, 73–78, 79
Pritchard, Phillip, 73

R

R101 airship, 112–26, 113 (ill.), 114 (ill.), 115 (ill.), 117 (ill.), 121 (ill.), 124 (ill.), 125 (ill.)
Rampton, H. G., 124 (ill.)
Raposa, Beverly, 131, 139
Repo, Don, 129–30, 131, 133–34, 135, 136, 137–38, 139, 141, 143
Reynolds, John, 171
Richardson, J., 124 (ill.)
Riley, John, 185 (ill.), 185–86
Roe, Ralph, 213
Rook, John, 65
Rowe, H., 124 (ill.)
Ruiz, Mercy, 139

S

Salem, USS, 228–30, 229 (ill.)
Sallie House (Atchison, KS), 199–206, 200 (ill.), 201 (ill.), 203 (ill.), 204 (ill.), 205 (ill.)
Schieffelin, Ed, 59, 61 (ill.), 67, 68, 68 (ill.)
Schrader, Dave, 50
Scott, George, 16 (ill.), 123, 124
Scott, S. E., 124 (ill.)
Serling, Robert J., 136
Shepton Mallet Prison (Somerset, England), 157–66, 158 (ill.), 159 (ill.), 162 (ill.), 163 (ill.), 165 (ill.)
The Shining, 191–92, 192 (ill.), 193, 194 (ill.), 195
Shippy, Steve, 138–40, 141, 143
Short, W. G. W., 124 (ill.)
Skirrid Mountain Inn (Llanvihangel Crucorney, Wales), 231–32 (ill.)
Smiley, "Chink," 63
Smith, Edward John, 111–12
Smith, Guy Eric, 100–101
Smith, Mabel, 100–101, 104–5
Smith, Trudi, 136 (ill.)
Sparrow, Margaret, 27
Stanley, Flora, 193, 196
Stanley, Freelan Oscar, 192 (ill.), 193, 193 (ill.)

Stanley Hotel (Estes Park, CO), 191–97, 192 (ill.), 194 (ill.), 196 (ill.), 197 (ill.)
Steff, M. H., 124 (ill.)
Stockstill, Albert, 130, 131–32, 137
Stodden, Mike, 8
Streisand Effect, 134–35
Stroud, Robert, 214–16, 215 (ill.)
Strudwick, Matt, 51
Sweney House (Gettysburg, PA), 176

T

Tabori, Paul, 105
Taylor, C., 124 (ill.)
Taylor, Troy, 5
Tennant, David, 163
Thompson, Paul, 52–53
Thomson, Christopher B., 114, 116, 123–24
Titanic, RMS, 111–12, 112 (ill.)
Tombstone, Arizona, 55–69, 59 (ill.), 61 (ill.), 62 (ill.), 63 (ill.), 65 (ill.), 68 (ill.)
Toronto Society for Psychical Research, 24, 28
Trimble, Isaac R., 182
triskaidekaphobia, 219–20
tuberculosis, 29–33
Turkel, Joe, 191
Turner, Andrew, 215

U–V

Underwood, Peter, 98, 105, 106, 162

V

Vanderdecken, 221
Villiers, Oliver, 123, 124

W

Wade, Jennie, 179 (ill.), 179–81
Warren, Ed, 50–51
Warren, Lorraine, 50–51, 51 (ill.)
Waverly Hills Sanatorium (Louisville, KY), 30 (ill.), 30–37, 32 (ill.), 34 (ill.), 35 (ill.), 36 (ill.)
White, Tim, 199
Wilkins, Bill, 48–49, 53
Wilkins, Ethel, 48
Williams, Delia, 64
Wilson, Bill, 93
Wilson, Colin, 76–77
Wilson, Elizabeth, 195
Wilson, Grant, 7
Wilson, Woodrow, 215
Wiseman, Richard, 109
Wright, Thomas, 5–6

Y

Yorke, William Howard, 225 (ill.)